From Molecule to Metaphor

From Molecule to Metaphor

A Neural Theory of Language

Jerome A. Feldman

A Bradford Book
The MIT Press
Cambridge, Massachusetts
London, England

First MIT Press paperback edition, 2008

MIT Press books may be purchased at special quantity discounts for business or sales promotional use. For information, please email special_sales@mitpress.mit.edu or write to Special Sales Department, The MIT Press, 55 Hayward Street, Cambridge, MA 02142.

This book was set in Stone Sans and Stone Serif by SNP Best-set Typesetter Ltd., Hong Kong and was printed and bound in the United States of America.

Library of Congress Cataloging-in-Publication Data

Feldman, Jerome A.
From molecule to metaphor : a neural theory of language / by Jerome A. Feldman.
    p.   cm.
Includes bibliographical references and index.
ISBN 978-0-262-06253-4 (hard : alk. paper)—978-0-262-56235-5 (pb. : alk. paper)
1. Language and languages—Philosophy. 2. Psycholinguistics. 3. Neurobiology.
4. Cognitive science. I. Title.

P107.F445   2006
401—dc22

                                                            2005058045

10 9 8 7 6 5

For Debby, my *sine qua non*.

Contents

Preface

I hear and I forget
I see and I remember
I do and I understand
—Attributed to Confucius, 500 BCE

Many years ago, I was browsing through books on learning how to draw. One of them said, after a brief introduction, put down this book and start drawing. This book is like that—it will frequently suggest a simple mental exercise to help you personally experience a phenomenon. If this appeals to you, you might like the book.

By now, virtually everyone agrees that the scientific explanation for human language and cognition will be based on our bodies, brains, and experiences. The major exception is Noam Chomsky whose dominance of twentieth-century linguistics is unparalleled in any other academic field. I will later quote from Chomsky's 1993 book, *Language and Thought*, and he repeatedly stated the same idea in his 2003 Berkeley lectures: "We don't know nearly enough about the brain for cognitive science to take it seriously." Chomsky has focused on linguistic *form*; since this book deals first with *meaning*, we won't encounter him again until chapter 22.

As a first mental exercise, try expressing to yourself what you know about how your own thoughts work. *How do our brains compute our minds?* When I ask Berkeley students, on the first day of class, to write a page on this question, most of the students express mystification. Even people who know a great deal about neuroscience, psychology, linguistics, philosophy, and artificial intelligence often have no clear idea of how the findings of these fields could combine to yield even a preliminary understanding of how language is embodied in us.

This book proposes to begin integrating current insights from many disciplines into a coherent *neural theory of language*. It might seem that no such effort is needed. Isn't language obviously a function of our brains—what else could it be? Certainly other human abilities such as motor control, hearing, and especially vision have been studied as neural systems for many decades. But language is still often treated as an abstract symbol system not particularly tied to human brains or experience.

A great deal of permanent value has been learned from formal studies of language, but it is surprising that the notion of disembodied language persists. This is partly an historical artifact, but it also arises from the fact that other animals share our visual and motor abilities but not our language skills. Much of the progress in neural theories of vision and motor control have come from invasive animal experiments that are thankfully prohibited on people. Until recently, very little has been known about how our brains process language.

Currently no one knows the details of how words or sentences are processed in the brain, and there is no known methodology for finding out. Many scientists believe it is premature (perhaps by centuries) to formulate explicit theories linking language to neural computation. Even theoreticians are usually content with suggestive models, which can't actually be right, but do suggest interesting experiments. However, the cognitive sciences reveal a great deal about how our brains produce language and thought. And we have a long and productive tradition, going back at least to the Greek atomic theories of matter, of postulating "bridging theories" in advance of the detailed evidence. Brian Greene's *The Elegant Universe* offers a wonderful description of the fundamental nature of matter, though science might never deliver experimental verification.

In contemporary science, it is not unusual to have quite extensive knowledge at both ends of a causal chain and to build and test theories to explicate the bridging links. For example, astrophysics is concerned with linking fundamental particle physics with astronomy. In economics and other social sciences, a principal concern is how individual preferences give rise to group behavior. Similarly, much of molecular biology is concerned with how genetic material yields the various proteins and resultant organisms. Higher levels of biology also try to develop bridging theories. We can see the search for a neural theory of language as one such attempt, albeit an unusually ambitious one. These bridging theories are often developed as computer simulations, and this book follows this tradition.

I treat the mind as a biological question—language and thought are adaptations that extend abilities we share with other animals. For well over a century, this has been the standard scientific approach to other mental capacities such as vision and motor control. But language and thought, even now, are usually studied as abstract formal systems that just happen to be implemented in our brains. Instead, we pursue the great ethologist Nico Tinbergen's (Tinbergen 1963) four questions that must be asked of any biological ability:

1. How does it work?
2. How does it improve fitness?
3. How does it develop and adapt?
4. How did it evolve?

The first three of these questions are covered in considerable detail. The origins of language are still largely unknown and are discussed briefly in chapter 26.

There is a sufficiently large gap between brain and language to contain ecological niches for many theories, especially if their proponents are satisfied to ignore inconvenient findings. Understanding language and thought requires combining findings from biology, computer science, linguistics, and psychology. A theory that seems perfectly adequate from one perspective may contradict what is known in another field. Problems that seem intractable in one discipline might be quite approachable from a different direction. Taking all the constraints seriously is the only way to get it right.

But this requires us to understand the essential ideas from several quite different scientific domains. In any of these fields, keeping up with technical advances and doing original work are extremely demanding pursuits and require focused effort. There are some endeavors at the boundaries between subfields, but very little scientific work that attempts to encompass the full range needed for our task. I will need to synthesize a bridging theory from separate fields, all of which have their focus elsewhere. My approach is to pick out key findings and theories from various disciplines and show how, in combination, they constrain the possible bridging theories of language to a narrow family of possibilities.

Each discussion is an oversimplification of some research field, often involving thousands of active investigators, and thus is inherently incomplete. The usual references suggest more detailed discussions of various points, but these are most useful as key words for search engines. By the time you read this book, important new developments will have occurred in each of these areas. Books for further reading are included for people who would like additional background in one or another direction.

While we are far from having a complete neural theory of language, enormous scientific advances have occurred in all the relevant fields. Taken together, these developments provide a framework in which everything we know fits together nicely. The goal of this book is simple: I would like you, at the end, to say, *This all makes sense. It could explain how people understand language.* I will make no attempt to convince you other theories are wrong—in fact, I assume that most of them are partially right. The book can be seen as part of a general effort to construct a Unified Cognitive Science that can guide the effort to understand our brains and minds. I try to present a story here that is consistent with all the existing scientific data and that also seems plausible to you as a description of your own mind.

Except for one thing. One part of our mental life is still scientifically inexplicable—subjective experience. Why do we experience everything in the way we do? The pleasure of beauty, the pain of disappointment, and even the awareness of being alive . . . these do not feel like they are reducible to neural firings and chemical reactions. Almost everyone believes that his or her own personal experience has a quality that goes beyond what this book, and science in general, can describe. If I had anything technical to say about subjective experience, it would be the highlight of the book, to say the least.

People use terms like *personal experience, subjective experience,* and *phenomenology* to label this idea. Philosophers have coined a technical term, *qualia,* to refer to these phenomena that are currently beyond scientific explanation. Antonio Damasio (Damasio 2003), who in my opinion is doing the best scientific work on subjective experience, distinguishes measurable *emotions* from subjective *feelings.* Aside from a brief discussion in chapter 26, this book focuses on what can be learned from studying the physiological and behavioral correlates of experience—that is, what can be measured and modeled objectively.

My undertaking of this quixotic enterprise came as the result of a year of explicit soul-searching around the time of my fortieth birthday. I had the good luck of entering the field of computer science in its infancy, and I believed this gave me the opportunity to move in almost any direction, exploiting insights into information processing not available to previous generations. My long-term interests in language and the brain and work on various computer systems including some of the earliest robots, led me to focus on the question that I just asked you—How does the brain compute the mind? Twenty-five years later, due to advances in all fields that were inconceivable to me at the time, the outlines of an answer seem to be emerging.

A Brief Guide to the Book

This book is designed to be read in order; each chapter provides some of the underpinnings for later ideas. But it should also be possible to look first at the parts that interest you most and then decide how much effort you wish to exert. Many forward and backward pointers are included to help integrate the material.

Information processing is my organizing theme. Language and thought are inherently about how information is acquired, used, and transmitted. Chapter 1 lays out some of the richness of language and its relation to experience. The central mechanism in my approach to the neural language problem is neural computation. Chapters 2 and 3 provide a general introduction to neural computation. Chapters 4 through 6 provide the minimal biological background on neurons, neural circuits, and how they develop. We focus on those properties of molecules, cells, and brain circuits that determine the character of our thinking and language.

Chapters 7 and 8 consider thought from the external perspective and look at the brain/mind as a behaving system. With all of this background, chapter 9 introduces the technical tools that are used to model how various components of language and thought are realized in the brain. A fair amount of mechanism is required for my approach, which involves building computational models that actually exhibit the required behavior while remaining consistent with the findings from all disciplines. I refer to such systems as *adequate* computational models, which I believe are the only hope for scientifically linking brain and behavior. There is no guarantee that an adequate model is correct, but any correct model must be adequate in the sense defined here.

The specific demonstrations begin with a study of how children learn their first words. This involves some general review (chapter 10) and a more thorough study of conceptual structure (chapter 11) needed for word learning. The first detailed model is presented in chapter 12, which describes Terry Regier's program that learns words for spatial relation concepts across languages. This theme of concrete word learning is then extended to cover words for simple actions in chapters 13 and 14, which describes David Bailey's demonstration system.

The next section extends the discussion to words for abstract and metaphorical concepts. In chapters 15 and 16, we look further at the structure of conceptual systems and how they arise through metaphorical mappings from direct experience. Chapter 17 takes the informal idea of understanding as imaginative *simulation* and shows how it can be made the basis for a concrete theory. This theory is shown in chapter 18 to be sufficiently rich to describe linguistic aspect—the shape of events. This is enough to capture the direct effects of hearing a sentence, but for the indirect consequences, we need one more computational abstraction of neural activity—belief networks, described in chapter 19. All of these ideas are brought together in Srinivas Narayanan's program for understanding news stories, discussed in chapter 20.

Chapters 21 through 25 are about language *form*, that is, grammar—how grammar is learned and how grammatical processing works. Chapter 21 lays out the basic facts about the form of language that any theory must explain. Chapter 22 is partly a digression; it discusses the hotbutton issues surrounding how much of human grammar is innate. We see that classical questions become much different in an explicitly embodied neural theory of language and that such theories can be expressed in standard formalisms (chapter 23).

Chapter 24 shows how the formalized version of neural grammar can be used scientifically and to build software systems for understanding natural language. The poster child for the entire theory is Nancy Chang's program (chapter 25) that models how children learn their early grammar—as explicit mappings (constructions) relating linguistic form to meaning. Chapter 26 discusses two questions that are not currently answerable: the evolution of language and the nature of subjective experience. Finally, chapter 27 summarizes the book and suggests that further progress will require a broadly based unified cognitive science. But the scientific progress to date does support a range of practical and intellectual applications and should allow us to understand ourselves a bit better.

A version of the material in this book has been taught to hundreds of undergraduate students at the University of California, Berkeley over the years. There were weekly assignments, and most of the students actually did them. The course did not work for all the students, but a significant number of them came out of the class with the basic insights of a neural theory of language. If you want to understand how our brains create thought and language, there is a fair chance that this book can help.

Acknowledgments

This book is a result of many years of collaborative research with students and other colleagues. For the last two decades, my constant partners in the NTL project have been George Lakoff, Srinivas Narayanan, and Lokendra Shastri; other colleagues who helped greatly include Dana Ballard, Julian Davidson, Rich Ivry, Roger Schank, Dan Slobin, Eve Sweetser, and David Zipser. As always, the students did the hard work. The doctoral students whose work has contributed most directly are David Bailey, Joe Becker, Ben Bergen, John Bryant, Nancy Chang, Paul Cooper, Ellen Dodge, Marc Ettlinger, Nigel Goddard, Olya Gurevich, Jim Horning, Eva Mok, Shweta Narayan, Srinivas Narayanan, Tom Olson, Terry Regier, Dan Sabbah, Lokendra Shastri, Steve Sinha, Andreas Stolcke, Susan Hollbach Weber, Carter Wendelken, and Gloria Yang—any new ideas in the book derive from this collaborative effort.

I imposed on various friends, relatives, and colleagues to read earlier and much worse versions of the book. Among those who provided valuable feedback were David Bailey, Joe Becker, Ben Bergen, John Bryant, Nancy Chang, David Feldman, Gary Feldman, Eric Grimson, Dan Jurafsky, Paul Kay, Ron Kay, Debby Kearney, George Lakoff, Jay McClelland, Christos Papadimitriou, Srinivas Narayanan, Steve Pinker, Terry Regier, Roger Schank, Phillip Tucker, Wolfgang Wahlster, and Steve Weber.

Versions of this material have been used in a regular undergraduate class at Berkeley and the students have been very forthcoming about problems with the ideas and their exposition. Shorter versions of the class were presented in Turin, Italy, and Guenne, Germany, yielding different, but equally valuable, criticism.

Much of the work was done while the U.S. government still knowingly encouraged basic research. Support from the National Science Foundation and the Department of Defense (ONR, ARDA, DARPA) is gratefully acknowledged. The Klaus Tschira Foundation has provided invaluable assistance for the work and preparation of this book.

None of this would have been possible without the support of Nelson Morgan, the director of the ICSI, and his outstanding staff, especially Maria Eugenia Quintana and Leah Hitchcock. At the MIT Press, Mary Avery, Tom Stone, and Katherine Almeida in particular were very helpful.

I   Embodied Information Processing

1 | The Mystery of Embodied Language

Each of us is the world's greatest expert on one human mind—our own. But Nature (or God if you'd prefer) did not endow us with the ability to comprehend how our minds work. You can't understand by introspection even something as basic as your eye movements as you read these words. Cognitive scientists can predict where most people will focus their gaze—almost everyone pauses at *read these words* because it is unusual to see a sentence that talks about itself. When it comes to the mental processes involved in understanding the meaning of the text, scientists cannot explain even the basics, such as how the meaning of a word is represented in the brain.

This book contains a good deal of technical detail on various scientific subjects, but the central theme of our story on language and thought is based on two simple related principles:

Thought is structured neural activity.

Language is inextricable from thought and experience.

All of our thought and language arises from our genetic endowment and from our experience. Language and culture are, of course, carried by the family and the community. But each child has to rebuild it all in his or her own mind. From the child's internal perspective, all social and cultural interactions start as additional inputs that must somehow be understood and incorporated using existing knowledge. This is more than a truism. A neural theory of language depends critically on looking at the problem from the perspective of the mind/brain that is learning and using language. The human brain is a system of neurons intricately linked together. Neurons work via electrochemistry. How can such a physical system—biological, chemical, and electrical—have *ideas* and communicate them through *language*? In other words, how does all of this biology, chemistry, and electricity give rise to thought and language?

The link between neurons and physical behavior is easy to see in a well-understood case such as the knee-jerk reflex—the lifting of your leg when your doctor taps below your kneecap. Neural connections run from the sensing neurons in the knee, through one link in the spinal cord, back to motor neurons that drive the leg muscles. Although the complete underlying chemistry is very complex, your doctor doesn't need to think about that. She can quickly see if your knee is functioning correctly by taking an information-processing perspective. The question doctors ask is, *Are the signals from the knee being effectively transmitted to the spinal cord, correctly received there, and appropriate signals being transmitted to the leg muscles?* From this perspective, the problem of behavior (whether your knee jerks) becomes an information-processing problem involving circuitry and signals. As we will see, this information-processing view also applies to *learned* automatic behaviors, like driving a car or understanding language.

Now imagine that your doctor, instead of tapping your knee, asks you to lift your leg. The link between an input signal (the doctor's words) and the output (lifting) now does involve the brain and is much more complex, but the neural information processing perspective is still the key to understanding the behavior. The sound waves produced by the doctor's speech strike your ear and are converted to frequency signals involving millions of neurons. Between these incoming neural signals and the neural command involved in volitionally lifting your leg, there is an enormous amount of neural information processing. This is the physical embodiment of your understanding of what the doctor says and what you choose to do about it. Should you decide to kick, a neural signal from the motor control region of your brain is sent to a circuit in your spinal cord, which will activate the lifting circuitry and muscles in your leg. This assumes that your doctor asked politely—if she were nasty or arrogant, you would be more likely to stomp out of the office or worse.

Many of the neural circuits used in moving are also used in *perceiving* motion. If you watch a video of someone else kicking, this activates some of the same brain circuits that you use for kicking with your own leg (Buccino et al. 2001). Of course, if *all* of your kicking circuitry were active, you would kick. Now imagine you are told a story about someone else kicking. Recent biological evidence suggests that you can understand such stories by imagining yourself kicking (Hauk et al. 2004; Tettamanti et al. 2005). Brain imaging studies reveal that much of the neural activity required for you to understand someone else moving his or her leg overlaps significantly with the activity involved in actually moving your own leg. More generally, we can say the following:

• Understanding language about perceiving and moving involves much of the same neural circuitry as do perceiving and moving themselves.
• Neural computation links our experience of hearing and speaking to the experience of perception, motion, and imagination.
⇒ So we need to know more about neural computation to understand language.

The brain is made up of some 100 billion neurons, each connected, on the average to thousands of other neurons. This comes to some 100 trillion connections. The neurons and their connections (axons, dendrites, and synapses) are biological structures that work by means of chemistry. We will learn a lot in the book about this magnificent structure and how it develops, but we need a few initial insights now. Any thought or action involves a significant fraction of the billions of neurons—the computation is massively parallel. The brain is self-controlling and self-modifying, that is, no central controller tells each part what to do and no external monitor guides its learning. Neural computation involves *continuously finding a best match* between the inputs and current brain state, including our goals.

The brain is constantly active, computing inferences, predictions, and actions with each evolving situation. There has been enormous evolutionary pressure toward brains that can respond fast and effectively in complex situations. For example, a common housefly can sense changes in air currents and quickly shift directions, which is why fly swatters have holes.

To help get a feel for how your best-match circuitry works, look for a minute or so at figure 1.1. This wire-frame cube can be seen in two different ways, with either corner A or corner G appearing closer to you. If you are having trouble seeing corner A as closer, focus on it and imagine it coming out of the paper toward you. This figure is called the Necker Cube, after the nineteenth-century Swiss naturalist Louis Necker, who discovered that the image will spontaneously flip between the two

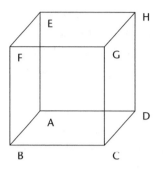

Figure 1.1
An ambiguous image; A or G can appear closer to you.

interpretations as you stare at it. We never see a mixture of the two versions—it's always one coherent whole (Gestalt).

This coherence principle also holds for language. If you read the sentence: Josh threw a ball, you picture him hurling a sphere, probably about the size of a baseball. But if you read, Josh threw a ball for charity, you are more likely to imagine him sponsoring a dance. As in the case of the Necker Cube, we always get one coherent reading at a time, although it can easily change. Consider the following: Josh threw a ball for charity, but missed the clown's nose. This takes us back to the original version.

The general properties of neural computation described earlier largely determine the nature of our language and thought, but there is still a significant conceptual gap. Thought involves ideas, feelings, and reasoning, and language somehow links those ideas, feelings, and reasoning to perceived and spoken sounds (or signs in the case of signed languages). We know all of this must be accomplished by a physical brain in a physical body. The question is, how?

This is not the standard *where* question, asking which parts of the brain are used in thought and language. It is misleading to talk about a brain *area* computing some function—areas don't compute, neural circuits do. It is like saying that U.S. cars are made by Detroit. The Detroit area is certainly important in automobile manufacture, but all cars have parts made in many places and some American cars are assembled in other places. Current technology is only able to crudely localize brain function, but by putting together findings from different kinds of studies, we are able to address the central question of how the circuitry underlying thought and language can work.

A quarter of a century ago, it was unimaginable that such questions about the neural basis of language could be answered scientifically. Yet today, the basic components of an answer are in place.

The Embodied Mind

One simple insight has driven much of the scientific study of how the structure and function of the brain results in thought and language. Human language and thought are crucially shaped by the properties of our bodies and the structure of our physical and social environment. Language and thought are not best studied as formal mathematics and logic, but as adaptations that enable creatures like us to thrive in a wide range of situations. This is essentially the same as the *principle of continuity* of the American pragmatists, most notably William James and John Dewey. It is unquestioned in contemporary science, except in the case of language.

The embodied approach entails several crucial questions. How much, and in exactly what ways, are thought and language products of our bodies? How, exactly, does our embodied nature shape the way we think and communicate? Here are some of the findings discussed in the course of this book:

• Concrete words and concepts directly label our embodied experience. Think of such short words in English as *knee*, *kick*, *ask*, *red*, *want*, *sad*.
• Spatial relations, for example, concepts expressed by words such as *in*, *through*, *above*, and *around*, can be seen as derived from specialized circuitry in the visual system: topographic maps of the visual field, orientation-sensitive cells.
• What is technically called "aspect" in linguistics—the way we conceptualize the structure of events, reason about events, and express events in language—appears to stem from the neural structure of our system of motor control.
• Abstract thought grows out of concrete embodied experiences, typically sensory-motor experiences. Much of abstract thought makes use of reasoning based on the underlying embodied experience.

• Our systems of abstract and metaphorical thought and language arise from everyday experiences and a basic neural learning mechanism.
• Grammar consists of neural circuitry pairing embodied concepts with sound (or sign). Grammar is not a separate faculty, but depends on embodied conceptual and phonological systems.
• Children first learn grammar by pairing sound combinations with familiar experiences.

Thought and language are thus very strongly shaped by the nature of our bodies, our brains, and our experience functioning in the everyday world.

What this means is that any approach to an embodied theory of language requires mechanisms of neural computation used for other purposes and adapted to thought and language—detailed structures in the visual system, the motor system, and basic neural learning mechanisms. This has profound consequences:

• Thought (including abstract thought) and language make use of important brain structures found in other mammals. Most of the brain mechanisms used in thought and language are not unique to human beings.
• Thought and language are neural systems. They work by neural computation, not formal symbol manipulation. The differences between these modes of computation and why they matter are examined as we go along.
• Thought and language are not disembodied symbol systems that happen to be realized in the human brain through its computation properties. Instead, thought and language are inherently embodied. They reflect the structure of human bodies and have the inherent properties of neural systems as well as the external physical and social environment.

The consequences of these findings for philosophy, politics, mathematics, and linguistics have been described elsewhere and are reprised in chapter 27. This book focuses on the scientific foundations of neural computation and embodied language and their consequences for how we think about our societies and ourselves.

The Integrated, Multimodal Nature of Language

Because language is complex, linguists have traditionally broken its study artificially into "levels" or "modules" given names such as phonetics, phonology, morphology, syntax, the lexicon, semantics, discourse, and pragmatics. Most linguists specialize in the study of just one level or at the border between two adjacent subfields. Such focused studies have told us a great deal about language and are still the norm.

However, real language is embodied, integrated, and multimodal. When your doctor asks you to lift your leg, your understanding involves a rich interaction among many neural systems. There is systematic structure to how all these components fit together to constitute language. The rules or patterns of language are called *constructions*, and these integrate different facets of language—for example, phonology, pragmatics, semantics, and syntax. A request construction might specify a grammatical form, an intonation pattern, pragmatic constraints, and the intended meaning. When your doctor asks you to lift your leg, all of these features are involved.

This integrated, multifaceted nature of language is hard to express in traditional theories, which focus on the separate levels and sometimes view each level as autonomous. But constructions can provide a natural description of the links between form and meaning that characterize the neural circuitry underlying real human language. They offer a high-level computational description of a neural theory of language (NTL).

An NTL does more than just provide a neural implementation of standard theories of thought and language. Rather it permits a more accurate and full account of our thought and language and the way they fit together. In particular, it allows the embodied and neural character of thought and language to take center stage. The neural theory of language described in this book helps us characterize the integrated, embodied nature of language. The following two concrete examples illustrate what this means.

Spinning Your Wheels
Imagine yourself trying to teach the meaning and usage of a phrase like "spinning your wheels" to a friend who knows English but comes from a culture where the phrase isn't used. Let's begin with the simplest, literal meaning of this idiomatic expression. If your friend's culture did not have cars, the task would be enormous. You would first have to explain what an automobile is, how it works, and how a car's wheels might spin in mud, in sand, or on ice without the car moving. One would also have to explain

the typical effect of this on the driver, namely, frustration at not being able to get the car to move. All of this is part of a knowledge structure called a *frame* that systematically relates cars, wheels, motion, attitudes, and so on to the situations in which the wheels are spinning but the car doesn't move. The expression "spinning your wheels" *evokes* the entire conceptual framework, with all the appropriate knowledge and attitudes.

The phrase "spinning your wheels" can be used either literally or metaphorically. In many cases, "spin your wheels" works in a simple and literal manner. *If you're spinning your wheels, don't step on the gas* is an expression that is probably new to you, but you can interpret it easily because the sentence connects directly to your own frustrating experiences or those you've seen in movies. But variations that are superficially just as simple are not allowed with this idiom, for example, *He's spinning her wheels* is not acceptable, although it could make sense (he might be driving her car) and it does fit a pattern found in other English idioms, for example, *He fixed her wagon.*

Spinning your wheels makes use of ordinary grammatical constructions of English. It is a verb phrase; it has a verb (spinning) followed by a noun phrase (possessive pronoun + wheels). The verb has a normal suffix –*ing*. The phrase can be modified by some of the standard grammar rules of English—one can say, *We used to be spinning our wheels.*

Also, the idiom is defined in relation to a knowledge frame with an image. In the image, there is a car whose drive wheels are spinning. The car is not moving. The driver of the car is trying to get the car to move, is putting a lot of energy into it, and is frustrated that the car is stuck. The most salient part of the scene is the spinning of the wheels of the car. The noun "wheels" refers to the wheels of the car and the verb "spin" refers to what the wheels are doing in the scene. These words become anchor points in metaphorical uses of the phrase.

For example, there is a general conceptual metaphor in which "achieving a purpose" is conceptualized as "reaching a destination" with *progress experienced as moving closer to the destination.* Consider the example, *I'm spinning my wheels working at this job.* The general metaphor is that "A career is a journey and career advancement is forward motion. If *you're spinning your wheels,* you are not moving, not making progress toward life goals, even though you are putting effort into it. The sentence implies that you are not advancing in your career. You are putting a lot of effort into it, not getting anywhere, and feel frustrated. Here, the metaphor maps the knowledge about the stuck-car scene onto the situation in which there is no advancement in your career.

The phrase "spinning your wheels" (like hundreds, if not thousands, of other motivated idioms in English) illustrates the multimodal nature of language. As an idiom, it is like a word of English; you have to learn it, and what you know about it does not follow from general rules. The words involved in the idiom (*spin* and *wheels*) have images that fit the salient part of a cultural image (a car spinning its wheels) with knowledge about the image (no motion, desire for motion, lots of effort, frustration). And the common metaphorical meanings make use of maps from this frame-and-scene semantics to various abstract domains (purposeful actions, careers, love relationships).

To know how to use "spinning your wheels" correctly, you need to have integrated knowledge involving at least grammar (the constructions), lexicon (the words), semantics (identity of the subject and the pronoun), a cultural image and associated knowledge, and standard conceptual metaphors. There must be precise linkages across all these modalities: the *ing* has to fit on the same verb (*spin*) that (a) precedes the noun phrase in the verb phrase construction, (b) has an image that fits into the wheel-spinning-on-a-car image, (c) is part of the cultural knowledge associated with the image, which entails lack of motion. Also, the lack of motion can stand as the base of at least three different metaphors: lack of progress in an activity, lack of advancement in a career, and lack of development in a relationship. The remarkable fact is that these metaphors are *productive*— we can apply them in novel situations and will be understood. For example, you will be spinning your wheels if you try to understand this book without doing the mental exercises.

Waltzing into a Recession
The waltz is a dance to music with a 1-2-3, 1-2-3, . . . rhythm. The dance partners move in sweeping circular paths, concentrating attention primarily on each other (rather than on where they are going). Ideally, it is a dance one enjoys and is swept up in. "To waltz" is to perform such a dance. When you waltz, you move; and, since verbs of motion can take directional modifiers (e.g., *onto the terrace*), there are sentences like "Harry and Sadie waltzed onto the terrace."

Now imagine reading the following sentence in the news: "France waltzed into a recession." Sentences like this are very common in news stories (check it out), and this one is immediately understandable, even though its subject is not animate and the path (*into a recession*) is abstract and does not indicate a physical direction. The use of *waltz* in this sentence appears to violate the rules of English—waltzing is done only by people. Why is this acceptable?

The answer has to do with the complex interaction between grammar and metaphor. In understanding the example sentence, a number of common metaphors are being used.

• *Countries* are metaphorically conceptualized as *people*. Since a person can be the agent of *waltz*, so can a metaphorical person.

• *Change* is metaphorically conceptualized as *motion*, with economic change as a special case. *More* is metaphorically *up* and *less is down*. In economics, an *increase in gross domestic product* is conceptualized as an *upward motion*, whereas a *decrease* is a *downward motion*. *States of an economy* are conceptualized metaphorically as *locations*, that is, bounded regions in space. A *recession* is thus a metaphorical *hole*: it is an economic state seen as a region in which the economy of a country is pulled downward for a significant length of time. When a country is in such a metaphorical hole, it tries to *climb out of it, pull itself out of it,* or induce another party to *help it get out*.

• To understand this sentence, the brain must activate these existing metaphorical structures to form what is called a "conceptual blend," consisting of all the metaphors linked together.

• In this sentence, *France* is a metaphorical person and *into a recession* metaphorically indicates a direction toward a physical location. Thus, with these metaphors, *waltz* fits within its normal grammatical constraints on the kind of subjects and modifiers fit with it.

• The connotation of the sentence follows from how the metaphors apply to our knowledge of waltzing. These metaphors connote that France was enjoying itself, that it was not paying attention to where it was going economically and, as a result, fell into the recession/hole.

Grammar is the study of the principles by which elements fit together in sentences to produce certain meanings. Here, the grammar of the sentence—what elements can fit with the verb *waltz* to form the sentence—

depends on the complex of metaphors used to understand what is being talked about, which can be quite subtle. Another common metaphorical use of *waltz* implies an easy achievement, as in *Josh waltzed into the end zone*. We don't accept this reading for "France waltzed into a recession," because we don't believe that countries have a goal of getting into recessions.

In general, we see that understanding a sentence involves finding the *best match* between what was spoken and our current mental state. The brain is inherently a best-match computer; its massively parallel, interconnected structure allows it to combine many factors in understanding a sentence (or image, etc.) as we saw with figure 1.1. Finding the best match for language input includes evoking metaphors, as we have seen in several examples. More details on how this works are presented in chapter 16.

You can see the productive aspect of language at work by substituting different verbs of motion in the example sentence, for example, *France stumbled into a recession*; *France rushed into a recession*; and so on. With almost any verb of motion you get a somewhat different image of France's economic progress. Each of these imagined situations is predictable from the meaning of the embodied action and the metaphors involved. We can also immediately understand *France is spinning its wheels on unemployment*.

This is language understanding in real life and is what this book tries to explain. The scientific explanation of language begins with the brain and neural computation.

The Three-Part Bridge

The bridge between neural structure and meaningful language rests on three pillars:

Neural computation   Our present understanding of how the general theory of computation can be applied to the structure and development of the neural circuitry of the brain. This background provides an account of what it means for the brain to compute, and how that computation differs crucially from the operation of a standard digital computer.

The embodied nature of thought and language   Using neural computation to account for what has been discovered about how thought and language are embodied, as in the preceding examples.

The integrated organization of language Language is organized in terms of *constructions*, each of which integrates many aspects—meaning, context, affect, phonological form, and so on. Language learning and use revolve around our ability to flexibly combine these multifaceted constructions.

The role of this bridge, as with any scientific theory, is to provide adequate descriptions, explanations, and predictions about natural phenomena. The natural phenomena we are studying are thought and language. The scientific technique I use is computational modeling, in particular, modeling using neural computation. An *adequate* model must actually exhibit the required behavior and be consistent with existing data from neuroscience, cognitive and developmental psychology, and cognitive linguistics. This book is a first attempt to explore the power of this approach.

The goal is to outline the whole story of how the brain gives rise to thought and language—enough to allow further scientific work to proceed along these lines. Currently we have nothing close to a complete neural computational model of thought and language, but such a model is the ultimate goal of the approach taken here.

One of the hardest parts of our journey of discovery is understanding the vehicle that is carrying us—the information processing perspective. Any explanation of language and thought will obviously involve some kind of information processing story. The tricky bit is that we need to use one kind of information processing system, conventional computing theory and programs, to discuss and model a quite different kind of information processing system, the brain. The following two chapters attempt to spell out both the necessity of using an information processing perspective and the critical importance of keeping the discussion grounded in the reality of the brain and human experience.

The Information Processing Perspective

Neuroscientists speak of neurons as processing information and communicating by sending and receiving signals. They also talk of neurons as performing computations. In fact, *neural computation* has become the standard way of thinking about how the brain works. But neurons are just cells, tiny biological entities that are alive and function by means of chemistry. Why can we say that neurons process information and perform computations?

Since neural computation and the information processing perspective on the brain are central to a neural theory of language, it is important that I say, in as simple, clear, and straightforward terms as possible, just what I, and others who study the brain, mean by neural computation. We are interested in a complex cell, the neuron, but it is easier to start by understanding a much simpler cell—the amoeba—in information processing terms.

Amoebas as Information Processors

The amoeba, one of the simplest and best known of living things, is depicted in figure 2.1. Amoebas are one-celled animals, somewhat smaller than a period on this page, that have remained essentially unchanged in their billion-year existence. Various members of the amoeba family live in a variety of environments including fresh and salt water, and the digestive systems of people with amoebic dysentery. Though primitive (the whole animal is a single cell), they exhibit many of the vital behaviors of all animals. Much about the way our neurons function can be learned from considering amoebas. We look at some of the details of cell structure and function in the next chapter. For now, I just want to discuss what is

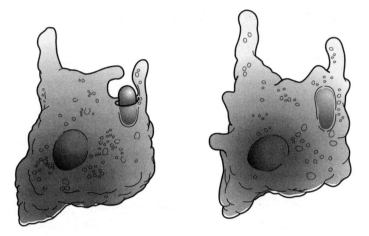

Figure 2.1
Drawings of an amoeba ingesting food.

involved in thinking about an amoeba from the information processing perspective.

Three Ways of Thinking about an Amoeba

A Chemical Factory
The amoeba is what it looks like—a tiny gelatinous blob of complex molecules. To even start talking about its behavior, we need a way to think about it—to conceptualize an amoeba in terms of something else we know how to think about. A simple and straightforward way to conceptualize the amoeba is from the chemical perspective, as a chemical plant—an organized system of about a million complex molecules. This view is required for many scientific purposes, but additional perspectives are needed for a full understanding.

A Creature with Needs, Desires, and Goals
The basic life problems of the amoeba are not very different from our own, as Antonio Damasio (Damasio 2003) states nicely:

All living organisms from the humble amoeba to the human are born with devices designed to solve *automatically*, no proper reasoning required, the basic problems of life. Those problems are: finding sources of energy; incorporating and transforming energy; maintaining a chemical balance of the interior compatible with the life process; maintaining the organism's structure by repairing its wear and tear; and fending off external agents of disease and physical injury.

The chemical perspective in itself doesn't help much when we are trying to understand the amoeba's behavior. A common way of modeling behavior is through a *personification* metaphor: try thinking of an amoeba as if it were a person with needs, desires, goals, and ways of satisfying them. Then think of yourself as that amoeba/person, and construct an imaginative simulation of what you would do if you were an amoeba with such needs, desires, and goals.

Imagine being a small aquatic blob, equipped with only crude feelers, trying to survive in a hostile environment. From such an *empathetic* perspective, one might say that the amoeba is trying to find food and avoid danger. It is hard to imagine really *being* an amoeba, because the amoeba has no coherent control. The membrane of the amoeba regularly pushes out in one direction or other. If the rest of the body flows behind, the whole amoeba moves—somewhat like the U.S. Congress.

To understand how the amoeba behaves, both the *chemical* and the *empathetic* perspectives are required at once. You need both the chemistry and the amoeba-as-person metaphor. Bringing such multiple perspectives to bear simultaneously is commonplace in science. Throughout this book, we use multiple perspectives. In what follows, we show how the *chemical* and *empathetic* perspectives work together to explain the amoeba's behavior. Words from the *empathetic* perspective (the amoeba-as-person metaphor) are indicated in italics.

It is no surprise that amoebas, like the rest of us animals, *need* to *eat*. But how does a one-celled animal know what to eat? If I were an amoeba, how would I *know* what to *eat*? Here is the answer from the chemical perspective: the amoeba's outer membrane contains complex molecules that react differently to different molecules in the environment. This general mechanism of chemical detectors in the cell membrane has evolved to play a central role in our immune and nervous systems.

For the amoeba, some membrane detectors match up well with amoeba-*food* (for example, bacteria). When the *food-detector* and amoeba-*food* molecules come together, the resulting chemical reaction leads to shape changes in the amoeba's membrane molecules, eventually resulting in the amoeba incorporating the potential *food*. Similarly, different membrane *detector* molecules react with amoeba-*hazard* molecules in the environment, causing reactions that retract amoeba tissue from the *threat*. That is about what we'd expect from a one-celled animal. The amoeba is a chemical system that reacts to chemicals that fit its irritant detectors differently from ones that activate its *food detectors*.

Although amoebas normally function as independent cells, certain species can (in times of famine) assemble themselves into a multicelled creature that can sense light and heat and that gives off amoeba spores, which can last indefinitely without food. The molecule that signals this need for community action, cAMP, is also a major messenger in our own cellular communication.

Here we have a reasonable, and comprehensible, account of amoeba behavior: from the amoeba-as-person perspective, we can conceptualize what the amoeba has to do. It *needs to eat* and *needs to avoid hazards* that *threaten it*. From a purely chemical perspective, of course, amoebas do not have needs, foods, avoidance behavior, or irritants. The chemical perspective allows for a description of how these life needs are satisfied.

The Information Processing Perspective

Now let's think about the amoeba from an information processing perspective. This is another generally useful way of talking about living things, and how they satisfy their needs and goals. It allows us to pose questions like the following:

• What information does the amoeba use to survive?
• How does it categorize the information inputs it gets, and how does it respond to each category?
• What is its reaction time?
• How does it know when to replicate by dividing?
• Can it remember and, if so, what is its memory capacity?
• Does it learn and, if so, how?
• Do amoebas communicate with one another?

As observers of amoebas, we may decide to ask such questions, and doing this requires an information processing perspective. From this perspective, the two types of chemical reactions (to food and to irritants) can be seen as enabling the amoeba to distinguish two kinds of inputs. In general, we always try to understand new things by relating them to familiar concepts.

The information processing stance is often useful because we have rich knowledge about computing, memory, and learning, and we can use this wisdom to help us understand what amoebas and other living things do.

An additional set of information processing questions concerns communication. Since amoebas do not reproduce sexually, they normally have nothing to communicate about, but other single-celled creatures, including yeast, do communicate using molecular signals.

Communication and Coordinated Evolution

Much smaller than an amoeba, a yeast cell makes its living by eating sugars (fermentation). The carbon dioxide released in this process is what makes bread rise and gives beer its carbonation. Yeast cells sometimes reproduce by division, as amoebas do. But they also can engage in sexual reproduction, and this requires communication among cells.

In general, communication between cells was a major evolutionary advance and a prerequisite for the appearance of multicelled creatures like ourselves. Individual cells, like the amoeba, survive by carefully controlling their internal chemistry and it goes against their nature to allow outside agitators. Of the 4 billion years since life began, about two-thirds was required to evolve the simplest multicellular organisms and their coordination mechanisms.

The basic mechanism of the communication is molecular matching. This is particularly simple in yeast, which release specific molecules (pheromones) from one cell that can interact with detecting molecules in the walls of other yeast cells (again as in figure 2.1). This can give rise to quite complex transformations in the receiving cell; dozens of steps of this chain are already known. As a result of pheromone recognition, a yeast cell can change its internal structure to reverse its gender so it can mate with the sending cell. This is an impressive sexual feat, even by California standards.

The emission and subsequent recognition of a signal molecule is the simplest form of communication among living things. The ability to recognize a molecular signal is a natural extension of specialized membrane molecules for detecting food and hazards, since it also involves molecular shape changes in the presence of interacting molecules.

But communication requires more than just having cells recognize things in their environment that are either good or bad for it. Communication occurs only when the sender and receiver agree on the nature of messages. This inherently requires coordinated evolution. The sex life of yeastkind depends on the coordinated evolution of at least three things:

1. a mechanism for releasing particular pheromone molecules when the cell's internal structure is in a mating state;
2. a detection mechanism tuned to just the right pheromone; and
3. a resulting action chain in the receiving cell.

If any of these is disrupted, communication and the resulting action will fail. There are, of course, also many other examples of coordinated evolution involving separate species, most famously among predators and prey. We are focusing here on explicit communication within a species. It is interesting to notice that even in this most rudimentary communication, the exact form of the message—the particular pheromone indicating readiness for reproduction—is fairly arbitrary. Other species evolved somewhat different pheromones, and it doesn't matter much which signal molecule is used as long as agreement regarding the message has coevolved. The much more elaborate mating signals of higher animals involve complex senses such as vision and hearing, but these intricate communication mechanisms must also be the products of coordinated evolution.

As in the case of the amoeba, we can often ignore consideration of the physical details and study communication from an information processing perspective, which specifies what counts as an input signal, output signal, recognition, reaction, memory, learning, communication, and so on. The information processing perspective is crucial in the next chapter as we look at yet another kind of cell: the neuron. As we will soon see, the idea of cells communicating information using small molecules as signals is also the necessary first step in making sense of neural computation.

But before we turn to *neural* information processing, we need to understand more about information processing in general and its use in computational modeling. Computer programs are the primary tools in formulating and testing theories of brain function and behavior.

Information Processing and Computers

This book is based on the idea that an appropriate information processing perspective allows us to understand the neural basis of language and thought. The amoeba and yeast examples illustrated information processing in a much simpler case than neural systems. One crucial point is that the information processing perspective is *always* metaphorically imposed—it is one way of understanding a complex system in terms of something completely well defined and very well understood. There is no abstract information in the neurons themselves; like amoebas, neurons are cells that work through chemistry.

An information processing metaphor creates an abstraction, in the sense that it abstracts away from—that is, ignores—any noninformational content of the physical system being studied, whether animate (like neurons) or electronic (like a computer). Any living system carries out specific physical processes in which distinctions are made toward satisfying needs and goals, and so it can be studied from the information processing perspective.

Information processing metaphors can be extremely powerful tools for understanding physical systems, particularly now that there are well-developed theories within computer science of how information is processed. The beauty of the information processing perspective is that it can be applied to any kind of system at all (e.g., an economic or social system, as well as a physical system), independently of how the information processing is actually carried out physically. A thermostat, an amoeba, a corporation, and the brain all can be analyzed using the same science.

However, we can't understand real animals or any other complex system using only the computational stance. Here is a simple example of the difference between the information processing abstraction and physical reality and how both are needed to understand what is going on. Take the telephone system. Ignore actual conversations for now and just think about how a connection is established when you place a call.

If you want to place a call, you have a wide range of choices. You can use phones connected by fixed wires, or cell phones, or combination systems like a cordless phone that sends radio signals to a fixed phone base. The most common methods use fixed wires to each phone and require us to enter the numbers either mechanically on a rotary phone or by pushing the buttons on a touch tone phone. But we can also enter the numbers by voice or through a computer system. Mobile phones communicate the numbers by local radio connections. An overseas call may go through many countries with different companies, different media, and different technologies.

These different physical systems work together because all of the technologies agree on an information processing abstraction—that a sequence of digits, however represented physically, specifies a purchase order for a telephone connection.

At one level, the telephone system depends on a shared information processing abstraction that works the same over all realizations. At another level, however, the physical details of how connections are made and messages transmitted become the central issue. It matters a lot to you whether the phone you are using is hard-wired or cellular; if it is hard-wired, you can't take it with you in your car or to annoy your fellow patrons at a local restaurant or on the train.

All of the science, engineering, manufacturing, and administrative effort in communication systems focuses on how the information processing abstraction is realized. There is currently an ongoing commercial and political battle of global proportions over the technical and economic details of how information is to be fed over high-speed links into your home. In short, a wide range of important questions cannot be addressed at all using an information processing abstraction alone. We will see that this is true of the human brain and mind. Nevertheless, the general idea of information processing is important and is best conveyed by looking at very simple abstract models.

Abstract Information Processing Models

The general idea of information processing goes back to long before computing machines existed. The word "computer" traditionally meant a person who performed computations. The word has, of course, come to refer to machines that perform computations. Much of the basic mathematical theory of information processing also came before electronic computers, but not by very much; it was developed in the 1930s and 1940s.

Information in the technical sense, and therefore information process-ing, is based on *detectable differences*. The amoeba is able to distinguish dif-ferent chemicals in its environment. The telephone system can distinguish one sequence of decimal digits from another. The core idea of information processing theory is a two-way (binary) distinction, universally written as 0 and 1. The distinction between the two symbols can be captured in a wide variety of physical systems, for example, holes in a punched card (a hole for 1, no hole for 0), magnetization of spots on a tape or disk (mag-netization for 1, none for 0), or dots and dashes in Morse code. An impor-tant fact is that, from the information processing perspective, this simple pair of symbols (0,1) is all we need to represent any message that can be written in any alphabet, however complex.

Any number written in decimal notation can be rewritten in binary nota-tion, using only 1s and 0s: $0 \rightarrow 0$, $1 \rightarrow 1$, $2 \rightarrow 10$, $3 \rightarrow 11$, $4 \rightarrow 100$, $5 \rightarrow 101$, and so on. Just as each number in the decimal system is the sum of digits times 10 to some power, each number in the binary system is the sum of digits times 2 to some power. For example

$$\text{Decimal } \mathbf{13} = \mathbf{1} * 10^1 + \mathbf{3} * 10^0 = \mathbf{1} * 10 + \mathbf{3} * 1 = 10 + 3 = 8 + 4 + 0 + 1$$
$$= \mathbf{1} * 8 + \mathbf{1} * 4 + \mathbf{0} * 2 + \mathbf{1} * 1 = \mathbf{1} * 2^3 + \mathbf{1} * 2^2 + \mathbf{0} * 2^1 + \mathbf{1} * 2^0$$
$$= \mathbf{1101} \text{ Binary}$$

It is equally easy to encode all the symbols on a keyboard as different binary sequences, and all computers do this. Thus, any manipulations that can be done with sequences of letters in an alphabet can be done equally well with the corresponding sequences of 1s and 0s by a real or abstract binary computer.

Within the information processing perspective, binary representations, being abstract, are *disembodied*. They are independent of any physical real-ization. Your telephone number is the same whether you are called from a wired phone or a cell phone, a rotary phone, a touch-tone phone, or a computer. But to understand how the phone system works, you need to know *how* the disembodied information is manifested in the type of phys-ical phone system you are using. Similarly, as we shall see, to understand how your brain works, the disembodied information processing perspec-tive is not enough. We need to know *how* that information is manifested in the physical brain. In short, we will need a way to map from an appro-priate information processing model to the relevant aspects of the brain.

Alan Turing, the British mathematician who developed the standard abstract model of computation, was keenly aware of the problem of embodiment, as we will see in later chapters. His abstract model of computation, now known as the Turing machine, has been used to develop some of our most profound insights into *disembodied* information processing. However, not all of his formalist successors have shared Turing's insight into the relationship between abstract computing and biological information processing. Part of the job of this book is to return to his insights about *embodied information processing* and to extend them.

Turing's idea for characterizing disembodied information processing was to define the simplest possible computing machine, in abstract mathematical terms, so that it would be easy to see what such machines could and could not do. One simplification he made was to use only two symbols, 0 and 1, as we just discussed. He also assumed that the abstract machine had as much storage as it would ever need, organized as a very long tape on which the 0 or 1 symbols could be read or written.

Turing assumed that the input and output of the machine also appear on this same memory tape, but it is simpler for us to assume there are separate tapes for input and output, as well as one for storage (or memory). For the machine to do something useful (like performing arithmetic computations), it needs some operations, but they can be surprisingly few. Turing assumed that the machine could read or write one symbol on each of the tapes (input, output, and memory) at a time (figure 2.2). For the machine to do anything at all, it needs the ability to move each tape in either direction, up or down, and that is almost all it needs. The one other requirement is the ability to have the machine's action depend on the symbol that it is reading. Called *conditional action*, this is essential for all information processing.

With this limited machinery, we can carry out a very broad class of computations. Let's start with an informal description of how a particular Turing machine might compute whether the number of consecutive zeros on its input tape was even or odd. Let's suppose that its input tape contained some string of zeros followed by a blank square marking the end of the sequence. We require that the machine should write a zero on its output tape if the string of zeros has even length and a 1 if the number of zeros in the input is odd. The following informal program will do the job:

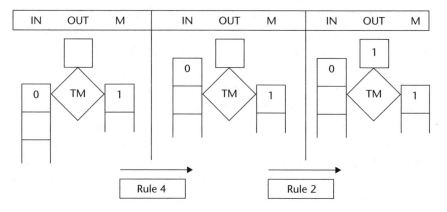

Figure 2.2
Operation of a Turing machine.

1. write the current memory tape position (*M*) to be 0;
2. if the current input tape position (*In*) is blank, then copy whatever symbol is in memory M onto the output tape and quit;
3. if the current input tape position *In* = 0, then flip *M* (that is, if *M* = 0 then change it to 1 and vice versa);
4. move the input tape upward so that the next square becomes the new *In*;
5. go back to line 2 and continue executing.

Let's first look at what this machine would do with a blank input tape. Following rule 1, it would first write a 0 on its memory tape, *M*, and then carry out rule 2. Since the input is blank, the machine will write the current memory value, which is 0, to the output tape and quit. This is just what we wanted; the machine correctly indicates that there was an even number of zeros on its input.

If the input tape had exactly one zero, the machine would again first set *M* to 0, obeying rule 1. The input is not blank, so the test in rule 2 is false. Let's follow the rest of the computation, using figure 2.2. Looking at rule 3, *In* does equal 0 and so the machine will flip *M*, writing a 1 there. This is shown on the left in the figure. Following rule 4, the machine then moves its input tape up, as depicted in the middle panel of the figure. Next, following rule 5, the machine loops back to rule 2. This time the input is blank so the machine copies *M* (which is now a 1) to the output tape and quits, as shown in the righthand panel of figure 2.2. This again produces the correct answer: there was an odd number of zeros (one of them) in the input and the output is 1, as required. You might want to check what happens if there are exactly two zeros on the input followed by the blank end marker.

A tiny example like this can convey much of the character of both information processing in general and the direct programming of electronic computers. The information processing perspective is appropriate for a device that has a purpose (internally driven for an animal or externally supplied for a machine) and a mechanism for carrying out that purpose. It would not make sense to interpret a cloud as an information processing system, although clouds can be thought of as having input (moisture), output (raindrops), storage (droplets), and processing (condensation of droplets to form raindrops). It is not the *purpose* of a cloud to produce raindrops. Clouds, like rocks, do not have purposes, although both do have *functions*.

The Turing machine model allows scientists to study information processing in the abstract, as operations on sequences of 0s and 1s. When we consider how a physical system (like an animal or robot) satisfies its needs and goals, performing some computations or other that get the job done isn't enough of an answer. Additional considerations are required, such as its *speed, storage capacity, reliability*, and its interaction with the physical world through *sensors* and *actuators*.

The use of a disembodied abstract information processing mechanism to model how a living thing satisfies its needs and goals requires, at the least, the following:

1. a conceptual model of the living system, that is, a model using familiar concepts;
2. an abstract information processing system; and
3. a precise mapping, preserving inferences, from the abstract information processing system to the conceptual model.

The mapping in item 3 allows one to make precise predictions about the system. It is through this mapping that one can think of the conceptual model as *an information processing model*. The mapping specifies precisely which aspects of the physical system being studied involve information processing. To the extent that the predictions hold, it makes scientific sense to say that the physical system is engaged in information processing.

Constructing such models is not easy. Writing programs that model the information processing aspects of a physical system is extremely demanding for any system of significant complexity. It is hard to be sure that a given complex program will always do what you want it to do. In fact, one of the main results of Turing's theory is that, in general, you can't prove that an arbitrary program does what it was designed for—or even that it will eventually stop.

The Program as Data—1s and 0s

As I mentioned earlier, the program itself can be written as a sequence of 1s and 0s. Here's how. Assume that the machine has an additional (fourth) tape for holding its instructions. Since the instructions are precise, formal rules, we can encode them compactly into symbols. For example, the first instruction above [Write the current memory tape position (M) to be 0] could be coded as: w M 0. Since any letter can be coded as a sequence of 1s and 0s, this instruction, and all other instructions, can be coded in binary notation as well. If the code for w was 1101101 and for M was 1010111, then the instruction would be the string for the instruction w M 0 would be 1101101 1010111 0, stored on the program tape.

The idea of programs being stored as data is quite beautiful and as important in practice as it is in theory. This means that, rather than designing a separate (Turing or electronic) machine for each purpose, we can construct a general-purpose machine that can read instructions from program memory and carry out the calculations they specify. Such a machine could be designed to first read a program from its input tape onto its program tape and then carry out the program on the remaining input. Called a Universal machine, this has played a large role in discussions about the nature of information processing in the brain as well as in computing theory and practice.

If a universal Turing machine had enough tape and time, it could do anything computable on any electronic machine, though it might take a huge number of computing steps—and a correspondingly very long time. This fact is sometimes taken to imply that all computing devices, including the brain, are essentially the same, so there is no reason to worry about the differences between electronic and biological information processing. This position, called *functionalism*, is discussed in the next chapter. But for animals who survive in the real world, the speed and flexibility of their computing mechanisms are crucial.

And the brain is not a universal computer. As wonderful as it is, the brain cannot do most of the computations that a universal computer could do. That is a good thing, since most of those computations are useless. The brain evolved to meet human needs using the bodies we have. The brain is a very special kind of information processing device. Its special properties determine the character of human thought and language, in ways that I talk about throughout this book. Nevertheless, universal digital computers play an important role in our story—they provide the conceptual basis and the modeling capability that allows us to *formulate and test theories* of how our brains do their information processing—the subject of the next chapter.

3 | Computational Models

Electronic digital computers have become an essential part of our civilization. The average person in an industrialized country will use computers many times each day—whether she is aware of it or not. A modern automobile, for example, has dozens of computers of differing size and complexity. The idea of a general-purpose computer has become the cornerstone of the information technology industry that is changing our world. The overwhelming bulk of the effort and cost of making modern computer chips is in their design and setting up the process for manufacturing and testing them. The incremental cost of making more chips of the same design and process is relatively small. What this means, in practice, is that it is usually much more expensive (in both effort and money) to use a custom-built chip than to program a more general one.

Our telephone example is typical. Until fairly recently, a phone call from Berkeley to Bombay required the commitment of dedicated switches and a hard-wired connection over the entire distance. All the switches and wires involved were reserved while you were connected, whether or not you were actually talking. At an intermediate stage, electronic computers replaced the switches linking the circuits. But with the information encoded as bits in computers, it is no longer necessary to reserve the circuit. Programs can break your message into digital packets and route them to their destination over a variety of (computer) pathways. This technology is so much more efficient that it, along with the demand for higher-speed connections, is leading a revolution in the telecommunications industry. Many other areas of life are also being transformed by the theory and practice of digital computation.

Simulation

Digital computers are, of course, used for a wide range of business, scientific, educational, and other applications. One task of particular interest to us is *simulation*. A computer simulation makes possible the study of a complex dynamic system by designing an information processing model of the system and running it as a program on a digital computer. This has been so successful in science that it has become the de facto third basic methodology of science, along with the traditional methodologies of theory and experiment. It is also a major component in the design of all complex physical systems. For example, the typical airplane or automobile is largely designed by simulation modeling on powerful computers. The current computer chips, with many millions of elements, could not be made at all without extensive simulations at many levels.

One computational simulation that is familiar to all of us is the weather map. The striking images of moving weather patterns we see on TV are the result of very complex computer simulations. Since the idea of simulation is central to this book, it is important to have some idea of how it works. We will take weather models as an example.

The basic idea behind a weather simulation is to model the behavior of the atmosphere over a selected region of the earth's surface. To do this, the atmosphere is modeled as if it were broken up into rectangular compartments or boxes. The size of each compartment is determined by the goals of the model and how much computing power is available. Since the simulation has to be fast enough to be useful, there is a tradeoff between the number of boxes and the speed of the computation. The simulation programs for various sizes of territory use different sized boxes. For example, current programs for the entire United States use boxes about a mile on a side.

The simulations start with an estimate of current conditions in the region of interest, including temperature, barometric pressure, humidity, cloud cover, wind speed and direction, and precipitation. One step of the simulation consists of using quite complex equations to predict the values for all the weather conditions a short time later (about a minute for local forecasts), taking into account the rotation of the earth and other factors. The results of each simulation step are used as input to the next step and can also be presented as a moving image for our viewing pleasure. The simplification that makes all this feasible is the assumption that conditions in any box at a given time are constant and depend only on the conditions in its directly neighboring boxes at the previous time step.

In the computational model, each box is represented by what we will call a *frame*—a structure consisting of a collection of parameters and their values. The parameters, for example, might be temperature, barometric pressure, humidity, degree of cloud cover, wind speed and direction, and precipitation over a previous length of time. The values of the parameters are numbers indicating measurements such as temperature and humidity. The compartments are quite large, and it is also not feasible to get accurate measurements of all the temperatures and other parameters that are needed. This helps explain why the predictions aren't always reliable.

Parameters and Simulations

In the weather case, we can clearly see an example of an interaction that will be of the utmost importance when we turn to computer simulations of neural systems: the interaction between *parameters* and simulations. The parameters and their values at a given time step are fixed. Initial values of parameters are data input to the dynamic simulation. That is, the simulation starts with specific values for the temperature, barometric pressure, humidity, and so on in each compartment. The rules of interaction between neighboring compartments are also fixed.

The simulation is carried out by a computer program. The program takes as input the fixed relations linking the compartments, together with the values for the parameters at the initial time step. The program computes predicted new values of the parameters for each compartment at the next time step. Then it takes the new values of the parameters as its new input to make the next prediction, and so on—until, as programmed, it displays the results we see on TV.

In a somewhat similar way, it is possible to simulate a neural network. The connections between neurons are specified, and each neural cell is represented by a collection of parameters at each time step. The parameters might include the values of inputs from other neurons, the multiplier effects of synapses, whether or not there is a spike, and the value of its intensity. The simulation program computes the values of the parameters at the next time step, as in the weather simulation. As we shall see, this neuron-by-neuron approach is powerful but is not feasible for modeling language understanding, which involves billions of neurons.

Evaluations of Simulation Models

It is easy to evaluate weather models, since they make predictions that can be readily checked. Evaluation is much more problematic for computational models in other domains. Such programs are used for many other simulations, including some that are largely replacing nuclear weapons tests. The advantages of such simulations are considerable, among them the fact that simulations do not poison the atmosphere as real tests do. The accuracy of those simulations has been questioned, however, leading to pressures from the military for real nuclear tests.

Cognitive scientists and neuroscientists also use computer simulations in their studies, at both the micro level of individual cells and the macro level of human behavior. Our little friends, the amoeba and yeast cells, have been the subject of various modeling studies. Here, even more than with weather models, there is a huge range of choices for the goals of a model. At one extreme, you could try to model the million-odd molecules in an amoeba and predict its behavior in detail. No one actually knows how to do this; we don't know enough about the molecules involved and couldn't simulate all their interactions if we did. At the other extreme, a model could study the behavior of colonies of amoebas and treat each individual as a unit described by a few parameters, as in the weather simulation. Intermediate models can be used to study the basic life processes of the amoeba at varying levels of detail. In the case of yeast, very large efforts has been made to model it in detail because, in important ways, it is like higher organisms (e.g., yeast can reproduce sexually).

Choosing what to model becomes enormously more complex when we try to use information processing models to understand the brain, which has billions of neurons, each rather more complex than an amoeba. Any direct modeling of neural circuits is complicated by the fact that a neuron can be affected by the thousands of other neurons that are connected to it. But models built at a coarser grain risk leaving out crucial details. A major purpose of the first section of this book is to establish a style of modeling *at the right level of detail* for studying thought and language. We suggest this is both feasible and informative, and such a modeling style reveals a great deal of crucial detail about how the brain is able to embody language and other mental functions.

Functionalism and the Chinese Room

No one believes that a computer simulation of a weather pattern is itself anything like the weather itself: the ever-changing clouds, the heat, the rain on your face, the oppressive humidity, and so on. The model is clearly distinct from the reality being modeled.

But when we use a computer program to simulate some function of the brain, we get into some delicate philosophical questions about exactly what is being done. One possibility is that, like the weather simulation, the computer is simply being used to carry out a formal, computational description of some process of the mind. The process is understood as being carried out by the physical brain, which is quite different from the program used to model it.

A second possibility, however, has become a major intellectual position within Anglo-American philosophy, generative linguistics, cognitive psychology, and artificial intelligence. This position is called *functionalism*. In its strong form, it claims that the way the mind is physically embodied in the brain is irrelevant to the study of mind. Functionalism as principle is the opposite of an embodiment theory, which suggests that everything important about language depends on the brain and body. There are also operational functionalists, such as Ray Jackendoff (Jackendoff 2003), who look forward to a neural theory but use functionalist models in their daily work. These researchers have contributed greatly to our understanding of language and thought. As we saw in the previous chapter, scientists always study nature using various perspectives, and a functional analysis is usually involved. Almost everyone (but see chapter 22) agrees that a functional level of description is needed for language and thought.

Philosophical *functionalism* holds that everything important about language and thought can be understood completely using information processing models, without looking at the brain at all. An even stronger position claims that any information processing system of sufficient complexity will automatically have all of the mental powers of the mind, including consciousness. This stance is also called strong artificial intelligence—there is *nothing* to the mind but abstract information processing.

It is important to distinguish the field of artificial intelligence (AI) in general from strong functionalist positions sometimes taken by some practitioners in that discipline. AI tends to be oriented to particular tasks. It asks what known computational techniques work best for performing that task, and it may seek to develop new techniques if that is necessary or interesting. AI in general does not try to model how human beings would carry out a task. There is, however, a subfield of AI called *cognitive modeling* that explicitly models human processing. By no means do all AI workers believe in strong AI—that they are creating fully conscious minds.

A famous case is the computer program Deep Blue, which in 1998 defeated the world chess champion. The Deep Blue program looks much more like our little Turing machine code in chapter 2 than the neural computation systems we describe later in this section. There is a wide range of such AI programs in use for solving complex planning and decision problems, transcribing speech, controlling robots, and so on. Engineers who build these AI systems consider animal brains one clue as to how to design them, but they feel free to use totally unbiological techniques when appropriate, as they should. There is no reason why a robot should not use wheels just because animals do not happen to have them.

The touchstone problem for functionalist claims has been understanding ordinary language by a computer. The standard test for machine understanding is called the Turing test, although the idea of using conversation to test another mind goes back at least to Descartes. Imagine that you are communicating in English with an unknown respondent by e-mail or some other written medium. If the other party were a computer program, how would you know? A program is said to pass the Turing test if you could not be sure whether or not it was a real person using only text interactions. Three related questions have been the subject of continuing heated debate:

1. Could a program pass the Turing test?
2. If it did pass, would it understand English?
3. Would it then have subjective experience (qualia)?

The first question is empirical, and there are continuing trials and contests on the Turing test; current programs can fool some of the people some of the time. The third question is the one that has most exercised philosophers—it is obviously related to the extreme functionalist and strong AI positions. For this book, the second question is the most important; if understanding can be disembodied, a major premise of the book is undermined—human language need not depend on its embodiment.

The philosopher John Searle proposed a thought experiment to test the idea of disembodied understanding of language, now famous as the Chinese Room, here is his description of it:

Suppose that I'm locked in a room and given a large batch of Chinese writing. Suppose furthermore (as is indeed the case) that I know no Chinese, either written or spoken, and that I'm not even confident that I could recognize Chinese writing as distinct from, say, Japanese writing or meaningless squiggles. To me, Chinese writing is just so many meaningless squiggles. Now suppose further that after this first batch of Chinese writing I am given a second batch of Chinese script together with a set of rules for correlating the second batch with the first batch. The rules are in English, and I understand these rules as well as any other native speaker of English. They enable me to correlate one set of formal symbols with another set of formal symbols, and all that "formal" means here is that I can identify the symbols entirely by their shapes.

Now suppose that I am given a third batch of Chinese symbols together with some instructions, again in English, that enable me to correlate elements of this third batch with the first two batches, and these rules instruct me how to give back certain sorts of Chinese symbols with certain sorts of shapes in response to certain sorts of shapes given me in the third batch. Unknown to me, the people who are giving me all these symbols call the first batch "a script," they call the second batch "a story," and they call the third batch "questions." Furthermore, they call the symbols I give back "answers to the questions," and the set of rules in English that they gave me they call "the program."

Suppose also that after a while I get so good at following the instructions for manipulating the Chinese symbols and the programmers get so good at writing the programs that from the external point of view that is, from the point of view of somebody outside the room in which I am locked, my answers to the questions are absolutely indistinguishable from those of Chinese speakers. Nobody just looking at my answers can tell that I don't speak a word of Chinese.

I produce the answers by manipulating uninterpreted formal symbols. As far as the Chinese is concerned, I simply behave like a computer; I perform computational operations on formally specified elements. For the purposes of Chinese, I am simply an instantiation of the computer program. (Searle 1980, p. 418)

Searle's point, of course, is that he might well be able to pass the Turing test in Chinese without understanding the language at all. This example has given rise to literally hundreds of papers and theses arguing almost every conceivable position. Most of the concern has been about question 3—is there some "system," maybe including Searle, the room, and the program, that has the full human experience in reading a Chinese story? We know that the brain is chemically linked to body states and that there is no scientific description of qualia, so no positive answer to question 3 is currently possible.

However, much more direct and behavioral tests are available for question 2—could the "system" fully understand Chinese? For one thing, no system that was cut off from the world could answer questions about anything that happened after the program was finished. Perhaps more strikingly, suppose the building that was housing the experiment caught fire and everyone needed to evacuate immediately. The person passing in the Chinese symbols could send this emergency message easily enough, but there would be no way for Searle to know it wasn't part of the experiment. He literally could not read Chinese to save his life. This seems to fail any test of what it means to understand language.

Let's look more closely at what is involved here—the fire example has nothing to do with subjective experience. It could well be that Searle's instruction book had some additional rules about emergencies, but these would need to be in a *language that he understood*. No symbol manipulation could link the Chinese characters to actions that Searle would need to take. So we have our answer to question 2—there are fundamental aspects of understanding that require embodiment. The example also doesn't depend on the emergency. If one Chinese input said: What color is this written in?, Searle or a program would be equally clueless on how to respond.

Notice that this also applies to a robot in the Chinese room—language understanding by a robot will require software relating to its body and its computational mechanisms. Modern functionalists include this kind of embodied connection to the world even when they deny the relevance of the brain. There is an active and productive effort on embodied AI, particularly in the group of Rod Brooks at MIT (Brooks 2003). Moving from an abstract to an embodied view of robot problem solving has yielded significant advances in pure and applied robotics. But our concern is with embodied language in *people* and for that we need both the functional information processing perspective and a fundamentally neural description of computation.

Neural Information Processing

The information processing stance is extremely common in the cognitive sciences and neuroscience, so much so that it rarely needs to be mentioned. It is simply implicit in much of the research done.

But there are many varieties of information processing, and a wide range of specific methodologies. When we get to problems as complex as modeling language, the details matter a great deal. Over the past two decades, computational neural modeling techniques have been developed through a large interdisciplinary effort involving biologists, psychologists, linguists, engineers, and mathematicians as well as computer scientists. These techniques have proven invaluable in helping to understand the neural basis of language and thought.

Neural information processing systems are sufficiently different from their electronic counterparts that it has proved necessary to develop special theories and simulation techniques for the neural case. As table 3.1 shows, neurons are a million times slower than electronic components. But each neuron is connected to thousands of others, most of which are active most of the time. In contrast, electronic computers are extremely fast, but have only local effects and only a tiny fraction of their elements are simultaneously active.

This difference in basic computational character has the most profound consequences for our project of modeling thought and language. Because the brain is richly connected and profusely activated, there is no such thing as an isolated or purely abstract thought. One idea automatically activates

Table 3.1
Some major differences between brains and digital computers

Brains	Computers
100,000,000,000 processing units	1–100 processing units
1000 operations/second	1,000,000,000 operations/second
Embodied	Abstract, disembodied
Fault tolerant	Frequently crashes
Graded, probabilistic signals	Binary, deterministic signals
Evolves and is self-organizing	Is explicitly designed
Learns	Is programmed

others. In addition, any input of language or perception is understood against a background of ongoing activity and is always contextual. This has long been understood informally and is central to modern psychological theories of memory and language processing, as we discuss in chapter 7. The main consequence of these findings will be that *mental structure parallels active neural structure*—connected concepts are neurally connected.

Another crucial property of our brain is its intimate link to our body. Digital computers are designed to compute general functions; brains evolved to control animal bodies. The link between sensation and action remains the dominant function of the human brain. Language and thought are refined means of connecting inputs to desired outputs and work through computational mechanisms based on the embodied brain.

Neural systems also differ from electronic systems (and the Turing machine) in that there is no separate program. Instructions as such do not exist, and control appears as patterns of activation in the network itself. This also has profound implications for learning. Neural systems appear to acquire knowledge in two ways, weight change (change at the synapses) and structural recruitment (the strengthening of a previously latent connection between active neural clusters), as will be discussed in chapter 9.

All neural learning is the result of activity in the network itself plus feedback about the quality of the result. It makes no biological sense to think of an omniscient rewiring mechanism that creates new connections in the brain. Connections may be strengthened or weakened, but the mechanisms for this must be local to the neurons involved, with some general feedback from the overall brain state on the effectiveness of their functioning.

Here is an additional important fact about neural computation and learning. Current evidence suggests there is *no erasing* in the adult brain. As we will see in Chapter 6, long term memory of facts, skills, or situations is captured by structural changes in the connections between neurons. There is no process for selectively reversing these changes. This is why it is so hard to alter your behavior patterns or to change the beliefs of others. The only known neural mechanisms for changing behavior involve inhibiting a pathway or bypassing it with a more active alternative.

This does not imply that repressed memories are always accurate. My memory of last week is spotty and research has shown that people misremember even important events like their wedding. Some neurons die naturally and trauma or disease can cause massive destruction. But the fact that there is no mechanism for selectively eliminating unwanted neural connections has a fundamental role in our mental life and institutions.

The combination of all these specifically neural computational features have given rise to repeated efforts over the last 60 years to develop a biologically plausible information-processing theory. The most recent efforts, dating from about 1980, have yielded a theory with profound scientific and applied ramifications.

In chapter 9, I describe in some detail these brainlike information-processing models, which form the technical underpinning for the rest of the book. But first we need to learn more about what is currently understood about the structure, development, and function of the brain. Starting from the common biochemistry of all living things, we will work from the bottom up, through individual neurons to large neural networks, and from there to the behavior of people. With this scientific background in place, we will be ready in chapter 9 to present the theory of neural computation, which combines the general idea of information processing with the known biological constraints. At that point, we will have the technical tools for neural and cognitive modeling to use in the remainder of the book.

II | **How the Brain Computes**

Simple animals like the amoeba must incorporate all life's functions within a single cell. We can choose to view such animals from the information-processing perspective and this is instructive, but limited. In higher animals, information processing is explicitly delegated to specialist cells— neurons.

Neurons, the heroes of this book, share many of the properties of their amoeboid ancestors. But rather than living independently like amoebas and other one-celled animals, neurons have evolved to function as part of a large, complex system of interacting cells. For comparison, the number of neurons in the human brain (estimated to be 10 to 100 billion) is of the same scale as the number of people on earth (6 billion). In the next section, we explore how these billions of neurons function together to constitute our brain, but first we should know more about them as individuals. We will start by looking in some detail at the lives of cells in general, continuing with the amoeba example from chapter 2.

Figure 2.1 depicted an amoeba in the process of enveloping some bit of organic matter. We saw earlier that the amoeba must recognize what it should ingest, but how does it do that? An amoeba can't see or think. It works by chemistry. Figure 4.1 is a general rendering of the outer wall of any animal cell, including a neuron or amoeba. The drawing shows a small piece of the wall of the cell in figure 2.1, magnified about a million times. Each blob in figure 4.1 represents a complex organic molecule. Zooming in another million times, we can look at the structure of one of these molecules, as stylized in figure 4.2. Even this is only an approximation, because each of the loops in the figure is made up of hundreds of individual atoms.

Returning to figure 4.1, we can see that a cell wall contains some very complex molecules, for example, the long one with the corkscrew piece

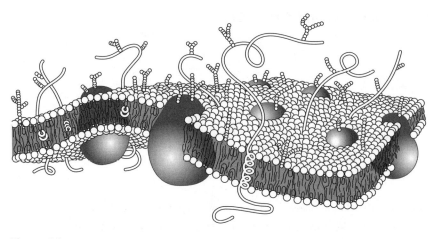

Figure 4.1
Drawing of a typical cell wall.

that protrudes through both the inside and the outside of the cell wall. Such specialized molecules are the sensors of a cell like the amoeba. They detect information about what is outside the cell and convey that information to the rest of the cell. A similar mechanism, with complex molecules extending through the cell wall, is the basis for much of the human immune system. To understand how these molecules detect information and convey it to the rest of the cell, we need to know a bit more about biochemical interactions.

Biochemistry, the study of chemical reactions in living things, is one of the most complicated and important fields of contemporary science. I won't say much about it in this book (and don't actually know that much), but even some simple general ideas can be of enormous value in understanding how neurons and other cells carry out their functions.

The central idea of biochemistry is structural matching. A complex protein molecule, like those depicted in figures 4.1 and 4.2, has an elaborate three-dimensional shape—like the most fantastic abstract sculpture. Various sections of one of these giant structures contain complex nooks and crannies into which pieces of other (large or small) molecules might fit. This is usually presented in biochemistry texts with a lock-and-key metaphor, but you can see that the structures involved are much more complex than any lock tumblers. The amoeba evolved to have membranes with this kind of protruding molecule that has segments (called binding

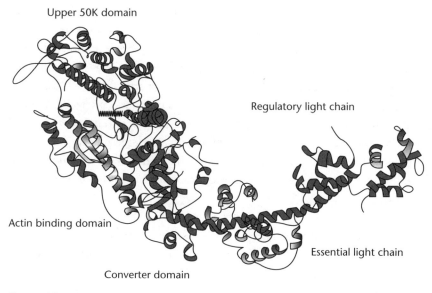

Upper 50K domain

Regulatory light chain

Actin binding domain

Essential light chain

Converter domain

Figure 4.2
Drawing of an actin molecule.

sites) that fit together with those of other organic substances that are particularly good or bad for amoebakind.

But molecular fitting is only the first part of the story. To understand the dynamic part of the binding process, the lock-and-key metaphor is too passive and must be abandoned. The large receptor molecules are not just inert matter; their shape and function results from the interplay between powerful basic forces of molecular attraction and repulsion. The key thing to envision is that, when two molecules do bind together, the balance of forces can change significantly—often leading to a major change in structure for the resulting combined molecule.

My best physical metaphor for this is to imagine elaborate abstract sculptures made of strong springs and magnets. Fitting two of these contraptions together could cause a total reconfiguration of shape and might even cause some pieces to break off and take on a new shape. This is what happens in molecular binding, but the forces involved are much stronger relative to the size of the molecules than could actually be built with magnets and springs. The changing shape of molecules is the basis for all animal action. Think of the forces exerted by leaping whales or frogs to get a feeling for the power involved. A frog can jump twenty times its length—equivalent to a 100-foot standing broad jump for a person.

The story so far makes it appear that interacting organic molecules just meet at random. This sometimes happens, but most of the mechanisms of cells are highly organized. There are specific subparts of the cell for carrying out various construction and reconstruction tasks as well as transportation networks, resembling microscopic railroads that allow material to move around the cell. Enzymes, which are also large protein molecules, bring specific molecules together in ways that can make their interactions a million times more efficient than they would be by just relying on chance collisions.

Most life processes, like the amoeba recognizing its food, happen repeatedly. They are iterative processes, with a sequence of states, returning to the initial state to begin the process again. This requires the coevolution of each complex chemical reaction together with a specific complementary chemical mechanism that restores the system to its previous state. All cells, including neurons, have elaborate mechanisms for controlling the many facets of their internal state.

Although it is not a direct part of our story, we should recall that all of these specialized protein molecules are specified in the genetic code and are constantly being generated in and around the cell nucleus. Particularly in one-celled animals such as the amoeba, the behavior of the creature depends largely on the shape and binding properties of the cell's protein molecules.

As a specific example, we can imagine that the long protein molecule protruding though the membrane in figure 4.1 evolved to signal the presence of a noxious substance to an amoeba. Following is one way this could be signaled. Suppose that when an offending substance becomes bound to some site on the sensor molecule outside the cell, the resulting forces cause the whole molecule to twist slightly. This could change the shape of the part of the molecule inside the cell wall. This shape change could, in turn, alter the binding properties of sites on the inside of the cell.

One common result of such an overall shape change is to cause a small molecule to split off from the inside portion of the sensor molecule to become a second messenger, delivering the news of the noxious substance to the inside of the cell. "Delivering the news" in chemical terms is again fitting—here the second messenger fits some other molecule, producing forces resulting in shape change, which in turn produces forces resulting in splitting off. Further processes of fitting, shape change, and splitting-off can constitute a chain of actions that leads to the nearby section of cell membrane retracting itself from the source of the irritation (that is, changing shape in just the right way), so that the amoeba is no longer in contact with the irritant.

Although it is a single cell, the amoeba can—from our metaphorical perspective—sense, categorize, and act. In higher animals like us, sensing is done by specialized cells, but the underlying mechanisms are similar. Our senses of taste and smell are based on chemical shape matching much like that of figure 4.1. Hearing, balance, and touch all depend on molecules that change shape under mechanical pressure, and vision makes use of molecules that are sensitive to light. Colors, which are an important part of the overall story in this book, rely on the fact that certain specialized pigment molecules change shape when exposed to particular wavelengths of light. Our retinas have three different types of receptor cells, each type sensitive to different wavelengths. All of these various sensor cells detect differences in essentially the same way—namely, via molecular shape change and the forces accompanying such change. This forms the common starting point—a sensory cell receiving a signal begins the processing of information.

In chapter 2, we looked at the life of the amoeba from a computational perspective, asking What information does the animal process as it goes through life? With our new understanding of molecular interactions, we can now look at the same information-processing functions from a biochemical perspective. It is completely appropriate to envision the amoeba as a complex chemical system and study the reactions in which it participates. However, because we are people, we cannot help but envision the life of an amoeba as a projection of our own desires and goals. So we, and even the most hard-nosed scientists, will also talk metaphorically about an amoeba "trying" to engulf food or to "avoid" a noxious substance.

Multiple Perspectives

A theory of how a cell functions—its needs and how it satisfies those needs—involves multiple perspectives. In thinking about the amoeba, we simultaneously envision (1) a chemical factory and (2) a small agent rather like ourselves with needs and ways of functioning to satisfy those needs.

The factory theory involves characterizing needs and their satisfaction in chemical terms.

Perspective 2 is an *embodied* perspective, based on our embodied experiences. Such experiences generate questions to be answered, and criteria for satisfactory answers to those questions. Not all questions we ask about ourselves make sense when speaking of an amoeba, but some important questions do—those that are about us as living beings functioning in an environment.

There is nothing unusual or exotic about maintaining several perspectives at the same time. Think of the many perspectives you have about your bicycle or car. Each is a mode of transportation, but also an investment, a source of pleasure, and possibly a status symbol. If it isn't functioning properly, you might start to think about the details of how it works or who could fix it for you.

The general ideas of multiple viewpoints and the embodied perspective lie at the core of much of science, yielding such questions as, "How can the immune system defend the body from attackers?" Not surprisingly, the theory of language in this book makes use of this common scientific practice. And as we shall see, the scientific practice of personalization itself arises from the standard way we conceptualize all abstract ideas—as mappings from our direct personal experience.

How Human Cells Sense and Signal

The same basic chemical mechanisms of structural matching and shape change underlie all the sensing, signaling, and motor actions in higher animals, including people. Before discussing neurons, we should look briefly at motor cells, which are of intermediate complexity. All animal motor activity, from our exquisitely articulate speech to the massive force of a whale flipping its tail, are based on one particular matching-and-shape-change system involving actin (figure 4.2) and myosin. The molecular binding of actin and myosin causes a shape change that, repeated across many molecules, causes muscle contraction. Since these actions repeat, each muscle cell needs to be restored to its relaxed state. This requires chemical energy, which is supplied by a particular small molecule, ATP. The energy is supplied when adenosine triphosphate (ATP) binds with a protein like actin and then changes to the related form, adenosine diphosphate (ADP). ADP is restored to ATP in a separate, evolutionarily ancient, cellular process. Our heroes, the neurons, will enter the scene as sources of the signals that start the whole process of muscle contraction.

The message telling a muscle cell to start contraction comes in chemical form. The walls of a muscle cell are also generally like those of the cell in figure 4.1 in that they have specialized molecules that can react to external chemicals and cause changes inside the cell. The signal from neuron to muscle cell is carried by a messenger—another small molecule, acetylcholine (ACh). Muscle cells have recognizer molecules (again as in figure 4.1) specialized for ACh. The match between ACh and a recognizer molecule opens a channel (cf. figure 4.4), which allows the chemical changes that cause the contraction. The transmission of signals from one neuron to another also employs ACh and other small specialized molecules, using similar mechanisms of recognition and subsequent action, as we will see in detail later in this chapter.

Signposts: From Neural Signals to Mind and Language

How signals are transmitted from neuron to neuron is a central part of our story. The macroscopic properties of mind and language arise, as we shall see, from the microscopic properties of neurons, and the mechanisms of neural signaling, neural adaptation, and neural growth. In the next three chapters, I describe these aspects of neural systems and how they help explain psychological findings on how we learn and process language.

The remainder of this chapter describes how neurons receive and transmit messages. In chapter 5, we examine some neural systems, including those for motor control and vision. Chapter 6 discusses how the magnificent apparatus of the brain is wired up during development and continues to adapt throughout life. With the basic biological background complete, we proceed in chapter 7 to the psychological level. This chapter focuses on psychology experiments that assess aspects of language behavior and how they fit the embodied perspective. It shows how our understanding of neural connectivity and signaling can apply at the macroscopic level, explaining a great deal about human linguistic and other behavior.

Chapter 8 abstracts even further, examining what has been observed about how children learn their first concepts and words. Finally, chapter

9 brings all of the background material together in a notation for computational modeling that will carry us through the rest of the book. In that chapter we develop enough background to talk concretely not only about what it means for the physical brain to compute, but also about how such embodied computation can give rise to ideas and language.

How Neurons Signal

In thinking about the signaling properties of neurons, the first thing to remember is that they are cells with all the life requirements of any other cell such as an amoeba. We see in chapter 6 that, as neurons grow and connect, they use essentially the same kind of chemical detection and reaction mechanisms described for the amoeba. All of the processes of making, transporting, and using proteins are essentially the same for neurons as they are for other cells. The basic requirements of life greatly constrain the signaling possibilities of neurons. Because of the chemical complexity, it takes about one-thousandth of a second for signal transmission between neurons—the circuits in a home computer are a million times faster.

Yet, nature has evolved beautiful mechanisms for transmitting signals fast enough, far enough, and extensively enough to support all we are and do. Transmission from neuron to neuron across synapses may be relatively slow, but evolution has outfitted us with neurons that convey signals quickly from our toes to the spinal cord: they are several feet long, although much narrower than an amoeba, and they provide quick transmission because, within a single neuron, there are no synaptic gaps to be crossed.

Despite slow transmission from neuron to neuron, the brain is more powerful than any electronic computer in important ways. This is because each neuron in the brain can receive signals from some 10,000 upstream neurons and has ways to combine their signals. Such massive connectivity, together with the ability to combine signals in a systematic fashion, compensates for slow transmission. This ability is what we mean when we speak of the information-processing capacity of neurons. These two functions—signal transmission and information combination—allow neurons to function as the physical basis for all of our thoughts and actions.

Let's look in more detail at how a neuron processes incoming information. Again, we employ three perspectives: the chemical perspective and the metaphorical view of a neuron as a worker doing its job as well as the

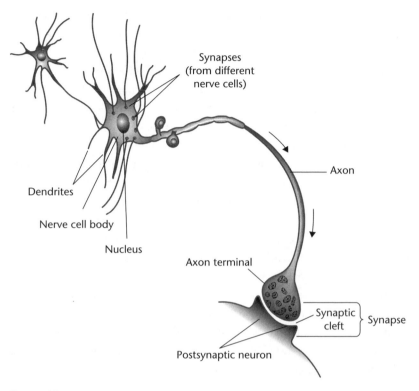

Figure 4.3
Drawing of a neuron and a synapse.

information processing perspective. Figure 4.3 depicts all the major players in neural computation. The centerpiece is one main neuron, shown with a connection from a smaller neuron at the upper left and several *synapses* onto its *dendrites* from other neurons, including the one at the upper left. The neuron's output is depicted as arrows along the axon, which is shown leading to a greatly exaggerated synapse on a downstream (postsynaptic) neuron. The two tiny cells just to the right of the cell body, near the beginning of the axon, provide the *myelin* insulation needed for rapid electrical signaling.

As in all cells, the neuron cell body contains a nucleus, which is involved in the manufacture of new molecules and vital life functions. From the information processing perspective, the dendrites are the input terminals and the axon is the single output cable of the neuron. The connections between pairs of neurons, *synapses*, are the crucial elements in memory and learning. I will describe all of these components and their interactions, starting with a detailed view of the synapse.

The lower right section of figure 4.3 depicts one synapse at a scale much larger than natural compared to the neuron. Each synapse links the output signal carried by the axon of an upstream neuron to a dendritic terminal of a downstream neuron. There is no physical contact; the small gap between the input and output connections is called the *synaptic cleft*. The chemical mechanism for signal transmission at a synapse is the movement of specialized molecules such as ACh across the synaptic cleft.

As in the case of molecular signals in yeast, the membrane of the post-synaptic neuron has specialized receptor molecules. Figure 4.4 is magnified 10 million times to depict two neural signal receptors in a typical neural synapse in an animal brain, showing its specialized receptors binding to a toxin, the leaflike structures at top left. The neuron's cell walls are basically like those shown in figure 4.1, with various detector molecules projecting from the inside to the outside of the cells. Like the amoeba's detector molecules, various receptor molecules of the neuron evolved to match the molecular structure of chemical signal molecules and change shape when reacting with them. Since this process is the key

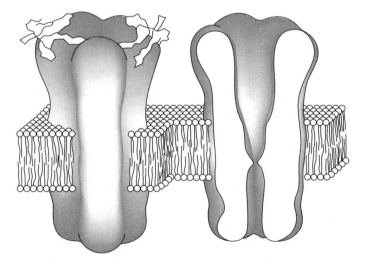

Figure 4.4
Drawing of a receptive channel, shown protruding through a cell wall. On the right, the channel is open, allowing neurotransmitters to enter the cell.

to both neural signaling and neural learning, we will look at it in more detail.

A crucial point to bear in mind is that neural signaling is all-or-none. Before turning to the chemistry of all-or-none signaling, let us think about this fact from the perspective of the neuron as an agent. We can think of the neuron as having the following job: to decide, about a hundred times per second, whether or not to send an output signal. Since this is a yes/no decision, the neuron can be seen as treating each of its (perhaps 10,000) inputs as voting for or against emitting a signal at this instant. Based on the perspective of the neuron as agent, these combined inputs are technically termed *excitatory* and *inhibitory* for positive and negative votes, respectively.

If that were all there was to it, the information processing would be easy: if the positive votes outnumber the negative votes by a big enough margin (called a *threshold*), then output a signal. But not all input votes get equal weight in this election; some count more than others. And, as in the United States, only a fraction of voters usually participates. There is also a time limit, so the neuron needs to compare the weighted sum of positive votes against the weighted negative votes arriving in an interval. If the positive total outweighs the negative total by a big enough margin, a signal is sent out.

Compelling evidence exists that learning depends on the change of synaptic weights; this modification is realized through several kinds of chemical changes involving protein synthesis at both the transmitting and receiving sides of the synapse. We look at this in more detail in chapter 6, which focuses on neural development and learning.

The voting metaphor uses arithmetic to model neural information processing. It is the arithmetic that really matters here, not the voting. We can see better what the arithmetic is modeling by looking at the electrical aspects of the neural signaling.

Molecules can be electrically neutral or have a positive (+) or negative (–) electrical charge. Ordinary batteries have separate electrically positive and negative sections. When a conducting path including, for example, the ignition system of your car or the chip circuitry in a calculator, connects these two sections, electrical current flows between them, providing power to make your car start or your calculator function. The transmission of a signal from one neuron to the next involves essentially the same electrical processes as a battery, but also some beautiful chemical interactions unique to neurons.

In a neuron, what we have called positive and negative votes are really ions—atoms with a positive or a negative charge. Positively charged ions function as votes for emitting a signal, while negatively charged ions are votes against. If the positively charged ions taken together outweigh the negatively charged ions by a sufficient amount, yielding a sufficiently large net positive charge, the neuron emits a signal that travels down its axon.

But it is not that simple. Positive ions are chemically distinct from negative ions. Each kind of signal has different *channels* embedded in the cell membrane and different signaling molecules that activate these channels. As we discussed, detector molecules in the neuron's wall react with signal molecules and change shape.

Rather than just releasing a single signal molecule inside the neuron, the neuron's detector molecule changes its shape to become a *channel*, through which many (either positive or negative) ions can flow. The opening of such a channel is depicted in figure 4.4. The positive ions involved are sodium and the negative ions are chloride, the two components of table salt (sodium chloride). The flow of ions into the cell depends on the shape of the channel molecule and also on a chemical imbalance between the inside and outside of the cell. If there are many more sodium ions outside the cell and an open channel that passes such ions, then a net flow of sodium ions to the inside will occur. Since these ions are positively charged, the overall charge of the neuron increases. We will return later to how the cell gets rid of the excess sodium and chloride ions so that the whole process can be repeated about a thousandth of a second (a millisecond) later.

We need one final chemical fact to complete the neural signaling story. The shape of some membrane molecules is affected by strong positive or negative electrical charges in their vicinity. This occurs because the electrical attraction between positive and negative ions continues when these ions become part of large molecules such as those in the walls of cells. Another evolutionary wonder is that some molecules in the cell walls change shape in just the right way when enough positive ions gather nearby inside the cell. This action is the chemical basis for the neuron's "decision" to send an output signal.

These special membrane molecules change shape to form additional channels allowing sodium ions to enter the cell, creating a positive feedback loop—more sodium ions lead to more open channels for sodium ions, and so on. This is where the all-or-none signaling mechanism of the neuron comes in. At a certain point, this process feeds on itself, producing the large electrical output signal known as a neural spike or *firing*.

The standard transmission of a neural signal down the axon to successor neurons is a slight variation on this sodium ion feedback loop. The output connection (axon) of the neuron (cf. figure 4.3) has the same charge-sensitive membrane molecules that led to the original firing. The molecules closest to the cell body are the first to feel the effects of all those positive sodium ions entering the cell, and themselves change shape to admit more sodium ions. This causes a shape change in the next set of molecules down the line, leading to more sodium coming through these channels, and so on. This chain reaction, like toppling dominoes, effectively sends a signal to downstream neurons.

This traveling wave mechanism of neural signaling is sufficient for short distances, but for longer signal paths, nature has also evolved a faster way to transmit signals relying on special insulating cells, called myelin glia. These grow around the axons of long-distance neurons, like the one shown in figure 4.3 or those connecting your knee to the spinal cord. The myelin allows for faster, purely electrical, signaling through the insulated sections of the axon. Every so often, the myelin insulation has a gap where sodium influx regenerates the spike.

The speed of these signals, like those of other computations by neurons, is measured in *milliseconds*, one-thousandths of a second. This transmission rate plays a central role in our reasoning about the neural basis of language. It takes about a millisecond for a neuron to decide whether or not to transmit a signal and also to reset itself for the next signal. There would be no evolutionary advantage to having one part of the process much faster than the other parts; all systems are limited by their slowest operation.

We can compare this with two other process speeds: the speed of human thought and the speed of digital computers. As I discuss in chapter 7, a wide range of experiments agree that people can react to stimuli in around 100 milliseconds, or a tenth of a second. This shows that the brain computes these reactions in no more than 100 neural time steps, telling us a great deal about what kind of computation is involved. In contrast, a standard digital computer carries out a basic operation in about a *nanosecond*, one-billionth of a second, which is a million times faster than the basic neural computation. Chapter 9 discusses in detail neural computation and its central role in explaining how the brain computes the mind.

Signals Across Synapses

The connection between the sending and the receiving neurons is not direct (they are, after all, separate cells that need their walls) and involves a narrow gap called a *synapse*, depicted nicely in figure 4.3. When I talked earlier about trillions of neural connections, I was referring to these synapses. One inherently slow step in neural systems involves the electrical signal in one neuron turning into a chemical signal that can interact with the channel molecules of the next neuron in a pathway.

Recall that the signal spreads down the axon of a signaling cell by a chain reaction of sodium channels opening, with positive sodium ions entering and building up an electrical change that then opens the adjacent channels. When this traveling electrical signal reaches the sending neuron's end of the synapse, it causes chemical changes that release small signal molecules called "transmitters" into the synapse, or gap (cf. figure 4.3). These chemical transmitters are released by means of a mechanism that is the reverse of the amoeba's enveloping of food; the transmitters are expelled from the cell through the membrane.

In the gap, these signal molecules move randomly, so it takes some time (again around a millisecond) before enough of them connect with receptor molecules of the receiving neuron to open the channels. This segment of the pathway is not inside any cell and is thus the most sensitive to chemical disruption. It will come as no surprise that most psychoactive drugs have their effects in the synaptic gap.

The recognition process on the receiving side of the synapse is described in figure 4.4, which depicts closed and open receptor channels. Several further important processes are involved, including the reuptake of transmitter molecules and additional signals that trigger learning by changing both the sending and the receiving sides of the synapse.

Another inherently slow part of neural signaling comes when the system resets the chemistry and membrane state between one signaling action and the next. All cells have mechanisms to maintain their chemical balance and the standard process of cell housekeeping suffices for the small amount of chloride and other bit players in neural firing. But the large flows of sodium ions require a special adaptation. In neural firing, sodium ions rush in quickly through open channels. The excess sodium then needs to be moved back out of the cell before the process can repeat. Evolution's solution to this problem is the "sodium pump." As you would guess from previous stories, sodium is removed by specialized molecules protruding through the cell wall, again as in figure 4.1. The pumping molecule has receptor sites for sodium on the section inside the cell. When these sites react with sodium ions, the pump molecule changes shape and orientation so that the sodium ions end up outside the cell, where they are released and wait around for a nearby channel to open.

The energy for all this action comes from the same workhorse ATP molecule that powers all such molecular magic. ATP is a small molecule that can be thought of as a tiny battery or coiled spring that is a floating source of energy for chemical reactions in the body. Many systems, including the sodium pump, have binding sites that ATP molecules fit into. When the bound ATP molecule changes to ADP, the energy released (like an uncoiling spring) can change the shape of the much larger host molecule. An important part of cell metabolism uses food energy to reset ADP to ATP for future use.

Where We Are in the Story

The neuron is a highly evolved cell of enormous beauty and complexity, but neurons do not work in isolation. In the next chapter, we explore how networks of interacting neurons enable the brain to carry out its functions.

But first, we should review where we are and how we got here. We have finished the third leg of a long journey to discover how the brain computes the mind. I began by laying out the problem and pointing to some commonplace properties of the mind and language that I hope to explain—the integrated, embodied, multimodal nature of language and thought. Chapters 2 and 3 introduced the computational stance, explained what is meant by an information processing model, and looked at animals and machines in terms of their information-processing behavior. It is hard to imagine any solution to our problem that is not computational in this general sense.

However, the general idea of computation is not enough; the properties of the mind depend fundamentally and in detail on the way the neural networks that are our brains carry out information processing. One important aspect of neural computation is that neurons, like all other cells, operate according to a few powerful principles of biochemistry—involving matching, shape change, and dissolution of specialized molecules. Within this general framework, this chapter showed how neurons compute whether to send a signal, and how such signals are propagated. The fact that the characteristic time scale for neural computation and signaling is about a millisecond remains a crucial point as we move on to consider networks of neurons, both small and large, in the next chapter.

Amazing as they are, neurons are useful only when they work together in networks or circuits. Although the neural circuits of the brain can be exceedingly complex, the basic ideas can be seen in even the simplest circuits, like the knee-jerk reflex shown in figure 5.1. The evolutionary function of the knee-jerk reflex is to allow rapid balance adjustments—to shift weight rapidly to the left leg when the right leg encounters difficulty. Figure 5.1 shows how this happens. The large oval on the top depicts the spinal cord, greatly magnified. Focusing on the right leg (on the left side of the figure), you can see two outgoing axon pathways, one (labeled –) that sends a negative signal to the extensor muscle on top of the right knee, and the other (labeled +) that sends a positive signal to the flexor muscle beneath the knee. The paired action of these two signals causes the right knee to bend inwards as the flexor is contracted and the extensor is loosened. If you like, you can recreate the story from previous chapters detailing how the neural signals are computed and transmitted, leading to muscle cell contraction through the actin–myacin mechanism. Our concern here is with the information processing aspects of this reflex and the more complicated circuits to come.

The important new information processing idea involves the long sensory axon pathway, shown on the far left. This leads back up from the knee to the control neurons in the spinal cord. When this pathway is activated (e.g., by tapping the right spot on the knee), a signal goes directly to the spinal cord, where it is shown connecting with four control neurons. Still focusing on the right leg, we see that the sensory signal connects, after one intermediate step, to the neurons that directly activate the appropriate leg muscles. This is the basic neural circuit for a *reflex*—a sensory neuron

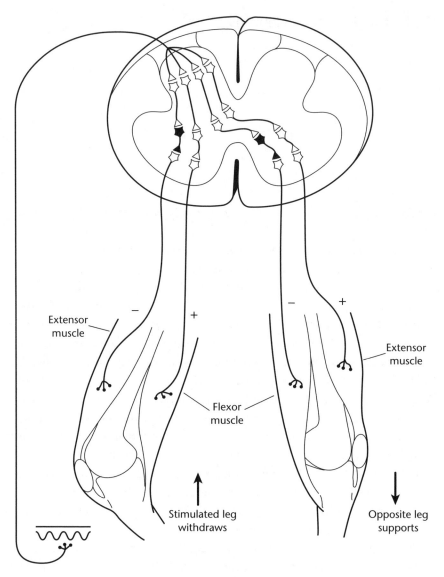

Figure 5.1
Drawing of the knee-jerk reflex.

connects quite directly to motor neurons. Obviously, this kind of circuit can be a lot faster than one that goes through the brain. But this link between sensing and action can't be modified by thought—it's just a reflex. This is our most important take-home lesson, but some of the details are also worth noting.

You will have noticed that the leftmost linking neuron is shown filled in black, as is another one in the circuit for the left leg. This is one way biologists depict *inhibitory* neurons, which send negative signals to their downstream neighbors, tending to reduce rather than increase their firing rate. Now we can see why the connection to the right extensor is labeled (−); the reflex reduces the amount of firing of that muscle. This hard-wired combination of tightening one muscle while relaxing its opposing muscle is a basic principle underlying all animal motor control.

We can see the same push-pull principle at work in the circuit for the left leg in figure 5.1. Here, the sensory signal from the right leg causes the simultaneous contraction (+) of the left extensor and relaxation (−) of the left flexor. The two muscles in each leg are coordinated and, in addition, the circuit coordinates the two legs, extending one leg while the other relaxes. Although this is not depicted in the figure, additional circuits modulate the knee-jerk reflex depending on what else your body is doing. The sharp tap by your doctor overrides the normal top-down brain control of your leg. This principle of layered or hierarchical control is universal in animals and is important for our discussion of embodied semantics theories, beginning in chapter 17.

The knee-jerk story is our first example of the link between sensation and action in people. This kind of direct neural connection is quite old in evolutionary time and not that different from the direct chemical link between sensation and action we saw in the amoeba. Reflex circuits like the knee-jerk appear in animals without brains. In people, these networks do not require signals to go up through the brain, which would slow everything down too much. So we now understand why we are not aware in advance of our reflex actions and cannot control them—they are hard-wired neural circuits. This also explains why your hand moves away from heat or pain before you are aware of the problem.

The Frog's Brain

Fixed reflex circuits, like the one shown in figure 5.1, are the most common kind of neural computing found in the nervous systems of many kinds of animal, including the frog. Some 4000 species of frog are found throughout the world, and they have adapted to a remarkable range of living conditions. They can be found just about anywhere there is fresh water, from the desert to the Arctic, on all continents except Antarctica. Though they thrive in warm, moist tropical climates, frogs also live in deserts and on high mountain slopes. The frogs that have been studied the most are the familiar ones from temperate climates that live in and out of water and catch their insect food with a long sticky tongue.

One of the original landmark papers in neural computation appeared in 1959 with the striking title, "What the Frog's Eye Tells the Frog's Brain." Its four authors included McCulloch and Pitts, who introduced the concept of abstract neurons in the early 1940s, and two biologists, Jerome Lettvin and Humberto Maturana, who we will meet again later in the book. They explored the frog's brain by using the standard technique of making thousands of measurements of individual neural responses (see chapter 4) to different visual images. The frog has direct neural connections from the retina to the brain, and it was generally believed that these connections just conveyed a copy of the image, like your TV cable.

Most of the frog's brain is organized in reflex circuits as in figure 5.1. A frog will normally snap at any small moving dark spot and jump away from any impending shadow. More interestingly, the frog's reflex circuitry for life-sustaining internal control of functions such as breathing and digestion is much the same as that found in all higher animals, including people. And frogs do have some ability to learn. As early as 1911, experiments showed frogs could learn that caterpillars were not edible and would then ignore them even when they moved.

Lettvin and colleagues (1959) discovered that the neurons of the frog's eye actually do quite a lot of computing, and this changed how scientists think about the brain. The results were that almost all the eye neurons signaled (were most active) when one of four particular visual conditions (*features*) occurred at a particular place in the visual environment. Some cells responded to local sharp edges and some to moving edges in the scene. A third kind of cell responded strongly to small dark convex moving objects and was most active when the objects moved irregularly. The authors were a bit cautious in calling these neurons "bug detectors," but later work confirmed that this was largely the case. The fourth kind of cell responded best when there was large local dimming, by either movement or overall darkening. Behavioral testing later showed that these cells indicated the possible presence of a predator and caused a reflex response of the frog jumping away.

Moving back from the details, it is worth considering why these findings had such a great impact. Lettvin and coworkers showed that extremely specific neural computations were being carried out in the frog's eye, and some of these calculations had immediate life consequences for the animal. These, and similar results by others, led to an explosion of interest in making detailed measurements of neural activity and in building theories of how these neural computations help explain the behavior of animals. It is obviously much more difficult to carry out this kind of neural modeling program for human language, but this is what I and other cognitive scientists are trying to do. It is also worth remembering that evolution builds on its past successes—much of the basic chemistry and many neural circuits from the frog continue to be recognizable in our own brains.

The wiring of the frog's brain also played a key role in my personal development. In the early 1970s, I was on a site review at the lab of Michael Arbib, one of the pioneers of neural modeling. Coming from a traditional computer science background, I kept wondering throughout the day of presentations how visual input got converted to symbols for reasoning in the frog's brain. I still remember my epiphany when it became clear that there was no symbolic form—the neural wiring directly connected perceptual categories to appropriate actions in physical space.

The Human Brain

Neurons are the heroes of this book, but it takes billions of them to achieve the miracle of the human mind. There are an estimated 10 billion to 100 billion neurons in the outer shell of the brain, where much of our higher mental functions are computed. This is the same magnitude as the number of people on earth (currently around 6 billion). It might be easier to think about billions of people working together than about a neural circuit of the same scale. So, to help us understand how the mind works, we will go through the mental exercise of trying to organize all of the people on the planet to work together as a simulation of the brain. This is the task that nature has solved in each of us. We will focus here on how the neural circuits could *function* and leave the next chapter to worry about how the wiring could be *laid down*.

To make our imaginary world/brain simulation more like a society of neurons, imagine that we are doing this around the year 1870—after the deployment of the telegraph but before telephones were invented in 1876. We can then imagine billions of people connected by telegraph lines that, like neurons, can transmit simple signals. The telegraph code is significantly richer because it allows both short signals (dots) and long ones (dashes) and so, as we saw in chapter 3, can encode any message at all. Neural signals, as described in chapter 4, all use the same signaling mechanism and this has important consequences for how the brain works. The information conveyed in a neural message is made up of just two components—the origin of the signal and its strength encoded as the number of spikes per second. Timing is also important; only neural signals that arrive at about the same time can be combined at the receiving end.

The hierarchical motor control circuits described earlier in this chapter could be organized fairly easily to be carried out by small groups of people—in fact, many business and government organizations work this way now—with e-mail playing the role of the limited information channel. We now know that specialized circuits in the brain coordinate complex motor activities, including learned ones. These specialized circuits are often modeled as computational *schemas*, and these will play an important part in our story, beginning with chapter 11.

Other mental functions, however, including vision, complex motor coordination, and language cannot be broken down into a hierarchy of simple tasks. Billions of neurons work together to achieve these functions.

To simulate this massively parallel computation, we need a division of labor, with various people/neurons specializing in different tasks. For concreteness, let's assign the people of China to model the visual system, with the coastal populations simulating the retina. It isn't hard to imagine each person on the coast looking out in a specific direction and sending telegraph messages about what he or she sees. However, it gets a lot harder when we try to decide how these millions of local sightings should be combined into an overall understanding of what is being seen. For example how would we determine what the overall weather pattern is along the coast? This simulation is designed to help us understand how the visual system is organized. More is known about vision than about any other brain function, so our modeling could get very specific.

As I discussed in chapter 4, people have specialized cells with pigment molecules that signal the color and amount of light falling on different parts of the eye. This information is combined and used in a wide variety of ways. One small circuit is a reflex, like the knee-jerk, that contracts the pupil when the light is too bright. But vision requires much more elaborate information processing, involving a number of computational ideas that we will need later. For example, one way the visual system avoids being flooded by data is by only transmitting *changes* in a scene. We have all experienced this phenomenon in hearing—a repetitive noise is disturbing for a while and then we stop noticing it.

The visual system has cells (as our simulation has people) that take signals from a collection of feature detectors and send an output if there is some pattern of interest. For example, a center-surround cell can signal when it sees a green center surrounded by red. A vertical-edge cell can signal when the detectors on its left report more brightness than those on its right. There are also intermediate cells that use memory to compare signals across time and report motion. All of these mechanisms are replicated millions of times and laid out in systematic maps in the brain—light at nearby points in space activates nearby neurons in the visual areas of the brain. This is just the kind of organization we would use to connect China as a vision machine. Systematic cortical maps have been created for vision, audition, and motor control, and these will feature prominently in our story.

Several more levels of visual processing are laid out as visual maps in the brain. Humans (unlike bats and owls, who have sonar) have no direct way to measure the distance to a remote object, but instead estimate distance using stereo vision from the two eyes and a score of other cues. Some brain areas specialize in distinguishing different textures and others respond best to complex patterns of motion. One remaining mystery (called the *binding problem*) is how we see the world as coherent scenes despite different brain areas computing color, motion, and other characteristics separately. From the information processing perspective, the best current hypothesis seems to be temporal and spatial synchronization: if units corresponding to the same area of the visual field are active at the same time, we perceive an integrated scene. We discuss temporal binding further in chapter 9.

The color system has played a particularly important role in the understanding of embodied language, and we will look at it a bit more closely. In addition to the general dim-light detectors (rods), the retina has three kinds of color-sensitive cells (cones), each with somewhat different pigment molecules that are most responsive to light in a particular range of wavelengths. Each of these pigment molecules changes shape when it is struck by the appropriate color of light, resulting in the emission of electrical signals. In the China metaphor, we could imagine teams of observers with three different colored filters on their telescopes. The color system has wiring that combines readings from several cones to register the hue of an external object and even compensates fairly well for different lighting conditions. For example, balanced activity of the "red" cones and "green" cones at a particular location will be seen as yellow. There are certain shades of red, blue, and so on that are particularly good at exciting human color cones, and these are easier to detect. As we will see in chapter 8, these optimal hues play an important role in the words for color in different languages. Discovering this link was a breakthrough in cognitive science in the 1960s. It was the first proof of the embodiment of word meaning, which is the foundation of any neural theory of language.

With all of this information about shape, motion, and color available, we can imagine wiring up some inland groups of people in China to detect various features of interest. Suppose that the design of the China–eye system used numerical signals corresponding to the differing strengths of neural connections. Each person in the system would then compute the weighted sum of all his or her incoming messages and could transmit an outgoing message as some higher or lower signal. For example, a person who had the job of detecting small blue things moving slowly north at one point in space might send a higher signal if inputs suggested strongly that this kind of target was present in his spot. Looking ahead to models of learning, every incoming signal could have a control so that each worker could learn which input signals were most reliable (led to good system results), and then increase the weight from those sources.

All this visual feature detection is fine, but the goal of perception is action—what is out there and what should I do about it? To continue with our China metaphor, we could have some region, say Tibet, specialized for recognizing faces and facial expressions. The workers of that area would receive inputs from earlier feature-detecting units and combine these to compute some face-specific features. Some small subset of these workers would have the job of recognizing, for example, that a particular face is being observed, that it is your boss, and that she is angry. The signal from these workers would presumably activate emotional and behavioral responses.

All living things need to classify their inputs and act on them as best they can. The *neural best-fit matching networks* of our brains are far from perfect; for example, we often initially mistake a stranger for someone we know. As we will see, the idea of making the best sense of complex input data is also important in understanding language processing. It is often useful to think of the brain as a system for finding solutions to complex computational problems involving many variables, which themselves are known only approximately. This kind of best-match computation is quite difficult and slow on electronic computers and hard to express in conventional programming languages, but it is essential in simulating theories that bridge brain and behavior. The *connectionist* computation models described in chapter 9 are a major advance in our ability to model the evidential and best-fit nature of neural systems.

To return to our world–brain metaphor, if some other place, say Kansas, were in charge of modeling the circuitry of the knee, the workers there would be connected as shown in figure 5.1. That is, each of the neurons in the figure could be modeled by one worker and each of the axons modeled by a telegraph wire.

But their work rules on combining input signals and emitting a higher or lower output signal would be identical to those of the Chinese vision workers. For those Kansans directly connected to simulated muscles, a high signal would indicate a strong contraction of the downstream muscle cell and a low signal would indicate relaxation.

We can see how the idea of neural computation allows scientists to make detailed models of brain operations. The crucial point is that such models are simple enough for people to understand and to simulate on computers, but they are sufficiently like neural functioning to yield scientific insights and possible clinical interventions.

Neuroscientists are making remarkable progress at working out the general architecture and quite a lot of the detailed circuitry of the human brain. Some of the most striking results come from studies of monkeys who, as our fellow primates, have quite similar brains. Many of these results come through recordings from individual neurons in the brains of awake, performing monkeys. Current experimental techniques allow this to be done in a relatively humane way, but it is not something that would or should be permissible on humans, except for specialized clinical purposes.

One of the most remarkable findings came about by accident in the lab of Giacomo Rizzolatti and his coworkers in Parma, Italy (Rizzolatti et al. 2001). They were recording from neurons in the frontal cortex of monkeys grasping various objects. One of the experimenters happened to pick up the target object while the recording was still in progress. To everyone's surprise, strong neural activity occurred in the supposedly *motor* neuron when the animal observed *someone else* grasping an object. These results have now been replicated many times and are quite robust and general.

So, some neurons are activated during both the execution of purposeful, goal-related hand actions, such as grasping, holding, or manipulating objects, and the observation of similar actions performed by another individual. These are called "mirror neurons." Mirror neurons do not fire when the monkey is just presented with an object that it can act on. Nor do they fire when the observed action is performed with a tool, such as pliers or pincers. Using similar techniques, physiologists have been able to work out quite a bit of the detailed circuitry that allows the monkey to recognize an object, decide what do with it, and carry out the appropriate movements.

While everyone agrees that monkeys' brains are quite like people's, there are clearly big differences, and it was not obvious that humans would have mirrorlike neural circuits that are active in both motor control and perception of the same operations. But the Parma group and others have provided convincing evidence, using some of the remarkable new methodologies now available, that we do indeed have multiple mirrorlike circuits (Buccino et al. 2001). The fact that specific human motor circuits are activated when we see or hear about the associated motions provides direct support for the NTL hypothesis that meaning is embodied.

Starting around 1980, a variety of new experimental techniques have greatly improved our ability to understand more about human brain structure and function. Figure 5.2 was made using a noninvasive technique called functional magnetic resonance imaging (fMRI). In general, MRI

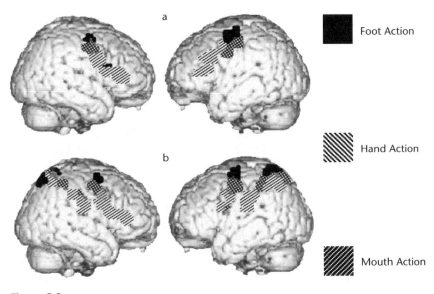

Foot Action

Hand Action

Mouth Action

Figure 5.2
Blood flow in brain while observing videos of actions. (*Source*: Buccino et al. *Eur J Neurosci*, 2001.)

techniques are based on the effects produced by molecules that are subject to a strong and rapidly changing magnetic field. Magnetically more susceptible molecules yield stronger effects and this, along with a prodigious amount of computing, enables the imaging of bodily structures. Functional imaging (fMRI) uses the magnetic properties of oxygen-carrying hemoglobin to compute brain areas that fire more strongly, and thus need more oxygen, during such neural activity as watching a video.

The top left image in figure 5.2 is the composite fMRI scan of the right side of the brain of a subject taken while he was *viewing* videos of human actions. The different areas represent regions of the brain that were most active during three different conditions. They are all in areas of the brain known to control *movement*, so this already confirms the general existence of mirrorlike neural systems in humans. The top right image depicts the left side of the same subject's brain while he was doing the task.

But there is much more. The motor cortex is well known to have somatotopic *maps* in which the circuits that control each particular body part are systematically distributed over the motor areas, like the visual maps in our China–brain model. Figure 5.2 shows that mirror activity also conforms to these maps. When the person viewed a video of someone biting, motor cortex parts normally used in mouth motions showed the greatest activation (in the lower parts of the brain, marked with a /// texture). Similarly, middle regions in the figure (marked with a \\\ texture) correspond to when the subject saw grasping (hand) actions. The higher brain regions that are marked in solid black were most activated when the subject saw kicking (foot) actions.

There is still more. Notice the different pattern of textured regions in the lower pair of the images; in particular, there are now two distinct bands of activity on each side of the brain. The videos used to generate the top pair of images all depicted actions *without a real object being acted on.* For the lower pair, subjects were shown videos where objects were being acted on: biting an apple, grasping a cup, or kicking a ball. This led to additional mirrorlike activation patterns in a distinct area of the brain. This area, which is further toward the back of the brain (the left in the lower left figure), is usually associated with vision and generally codes something about the position of objects in space. Again, the textured markings show the activation patterns are segregated along the lines of which effector is being used. When the video showed an object being kicked, the foot subarea (upper part, marked in solid black) of this brain region was most active. This is a remarkably detailed confirmation of the presence in humans of perception–action circuits like those mapped out in detail for monkeys.

Everyone involved in brain studies believes that something like this kind of information processing happens throughout the brain. But much less is known about language and other higher-level thinking than about the visual and motor control networks described here. We do know that there are parts of the brain where cells are active for specific objects or actions, indicating specialization. And we also know there are not enough neurons in the brain to provide a separate detector cell for any situation that we might encounter, so some more complex code must be used. We will return in chapter 9 to this question of how concepts are represented in our neural machinery. In the next chapter, we focus on another classic mystery that is rapidly being revealed—how the elaborate wiring of the brain is established during development and how it changes with experience.

Long before scientists mapped out the intricacies of the brain, people wondered how something as complex as the human mind could arise. This question has also been a core concern of philosophers over the ages. In keeping with their generally disputatious style, the question of the origins of mind was posed as a black/white controversy over whether the mind was shaped by inheritance (*nature*) or experience (*nurture*).

Developmental biologists and psychologists have learned an enormous amount about how people grow and learn. Just as you would expect, human development involves continuous and intricate interplay of genetic and environmental factors, and scientists in these fields have long abandoned the notion that there is an absolute answer to the nature/nurture question.

For reasons that will become clear later, however, controversy still rages among some linguists and philosophers over the extent to which language (which means grammar in this debate) is *innate*. We discuss this issue in detail in chapter 22, but some general ideas can be laid out in advance.

Two major scientific innovations of the last few years have led to a new view of the relationship between prior structure and experience. The traditional wisdom was that *development* should be associated with structural change—obviously in the body, but also in the brain and mind. *Learning*, on the other hand, was viewed as a gradual process of adding skills and knowledge. Development was associated with structural change, and learning was viewed as a cumulative process. These ideas are fine, but recent results show that we must also construe learning as structural change and development as a cumulative process. Here's why.

It is now clear that learning and permanent memory in animals comes about through the strengthening of neural connections (synapses). Some of the evidence for these facts are discussed in this chapter. When the strength of connections between neurons is modified, we have a fundamental structural change. The neural network is now different and will respond differently to new experience. That is, *learning does not add knowledge to an unchanging system—it changes the system.*

The other new findings come from the level of gene expression. Until fairly recently, scientists thought of the genetic code as a kind of template for making the proteins needed for various bodily functions. Newer findings show it is much more than that. In protein synthesis it matters not just which genes are involved, but also which are *expressed*, that is, actually used to make proteins. Every cell has the same genetic information; other factors determine exactly which proteins are synthesized. The modern view of this process is more like a computer program than a stencil. Often the role of one protein is to facilitate or block the expression of genetic material in the synthesis of some other proteins. Development, even at this most fundamental level, is thus also a cumulative process.

With these new scientific insights, there seems to be no principled reason to talk about separate notions of development (genetic, nature) and learning (experience, nurture). Both processes are cumulative, and both are realized by structural change. The commonality is particularly clear in cases of recovery from brain damage, which can involve both adaptation and new growth. This evolving new picture can be captured with the idea of a structure–experience–adaptation (SEA) cycle. At any time, a system (such as a person) has some structure. As experience is accumulated, this leads through adaptation to a modified system structure, and the cycle continues.

The structure of a system at any time determines what it *can* experience. If you don't know the language being spoken, you will miss a lot of a conversation. Given its current state and its (social and physical) environment, a system (e.g., a person) will have experiences, some self-initiated and others not. Some of these experiences will lead to structural changes.

The idea of *adaptation* entails some notion of improvement, for example, in enhanced survival. We are interested in the cases in which there is an idea of system performance and a way of evaluating whether a structural change is likely to lead to improved performance. It can be quite difficult for a system, at any level, to evaluate how to adapt to an experience, and I will discuss how the brain seems to do this. The criteria for what counts

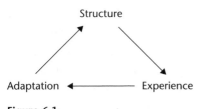

Figure 6.1
The SEA cycle.

as performance improvement might themselves be controversial, as in the case of political systems, but we won't concern ourselves with that until the end of the book.

The SEA cycle (figure 6.1) can be seen as a model of the development of systems over a wide range of time and complexity scales—from molecules to individuals to societies and species. It seems to help liberate our thinking from a variety of classical dilemmas, such as the nature–nurture controversy. However, anything so general must be used with caution. For example, the SEA cycle does not suggest that all adaptations are small and incremental. Some experiences are clearly life-changing while others are insignificant.

All of these general considerations on the relation of structure to learning will become important later in our discussion. For now, our focus is on understanding the basic processes of neural development.

Of course, human development begins with a single fertilized cell in the mother's womb. We will skip over the first 6 weeks of cell division and reorganization, except to note that, even at this stage, genetic and environmental influences interact—normal development requires an appropriate chemical environment in the womb. Our story picks up after the point of separation when the cells destined to be ancestors of neural tissue are segregated from those that will generate internal organs, muscle, skin, and other parts of an individual. The cells that will become our nervous system form a distinct neural "plate," which over time folds in on itself to become a neural tube running the length of the embryo, following a pattern that is basically the same for all neural animals. This is the general story, but what interests us is how the billions of individual neurons in the brain and nervous system become connected in a way that creates our mental life. This has been most thoroughly studied in the visual system.

As we saw in the last chapter, one striking property of the visual system is the large number of topographic maps in the brain, corresponding to various visual properties. At least a couple of dozen distinct visual areas with spatial structure are organized according to function. All of the sensory and motor areas of the brain have this kind of systematic map structure (c.f. figure 5.2). For example, the brain's representation of skin contact (touch) is laid out as a map of the body, with more sensitive areas represented by more neurons, and thus larger areas of the map. The auditory system has maps laid out according to tone qualities, and other factors. One question we are asking in this chapter is: How do all these intricate maps get wired as part of neural development?

Nature's solution to the initial wiring problem is quite elegant and harks back to simple one-celled animals like our old friend, the amoeba. Recall that an amoeba has a variety of complex sensing molecules penetrating its cell membrane. As part of its survival, an amoeba has chemical mechanisms that cause it to move its blobby body toward food and away from harmful substances. Neurons are also cells and, in early development, behave somewhat like an amoeba in approaching and avoiding various chemicals. But rather than the whole cell moving, neural growth involves the cell's connecting pathway (axon) reaching out toward its downstream partner neurons.

The basic layout of visual and other maps is established during development by billions of neurons each separately following a pattern of chemical markers to its predestined brain region and specific subareas within that region. For example, a retinal cell that responds best to red light in the upper left of the visual field will connect to cells in the brain that are tuned to the same properties and these cells, in turn, will link to other cells that use these particular properties. In the course of development, detector molecules in the growing neuron interact with guide molecules to route the connection to the right general destination, sometimes over long distances as in the connection from the spinal cord to the knee. This will get neural connections to the right general area, but aligning the millions of neurons in visual and other neural maps also involves continuous chemical *gradients*, again using mechanisms that are very old in evolutionary terms.

I have talked about amoebas and other cells approaching food and avoiding pollution. They can actually do a bit better by being sensitive to not only the presence of good and bad molecules, but also their concentration. It makes a lot of sense for an animal that evolved in water to have mechanisms for preferentially moving in the direction where the most food molecules are. This gradient-following behavior tends to bring the animal to ever richer pastures, by its standards.

For the task of wiring up visual maps, gradient following greatly simplifies nature's information processing requirements. The axon of a developing visual neuron will follow the gradient of a marker chemical related to its destination, analogous to the amoeba's moving in the direction of food. A neuron destined for the upper left section of the scene in a visual map will therefore follow two separate chemical gradients that mark areas corresponding to leftness and to higher elevation in the target map. When an axon tip gets to an appropriately marked destination cell, this contact starts a process that develops rudimentary synapses (discussed in chapter 4). Local competition among neural axons with similar marker profiles produces some further tuning at the destination. For example, each human muscle fiber ends up with exactly one incoming neural connection, and this greatly facilitates fine motor control.

With enough poetic license, we can think about the neural wiring problem in terms of the world-as-brain simulation from the previous chapter. Real neurons find their own connections, but we can imagine wiring crews trying to link up the right workers in, for example, the China simulation of the visual system. The analogy to the chemical target markers might be a latitude and longitude goal for each set of wire connections. The wiring crews would follow local or global directions, linking to houses in the right general area. We could model local competition as a limited number of connections per house. Later development and learning could be modeled as strengthening some connections and abandoning others.

It would be amazing if this kind of chemical scramble could produce the exact wiring needed for all of our elaborate perception, thinking, and acting. In fact, the initial wiring is only approximate and leaves each neuronal axon connected to several places in the neighborhood of each of its eventual partner neurons. A second, *activity-dependent* mechanism is required to complete the development process. We know that babies become physically very active in the womb in the late prenatal period, but it has only recently become clear how crucial this activity is to neural development. Moreover, of course, humans develop tremendously after birth, and some people continue to learn even in adulthood.

The growth processes that follow chemical gradients to produce our initial neural wiring do remarkably well, but not nearly well enough. What is needed for survival are circuits with highly tuned and coordinated activity for carrying out our perceptions, actions, and thoughts. The initial chemical wiring actually produces many more connections and somewhat more neurons than are present in adult brains. The detailed tuning of neural connections is done by eliminating the extra links as well as strengthening functional synapses. This has been known for decades.

What is new is the realization of how important *activity* is in the prenatal process of tuning neural connections. Although the details are far from complete, the general idea is clear and eminently logical. Development must result in coordinated networks for vital functions. The knee-reflex circuit of chapter 5 would be a simple example of such a circuit. Assuming that the initial wiring was successful and the proper connections are in place, it is just a question of eliminating the useless ones. This is done by strengthening connections that work well together and weakening the others. The same basic mechanisms underlie adult learning and will be an important part of our account.

But in the womb, what provides the feedback to establish which are the right neural circuits to strengthen? This problem doesn't seem to be too difficult for motor circuits—the feedback and control networks for basic physical actions can be refined as the infant moves its limbs and, indeed, this is what happens. However, there is no vision in the womb. Recent research shows that systematic moving patterns of activity are spontaneously generated prenatally in the retina. A predictable test pattern, changing systematically over time, provides excellent training data for tuning the connections between visual maps (Stellwagen & Schatz 2002).

The prenatal development of the auditory system is also interesting and is directly relevant to embodied language. Research indicates that infants, immediately after birth, preferentially recognize the sounds of their native language over others. The assumption is that activity-dependent tuning mechanisms, similar to those for vision and motor control, work with speech signals perceived in the womb.

The prenatal tuning of neural connections using simulated activity can work quite well; a newborn colt or calf is essentially functional at birth. This is necessary because the herd is always on the move. But many animals, including people, do much of their development after birth, and activity-dependent mechanisms can exploit experience in the real world beyond the womb. In fact, such experience is absolutely necessary for normal development. Early experiments with kittens showed that there are fairly short critical periods during which animals deprived of visual input could forever lose their ability to see motion, vertical lines, and so on. For a similar reason, if a human child has one weak eye, the doctor will sometimes place a patch over the stronger one, forcing the weaker eye to gain experience.

Both growth and death of neural connections occur after birth, and current theory suggests no absolute demarcation between neural development and adult learning. The number of human synapses reaches its peak at around year 3 and the adult count is roughly the same as at birth. Recent discoveries suggest that some new neurons are even generated during human adulthood, reversing a longstanding belief to the contrary.

One more wrinkle to the basic neural wiring story becomes important in recovery from injury. I depicted the tuning competition as eliminating the less valuable connections, and this is largely accurate. But there is also a mechanism whereby functioning neural connections actively inhibit rival connections without destroying them physically. If an injury causes the original winner neuron to die, understudy neurons with connections are "released from inhibition" and can help restore lost function. As best we can tell, the processes of recovery from neural insult follow the same basic patterns as the original wiring and tuning mechanisms.

I have suggested that some elements of language learning begin in the womb, where newborns are more sensitive to the sounds of their mother's language. Although children don't say their first words until they are about a year old, our embodied perspective suggests that the development and learning in the first year is essential for language acquisition. I will have a lot more to say about language learning later. For now, I close this chapter with a brief discussion of the biology of adult learning realized as changes in the strength of neural connections. The emerging understanding of neural learning is important for the models we will use in later chapters.

Learning and Memory

We usually think of *memory* as what we have learned. This is fine for memory of facts or episodes, but we also learn *skills* and this kind of learning turns out to be quite different. Certain brain injuries involving the hippocampal region of the brain render their victims incapable of learning any new facts, situations, or faces. Nevertheless, these people can still learn new skills, including relatively abstract skills such as solving puzzles. One famous example involves a patient who became very good at the Towers puzzle, which requires you to move a stack of rings of decreasing size from one peg to another, using one intermediate peg and never placing a larger ring on a smaller one. On each trial, the patient thought the puzzle was new and was surprised that he knew how to solve it. This, and other evidence, strongly suggests that skill learning differs from learning about new situations and facts.

Another important difference between skill and fact learning is the number of lessons needed. You can learn a new fact, such as "George Lakoff was born in Bayonne, New Jersey," from one instance, if it is interesting or important to you. Learning a new skill, such as pronunciation in a new language, requires extensive practice, even with expert tutelage. The biological basis for learning is one of the hottest topics in contemporary science and, while much remains to be discovered, a number of the basic mechanisms are now known, and this can help us understand how language and other skills are learned.

Short-term memory is known to have a different biological basis from long-term memory of either facts or skills. To illustrate this: at the end of this very sentence, close your eyes and see how much of the exact wording you can remember. After you come back to the text, try it again and compare how well you recall the first sentence. We now know that this kind of short-term memory depends on ongoing electrical activity in the brain. You can keep something in mind by rehearsing it, but this interferes with your thinking about anything else. Should you try to recall the first sentence of this chapter, you would probably come up with nothing at all, despite the manifest brilliance of the prose.

Nevertheless, we do recall memories from decades past. These long-term memories are known to be based on structural changes in the synaptic connections between neurons. Such permanent changes require constructing new protein molecules and establishing them in the membranes of the synapses connecting neurons, and this can take several hours. Thus, there is a huge time gap between short-term memory that lasts for only a few seconds and long-term memory that takes hours to build. In addition to bridging the time gap, the brain needs mechanisms for converting the content of a memory from electrical to structural form.

This so-called mystery of intermediate memory is not completely solved, but some of the key bridging steps have been discovered recently. To understand them, we hark back to the story of neural transmission and signaling from chapter 4. Recall that a key step in neural communication was the movement of small transmitter molecules across the narrow synaptic gap between communicating neurons. We saw that there are receptor molecules (see figure 4.4) in the cell wall on the receiving side of the synaptic gap, and these receptors change shape when a transmitter molecule arrives. The main result of this shape change is the opening of a channel allowing charged molecules to rush into the cell and, if there is enough net positive activation, cause the receiving cell to fire as well, sending a signal to its downstream neighbors. This is the basic picture, but a lot more is happening, some of it crucial for neural learning. In addition to the small neural signaling molecules, a number of other molecules pass in both directions between the sending and receiving neurons at the synapse, and additional molecules enter the cells from the surrounding environment.

The key idea underlying theories of neural learning goes back to the Canadian psychologist Donald Hebb, who formulated Hebb's rule around 1950. From an information processing perspective, the goal of the system is to increase the strength of the effective neural connections. Hebb proposed, and recent research has confirmed, that this can be achieved by means of a simple rule: each time a particular synaptic connection is active, see if the receiving cell also becomes active. If it does, the connection contributed to the success (firing) of the receiving cell and should be strengthened; if the receiving cell was not active in this time period, our synapse was bucking the trend and should be weakened.

Elegant chemical processes realize Hebbian learning within two distinct time scales, providing the temporal and structural bridge from short-term electrical memory, through intermediate memory, to long-term structural memory. In addition to the synaptic sodium and chloride channels responsible for neural signaling, there are also calcium-based channels that facilitate learning. As Hebb suggested, when a receiving neuron fires, chemical changes take place at each synapse that was active shortly before the great event. These changes *potentiate* (make more potent) each of the winning synapses for an intermediate period, lasting from hours to days. Repetition of a pattern of successful firing also triggers additional intra-cellular changes that lead, in time, to an increased number of receptor channels associated with successful synapses—the requisite structural change for long-term memory. Related processes weaken synapses and also strengthen *pairs* of synapses that are active at about the same time.

This sequence of events is now accepted as the general solution to the problems of the temporal and structural gaps between short- and long-term memory. However, what is stored as memory of *situations*, like your grad-uation or your last lunch? The hippocampal area is known to play a central role in forming and possibly retrieving memories of past situations. The intermediate-term potentiation of synapses is quite pronounced in this brain region, forming the basis for the standard theory of situational memory, which has considerable experimental support.

Think about an old situation that you still remember well. Your memory will include multiple modalities—vision, emotion, sound, smell, and others. The standard theory is that memories in each particular modality activate much of the brain circuitry that was involved in the original expe-rience. It is generally agreed that the hippocampal area contains circuitry that can bind the various aspects of an important experience into a coher-ent memory. This process is believed to involve the calcium-based poten-tiation we just discussed.

The retrieval of long-term situational memory (Nadel et al. 2000) remains controversial. One theory suggests that the hippocampal area retains its binding function throughout life. The other theory is that the neural connections binding experiences into a long-term memory trace are transferred to the cortical areas involved, freeing the hippocampal neurons to form new memories. In either case, permanent weight changes are needed to consolidate a memory. There is general agreement and consid-erable evidence that dreaming is important in consolidating memory and involves simulating experiences.

Let's look at Hebbian learning from the perspective of a person working as a unit in the world–brain simulation from the previous chapter. The worker would like to turn up the strength of his most important incoming signals, if he could figure out how to do this. The Hebbian learning rule tells him how to do it. Each time you send out a strong signal, increase the strength of all of your inputs that were recently strong, and thus contributed to your own strong output. You could also decrease the strength of any inputs that were not active when your output was strong. This "rich get richer" learning rule will eventually lead to some inputs dominating the process. This is essentially the same mechanism we discussed as the key to the fine-tuning role in neural development. This idea of strengthening connections that are correlated with subsequent action is very natural and consistent with the general idea of reinforcing successful behavior.

The activity-dependent tuning of the developing nervous system, as well as postnatal learning and development, do well by following such a rule. Unsurprisingly, many computational systems for engineering tasks incorporate versions of Hebb's rule. However, there is an important caveat, and you may have already spotted it. What happens if a particular neural circuit fires, but the result is very bad for the animal, like eating something sickening? A pure invocation of Hebb's rule would strengthen all participating connections, which can't be good. On the other hand, just weakening all the active connections involved isn't correct. Much of the neural activity was just recognizing the situation; we would like to change only those connections that led to the wrong decision.

No one knows how to specify a learning rule that will change exactly the offending connections when an error occurs. Computer systems, and presumably nature as well, rely on statistical learning rules that tend to make the right changes over time. You might learn that you were allergic to walnuts by noticing over time that you broke out whenever you ate something containing them. Neural computation learning rules use essentially the same principle, and we learn more about this in chapter 9.

Given that some form of Hebb's rule would be a good thing, what do we know about how it is realized in the brain? Two problems need to be addressed. First the system must figure out which connections to strengthen. It also must bridge the time interval between electrical short-term memory and the structural changes required for long-term memory. Notice first that changing connection strengths every few seconds wouldn't work well, even if it were physically possible. It makes information processing sense to make structural changes only when a connection has often proven reliable. Recent discoveries suggest at least part of how all this happens, as follows.

Another result of coordinated activity at a synapse is to take in molecules that signal the receiving cell to manufacture additional receptor molecules. Similarly, the sending side of the synapse absorbs molecules that signal the upstream cell to provide more transmitter molecules for this synapse. Both local and global reinforcement signals (different molecules) also convey information on the success or failure of recent activity.

Of course, all these processes are much more complicated than I have suggested here, and many gaps in our knowledge persist. But for our purposes, the important lesson is that neural learning is moving from a mystery to standard science. Certainly, we know enough about the details of neural adaptation to shape theories of how our brains learn skills, including language, and how we acquire and use knowledge. Contemporary theories of learning are also heavily influenced by *psychological* findings, some of which are described in the next chapter.

III How the Mind Computes

Up to this point, we have been studying the mind by looking at its neural and chemical structure, and have said very little about language or any other behavior. Historically, psychologists were studying and modeling human behavior long before anyone understood much about the underlying neural structures. Any plausible model of language learning and use must agree with established psychological and psycholinguistic data as well as what is known from neurobiology.

As an introductory exercise to behavioral studies, please name (preferably aloud) the font type (bold, italic, caps, or lower) for each word in the first column of table 7.1, followed by the font type for the words of the second column. You may have noticed that it was rather harder to pronounce the font type in the second column, because the printed name conflicts with the actual font type. This is the famous Stroop effect, named for James Stroop who discovered it in 1935, using color words printed in different colors. Such experiments have taught us a great deal about human language and thought. One immediate lesson of the effect is that the brain does not separate words into form and meaning. The Stroop effect is so reliable that it is now a major tool in investigating which brain regions are most active in resolving conflicting information.

A vast array of demonstrations of the subliminal effects of language on action and vice versa now exist. One of the most striking examples comes from the lab of psychologist John Bargh (Bargh et al. 1996). They reported an experiment that cleverly primed participants with the idea of being elderly. They did this by having the participants convert word jumbles into sentences. Several of the trials had words associated with the elderly, such as *old*, *retired*, and *wrinkle*. When they were finished, the participants were informed that the experiment was over and they could leave. However, the

Table 7.1
Font type words in different fonts

lower	**lower**
italic	ITALIC
CAPS	caps
lower	LOWER
bold	*bold*
italic	**italic**
CAPS	*caps*

real data collection had only just begun. As the participants left the lab, a collaborator in the hallway recorded the time it took each person to walk from the lab to the elevator. Participants who had been given the words related to old age walked significantly slower than participants who had done a version of the word jumble task that did not prime the elderly stereotype. This result sounds unlikely, but the finding has since been replicated by a number of labs. Thus, it appears that unconsciously activating a concept may influence motor processes (e.g., walking) related to that concept.

In a striking demonstration of the effect of motor actions on language understanding, John Cacioppo had subjects evaluate abstract ideographs while using their hands and forearms to pull something toward themselves or push it away (Cacioppo et al. 1993). The pulling-toward-the-self motion was hypothesized to activate a concept of acceptance and the pushing-away motion to prime a concept of avoidance or rejection. When the participants were asked to rate the ideographs on a likeability scale, the images that had been viewed during a pulling motion received significantly more favorable ratings than those that had been viewed during a pushing motion. Any theory or model of embodied language understanding will need to be consistent with these and related behavioral results from psychologists such as Arthur Glenberg and Brian MacWhinney.

There are also a number of techniques for directly measuring the effects of language on thought. Much of the recent work depends on delicate timing experiments, often also involving recording eye movements. One kind of psychological experiment that is especially important for language understanding involves measuring human reaction times in different circumstances. Figure 7.1 depicts a typical experimental setup from the 1970s, when this work was started (Tanenhaus et al. 1979). A subject sits in front

Figure 7.1
Setup for a priming experiment. (Source: Tanenhaus, M., et al. *Journal of Verbal Learning and Verbal Behaviour* 18:427–440, 1979)

of a display on which English words and nonsense words appear briefly. The subject is asked to press one key if the flashed image is an English word and a different key if it is not—and to do this as rapidly and accurately as possible. Psychologists (and we) are interested in both the amount of time required to carry out this task and variations in time and accuracy under different conditions.

Let's first look at how long it takes, on average, to do one of these perception-reaction tasks (this can be important in driving safety). How fast can you engage the brakes after seeing an obstacle in your path? It takes about half a second. You can compute how far your car will go while you are reacting and how much further it goes after the brakes are engaged—together the total distance traveled. At 60 mph in good road conditions, the car will go about 150 feet before stopping.

This kind of calculation can help us understand some basic facts about how the brain computes. We saw in chapter 3 that the time for each of the basic processes in neural firing and signaling is about one-thousandth of a second, or one millisecond. Let's compare this with the average human reaction time of half a second, 500 milliseconds. We first observe that the speed of human response rules out any possibility that the basic operations of thought are carried out by hormones or some other non-neural mechanisms—all of these are thousands of times too slow. The reaction time includes the time for the image information to get from the eyes back to the brain and the time for the motor signals to reach the muscles and contract them. This doesn't leave very much time for the brain to do whatever processing is needed to decide which button to push or whether to slam on the brakes.

If we think of each neural action as one computing step, then our brain is able to compute the correct reaction in around 100 steps. By way of contrast, computer programs (which aren't nearly as accurate in this kind of task anyway) take many millions of time steps to recognize an image. This discrepancy is one of the main factors leading computer scientists to conclude that neural computation is radically different from ordinary computing. The resulting research into how the brain computes is the keystone of the bridge between brain and mind, and is discussed in chapter 9.

While the general human reaction time is around 500 milliseconds, the exact time for a given task depends on many factors and psychologists exploit this fact to study various properties of the mind. The particular experiment depicted in figure 7.1 concerns the effects of the subject *hearing* various words at about the same time she is trying to decide whether or not a flashed letter sequence (e.g., flower) is a word of English. The experiment measured the time required to respond and the number of errors made.

Earlier work had shown that you could both improve the speed and reduce the probability of error in such a visual reaction task by having the subject hear the target word around the time the image was flashed. This is a special case of the general phenomenon of *priming*, in which some previous experience can change the way we react to a visual or other input. You know this from everyday life. When you are planning to buy a car, you are much more likely to notice similar cars, without consciously setting out to do so. Various priming experiments have contributed greatly to what we know about language and the mind.

Knowing that hearing a target word shortly before it is shown improves performance, scientists tested whether this priming effect would also work for words that were related to the unknown target word in sound or meaning. For example, would hearing the word "rose" make one recognize faster that "flower" is an English word? The answer is, this kind of semantic priming effect does, indeed, work—the average time for recognition is a few percentage points faster when primed by a semantically related word. Psychologists specialize in ensuring that these kinds of experiments are reliable, and semantic priming has been replicated hundreds of times. The priming effect is essentially the same as our common experience that one word will often make us think of semantically related words. But the particular experiment illustrated in figure 7.1 went further, yielding results that were both surprising and very revealing about how words and concepts are represented in the brain.

In this landmark experiment, Tannenhaus and others used recorded speech cues that were complete English sentences, like "They all rose," as a possible prime for "flower." The point is that in this sentence, the word "rose" denotes an action, *getting up*, that has no close link at all to the target word "flower." Try to guess whether this made determining whether the flashed letter sequence "flower" was an English word faster, slower, or had no effect.

The answer depends on the relative timing of the speech and visual inputs. If the misleading sentence was timed so that the word "rose" appeared at the same time as the flash, it did make recognition of "flower" a bit faster, so there was a priming effect even when the prime only sounded like a word related to the target. The standard explanation of this result is shown pictorially in figure 7.2. The boxes in the figure all depict concepts in the mind and the lines represent various connections between concepts. Psychologists building such models do not postulate specific neural structures in these diagrams; the links model activation effects the scientists see in their experiments. But these effects occur too fast to be mediated by some complex extra processing and must be directly realized by neural circuits.

The bottom box in figure 7.2 depicts the sound of a spoken word, "rose," in a phonetic alphabet. We know that the auditory system computes something roughly equivalent to this as one instance of the brain's general

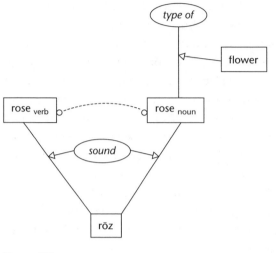

Figure 7.2
Priming model.

best-fit pattern matching. A crucial assumption is that the mental code for the sound, "roz," is mentally connected to both the noun (a flower) and the verb (the past tense of *rise*) that share that sound. The notation used to show connections with small triangles doesn't matter here, but will become important in later chapters.

The standard story in psychology is that a given sound, like "roz," is linked to all words with that sound; when the sound is recognized, it activates all of these words at once. In this case, activating the bottom node in figure 7.2 leads to activation of both the noun and verb meanings of "rose." When the noun rose is activated, the activation can spread (through the semantic link in the upper right of figure 7.2) to the node representing "flower." If the target string that the subject is trying to label as a word happens to be "flower," the extra activation from below constitutes priming and results in faster recognition.

The psychological literature is filled with discussions of priming, spreading activation, and related ideas. There is usually no specification of how mental connections and spreading mental activation map to neural connections and neural firing. Bridging this gap is an important goal of this book that I will return to shortly.

However, we will first consider another finding from the experiment of figure 7.1. We have seen that priming, even with the wrong meaning, can have a positive effect if the prime coincides with the display of the target string. However, if a verbal cue with the wrong meaning precedes the target by some 200 milliseconds, it can actually make the reaction time slower than if a totally unrelated word is used. To understand how this can happen, we go back to figure 7.2 and look at the dotted link connecting the two rival meanings of "rose." The circular tips on that link indicate negative connections, following the general convention in biology, cognitive science, and neural computation. As the notation suggests, the two rival meanings of a word are connected in such a way that increasing the activation of one decreases the activation of the other. This idea of mutual inhibition is very common in neural systems and is widely used in models such as those I will discuss later. If we assume that the words are linked in this way, then the negative effect of a false prime can be explained nicely. As the correct (verb) meaning of "rose" becomes more active, the noun meaning is reduced in activation, making recognition of the semantically related word "flower" harder.

A wide range of psychological findings can be explained using models that have mechanisms no more complicated than those in figure 7.2, although the full models can get intricate. The general idea of mental concept nodes that are connected by positively and negatively weighted links and have varying degrees of activation has proved to be very powerful in cognitive science. The graded activity of neurons and the way they combine multiple weighted inputs can be approximated, at the computational level, by probability theory. Later I will discuss how probabilistic and other abstract models of neural computation apply in a broad range of applied and scientific studies. For example, such models are widely used to describe how people normally produce speech and how various stress conditions lead to characteristic speech errors. Such spreading activation theories of mental function also provide the basis for linking brain to mind.

The core idea is remarkably simple—*mental connections are active neural connections*. There is every reason to believe that ideas, concepts, and the like are represented by neural activity. The exact circuitry involved is uncertain, but it suffices for us to assume that some stable connection pattern is associated with each word, concept, schema, and so on. I will often use a shorthand notation in which individual nodes in a connection diagram are labeled with names of concepts and so forth. This is not intended to suggest that there is a single dedicated neuron for each concept; that is impossible for reasons I explain in chapter 9. However, the notation is intended to imply that specific connection patterns are associated with particular mental constructions, as a wide range of experiments show.

The priming effects of neural activation can be deep and subtle. You may have noticed a tendency in writing to reuse exactly the same word several times, even though it is not good style. The obvious explanation for this is that the neural circuitry for a recently used word is active and thus tends to win the competition with other terms conveying the same notion. A similar unconscious priming effect can be shown in the choice of grammatical form used to express ideas.

English, like other languages, has several ways of expressing the same thought. For example, you can say either

(a) John gave the book to Mary.

(b) John gave Mary the book.

Different syntactic forms sometimes convey subtle differences, but often it is just a question of style. Some recent psychological experiments have shown that activation priming can affect the choice of style without the speaker being at all aware of it (F. Chang et al. 2000).

In these experiments, a subject is asked to describe what is happening in a cartoonlike drawing of a simple scene. For our two example sentences, the scene could be a male figure handing a book to a female figure. The goal of the experiment is to test the effects of the subject's recent experience on choosing either form (a) or form (b) to describe the scene. Before he or she is asked to describe the scenes, the subject is presented with some example scenes along with descriptions. If the training examples were presented in form (a), the subject also tended to use this form. Similarly, a subject instructed with examples of form (b) tended to give descriptions in that form.

Psychologists explain the results of these experiments in terms of spreading activation. As in the previous examples, residual activation in the circuits for one grammatical form gives that form competitive advantage in structuring the output sentence. Many other examples of subtle psychological effects are best explained as results of neural activation and there is now general agreement that specific neural activation patterns characterize each of our myriad mental processes.

No one has established experimentally how words and concepts are represented by neural structure and activity, and this is a lively domain of modeling and theorizing. You may have heard theories that suggest all of our concepts are completely distributed like a hologram over large sections of the brain. Such systems of representation have interesting mathematical properties and they are useful in applied computing, but we know our brains are not organized this way. Existing studies have eliminated the two extreme possibilities: either that each concept is concentrated in a single neuron or that all concepts are spread over the same neurons. But, there are still many theories of the neural representation of knowledge. Fortunately for us, all of the realistic possibilities are consistent with the relatively general requirements of a neural theory of language.

Sufficient progress has been made in the relevant areas of biology, psychology, and linguistics for scientists to formulate and test specific hypotheses involving neural theories of language. One recent example involves the mirror circuitry described in figure 5.2, which showed the activation of various brain areas while subjects were viewing simplified action videos. Recall that the evidence from this figure suggests that *viewing* an action, such as kicking, leads to increased brain response in related *motor control* areas. Would these same motor control areas be activated by *reading* or *hearing* about functions such as kicking? Some experiments aimed at resolving this question are using fMRI imaging as well as behavioral measures.

These behavioral experiments use differences in reaction time, but rely on *interference* rather than priming (Bergen et al. 2003). The basic task is very simple—the subject is shown a cartoon drawing followed by a single word and asked to indicate whether or not the word is a good caption for the drawing. Please look at the three labels in figure 7.3 and see if any one of them seems a bit harder to decide than the other two. Not everyone notices the difference, but response times to examples like the third one are reliably slower when measured experimentally. This is predicted by the following reasoning: it is quite easy to respond to pairs where the word and drawing fit together well; what's interesting is the time it takes the subject to report a mismatch. In the third example of figure 7.3, KICK, the word does not fit the cartoon drawing, but is the name of another action using the same effector (mouth, hand, or foot as in the brain images of figure 5.2). Suppose, as the theory suggests, that both the pictures and

Is the word a good label for the drawing?

- RUN

- DRINK

- KICK

Figure 7.3
Matching words to an image.

the words activate the same motor circuits. Reporting a mismatch between a cartoon of *running* and a word such as *kick* that also involves the feet should then be somewhat slower. When different effectors are involved, as in the middle example (DRINK), reporting a mismatch is measurably easier. Additional recent experiments using word pairs instead of images yield similar results.

So, considerable converging evidence supports the neural embodiment of language and thought. In this book, we invoke detailed circuitry when it is known, as in the knee-jerk reflex (chapter 5) or color perception (chapter 8), but are usually content with general descriptions and diagrams. While the details remain unclear, the general idea that *mental connections are active neural connections* is universally accepted and is the foundation for much research in various fields of psychology, including psycholinguistics and cognitive psychology.

This way of linking the mind to the brain is central to our story, but it must be spelled out with precision. The connectionist and neural formalisms described in chapter 9 provide us with the technical tools we need to understand the detailed computational models that bridge molecule to metaphor. But before getting into the computational details, we need to learn more about human words and concepts, and their embodiment.

8   Embodied Concepts and Their Words

The first seven chapters summarized our magnificent neural machinery, how it develops, and how it can be studied as an information processing system. Almost all of that discussion applies to animals in general and there is much more to be learned by studying animals as information processing systems, adapting to their environment and goals. But this book is about one special adaptation, *language*, that is unique to humans. Human *conceptual systems* are inextricably linked to language. These have been studied in various branches of cognitive science, usually without a specific concern for neural embodiment.

The driving question of the book remains: "How is the brain able to learn and understand language?" In chapters 8 through 14, we examine what is known about the learning and use of *concrete* words and concepts. This chapter reviews some of the basic findings on how people learn and represent concepts. In chapter 9, I describe the technology of neural computation needed to bridge between the biology of chapters 4 through 6 and the behavioral findings of chapters 7 and 8. Chapters 10 through 12 explain our core embodied words and concepts and present a computational model of how they might be learned. Then, in chapters 13 and 14, I illustrate the active schemas underlying *verbs* and demonstrate a biologically plausible model of how children might learn them.

Chapters 15 through 19 extend these ideas to *abstract* concepts and to more complex conceptual combinations. Chapter 20 brings all these ideas together in a biologically plausible model of how people understand metaphorical language in *news stories*. Finally, in chapters 21 through 27, I show how the embodied neural approach to language explains *grammar*—the rules that link form to meaning—and how children learn grammar.

Most of the data that I use comes from cognitive science and was largely developed without a specific concern for its neural substrate. However, as neural embodiment is our central focus, I relate the behavioral data to the brain. In some instances detailed physiological or computational modeling results support the bridging hypotheses linking behaviors to the brain, but in other cases there are only plausibility arguments based on general principles of computation and neuroscience.

The basis for concepts is *categorization*. As we saw in chapter 2, the amoeba categorizes. It can tell food from nonfood chemically, and this is a simple form of categorization. The visual system of the frog evolved to categorize scenes into ones involving potential prey, predators, shelter, and so on. People have 100 million detectors in the retina and only 1 million fibers going to the brain. This reduction of 100 to 1 involves lumping together different combinations of light patterns. Categorization occurs whenever a lot of data are boiled down to a few values. This happens in the retina and everywhere else in the brain, wherever a number of neurons signal to another neuron. Categorization is not just a function of language. All living systems categorize.

Some philosophical traditions ask us to rise above our human categorizations and see the world as it *really is*, assuming some basic structure of nature that is independent of people. However, this is impossible for neural beings who evolved to do best-fit matching of input to the current context and goals. We have good reason to believe that there is a real physical world, but not that there is a privileged way of categorizing it. People evolved to develop categories that match their situation and needs. These must be consistent with the facts about the physical and social environment or they wouldn't be of any use. But my categorization of trees is not at all like that of an arborist.

Besides the simple categories linked directly to perception and action, there are also more complex conceptual categories. The major concern in this book is with how people connect low-level information at the neural level with higher-level conceptual categories such as house, ugly, ask, truth. Walking down the street, we categorize the pavement versus the street, things that move versus things that stand still, things to step on versus things not to step on, people you know versus people you don't know, dangerous versus nondangerous things. How can a neural system form conceptual categories? To answer this question, we need to know more about conceptual categories.

When a neural system is categorizing, we would not expect categories to be all or none, because neural systems have weighted connections and degrees of firing—we naturally think of degrees of beauty or truth. That doesn't mean that you can never have all-or-none categorization, because neural systems also have thresholds above which they do fire and below which they don't. In addition, mutual inhibition in a system can yield all-or-nothing behavior as in the forced-choice experiments of the previous chapter. People routinely make binary decisions (e.g., Is the displayed string of letters an English word?) even when they are not sure.

So it is natural to have all-or-nothing categories, and it is also natural to have graded categories. What is it about neural systems that gives rise to the nature of human categories? The purpose of this chapter is to explain the little we know about that question and a lot of what we know about higher-level conceptual categories.

In the classical treatment dating back to the Greeks, categories were defined sets of necessary and sufficient (all or none) conditions, as in a mathematical definition. The assumption has been that all categories are like this. When we do mathematics, we can make up these kinds of categories and understand them, but we shouldn't expect all of our naturally learned categories to consist of necessary and sufficient conditions. People evolved to have some all-or-none responses to categories seen as danger, flight, mating, and so forth. However, we have also evolved to see things in degrees.

The structure of most categories is graded. Eleanor Rosch, among others, has done studies in which she gave subjects cues such as "A robin is a bird," "A chicken is a bird," "A pelican is a bird." She asked the subjects to respond true or false to each statement. The responses of true were faster for the statements involving a robin than for those with chicken or pelican. While each of these kinds of birds is definitely a bird, the robin is a better example of a bird than a chicken or pelican. So the category is graded. This is an instance of an all-or-none category with clear boundaries that still has gradations within it. The examples are clearly all birds, but some are seen as more *typical* than others (Rosch 1973).

This result also applies to numbers. For instance, good examples of odd numbers are 3, 5, and 7. But 4987 is not such a great example. This effect comes from our greater familiarity with and ease of manipulation of the lower numbers. As a general point, the kind of reasoning or processing that you usually do with particular members of a category has an effect on the structure of the category.

There are also examples of cognitive reference points in the numbers: 100 and 1000, are cognitive reference points. In a true/false response test: "99 is close to 100" is always much easier than "100 is close to 99." A cognitive reference point is a standard, which has a special cognitive status. It is a *prototype*. Many categories have prototypical elements—for example, if asked to think of a tool, most Americans will pick a hammer or screwdriver, not a shovel or a wrench.

Colors present an interesting example of categories with prototypical members. People all over the world largely agree that a prototypical red is rather like the color of a fire engine and not any of the many other shades of red. These *focal colors* are universal because they depend on the detailed physiological mechanisms of color vision, which were discussed in chapter 4. We will look at this phenomenon in more detail later in this chapter.

Several kinds of prototypes exist, each involving different styles of reasoning. The cognitive reference point is used to make estimates and also for location in semantic space. Graded prototypes are used for linear scale reasoning. For instance, how tall is someone? If A is taller than B and B is taller than C, then A is taller than C. Social stereotypes are used for snap judgments, sometimes made about people in a social context, and they are challengeable. Examples include "Blondes are dumb," and "Computer science students are geeks." The way people are categorized within their society can have a profound influence on their lives—consider caste and racial categories or medical diagnoses (Bowker and Star 1999).

Typical case prototypes are used for easy reasoning about common cases. For instance, if someone says that there's a bird outside, we expect to see a small songbird, not a great auk or an ostrich. In an experiment, Lance Rips (1995) told a group of subjects that all the robins on an island got a certain disease and asked them if they would expect the ducks to get it. Then he told another group of subjects that all the ducks on this island had a certain disease and asked if they would expect the robins to get it. The subjects were more likely to expect the ducks to catch a disease from the robins (a typical bird) than vice versa. The inference goes from the typical case to the category as a whole, in a way the typical case stands for the category as a whole.

Ideal case prototypes are used for standards of judgment or comparison. They are different from typical prototypes as in the typical husband versus the ideal husband or the typical used car versus the ideal used car. Paragon exemplars are ideal individual cases. Nelson Mandela is a paragon exemplar for politics. Paragon exemplars are used for describing a person/thing as excellent; for instance, "That is the Cadillac of vacuum cleaners." The antiparagon exemplar is the worst individual case of a category. Richard Nixon is an antiparagon exemplar for politics. Extreme exemplars are the actual members of a category that we perceive to be the best or the worst members of that category. Commercials use paragons and antiparagons a lot. In reasoning you also use these prototypes as positive and negative role models.

Salient examples are used to make probability judgments. For instance, after a famous DC-10 crash, people judged all DC-10s to be unsafe and wouldn't travel on them, even though DC-10s had the best overall safety record at the time. After the mad cow disease scare, fewer people would eat beef. The probability judgments are often based on prominent examples, not rational calculations.

Radial categories are very complex, particularly interesting categories. One famous example of a radial category is "mother." What counts as a mother? The typical cases of mother are marked by birth, nurturance, genetics, marriage, and culture. All of these features apply in the central case, but in many cases, such as "stepmother," only some of the roles apply. Some cases may have only one feature. For instance, the woman who donates genetic material to a child, but doesn't give birth to or raise the child is a kind of mother who satisfies only the genetic feature.

These criteria are important to understanding what a mother is. For instance, a working mother is defined relative to nurturance. A woman who gave up her child for adoption but is still working is not a working mother. The term "working mother" presupposes that the mother is raising the child. If a particular case satisfies all the criteria, it is a central case of the category. If only some of the criteria hold, the case is a less central member of the category, but for certain purposes only one criterion needs to be satisfied for something to be a member of the category.

Another kind of radial category has one central case (as opposed to a set of models) with other cases as its extensions, for example "harm." The central kind of harm is physical, but there is also emotional, financial, and social harm, which are metaphorical extensions of the central case. We will explore the embodiment of metaphorical language in chapters 16 and 20.

Radial categories have gradations; members are better or worse examples of the category. A purely genetic mother, for instance, is not a great example of the mother category. Because the central case in radial categories provides the basis for extension to less central category members, we often use it cognitively. The central mother has all of the genetic, birth, nurturing, and cultural features. In radial categories, better examples have more features of the central case and worse examples have fewer features.

Studying categories helps us address the question, given our neural system, how can we get such complicated structures, with so many forms of reasoning? The answer needs to cover all of the forms of reasoning and types of cognition involved. We need a theory that can account for the totality of evidence from experimentation and other means of investigation.

How do basic level categories arise? Brent Berlin worked on how native people in Chiapas categorize plants (Berlin et al. 1973). With a botanist, he examined how plants were named and identified, first looking at how many plants people could name accurately according to the botanist. He found that people sometimes used one name for a plant when it was identified from a distance and another when it was identified from close up. The people were able to identify 800 to 900 species of plants. At the genus level of biological categorization, the botanist determined that the people of Chiapas were 90 to 95 percent accurate in identifying the plants. At the species and subspecies level, though, they were only about 35 to 50 percent accurate. Above the level of genus, there was much less accuracy. The genus level of distinction is most important for ritual and culture, and the words to describe the genus level are much shorter.

In Chiapas, the botanists found that there was usually only one species of a plant in each ecological niche, but all the plants in a niche looked pretty much alike. The genus involves differences we can see, while the species distinction involves breeding, which is not easy to see. So, it is easiest for us to distinguish between things at the genus level. For instance, it is easy for us to tell sheep from goats, redwoods from live oaks, but harder to distinguish coast redwoods from giant sequoias.

Berlin looked for defining characteristics of the genus and noticed that they support gestalt perception; we can pick them out from a distance. He also found that children learn the distinction between genera earlier than the distinction between species. Basic levels are optimal for interacting with the world with our bodies, perceptual systems, motor systems, and so on. That means the basic levels are not defined by the external world, but by our interactions in it. Much of this ability has to do with the structure of our bodies and our brains. We have evolved to make certain perceptual distinctions and carry out various motor programs; it is no surprise that these distinctions play a prominent role in the way we form categories. The general term for this is *affordances*; we categorize the world around us the possibilities it affords us.

Eleanor Rosch found that this categorization happens with ordinary objects around us. If you look at a hierarchy of categories, such as furniture > chair > rocking chair, the middle of the hierarchy is a *basic* level category. In general, basic level categories have mental images associated with them. Chairs evoke an image, but generalized furniture doesn't. We have motor programs for interacting with these things. For instance, we have standard motor programs for interacting with a chair, but there's no motor program for interacting in general with furniture. In addition, much of our knowledge is organized at the basic level. We know a great deal about how to interact with chairs and tables, but little about furniture in general. Aside from a few very general categories such as animals and vehicles, children learn basic level distinctions first.

Let's look more carefully at words and how we learn them. A central question is the relationship between words and the world. The traditional view was that the world determines which concepts are needed and words are arbitrary labels different languages use for the fixed set of concepts that the world provides. But common sense tells us that our concepts depend on how we interact with the world. This can differ widely among cultures and professions. Nevertheless, all people share the same underlying physiology and we now know that many concepts and their words are determined directly by their embodiment. For example, think of the short words in English—hand, hear, hit, hot, hungry, happy.

The central insight is that the interaction of people with their physical and social environment defines various *semantic spaces*, such as the space of colors, emotions, or dance steps. Languages differ in how they talk about each of these semantic spaces, but all languages must have ways of expressing the conceptual primitives that all people share.

The paradigm example involves the words for colors in the languages of the world. Berlin and Kay (Berlin et al. 1969) showed that, in languages around the world, basic color terms had essentially the same focal colors, even though boundaries around color categories varied. The neurophysiology of color vision was seen as directly providing the best explanation. There are now a number of competing explanations for the commonality of focal colors, but they all are based on embodiment (Kay et al. 2005).

The eleven basic color terms in English are red, blue, yellow, green, brown, orange, purple, pink, gray, white, black. The basic color terms are all short words; they are not based on a color of a thing in the world, such as gold, copper, or blonde; they are not subsets of other colors, such as scarlet, which is a kind of red; and they are in general use. Languages have from two to twelve basic color terms. The New Guinean language Dani has two, Russian and Turkish have twelve.

In the 1950s, color names were believed to be arbitrary in different languages. The assumption was that you couldn't predict the ranges of these different color terms. Paul Kay and Brent Berlin did a study in which they asked where the boundaries of color terms were and also what colors from a color chart were the best examples of each term. Between their own experiments and the literature, they surveyed about 100 languages. They found that the boundaries for different languages were somewhat different, but the best examples were quite similar. This study has since been greatly expanded and the basic result confirmed (Kay et al. 2005).

For instance, if a language has one color term that covers both blue and green, the best examples selected for that color are usually either central blue or central green. Central blue and central green are the same hues chosen by English speakers as the best examples of blue and green, respectively. Some variability in the central colors may be caused in part by gender differences. Do not argue with someone of the opposite gender over whether something looks blue or green. In some cultures, certain colors may be environmentally very prominent (such as the color of a certain type of plant), and these colors may be chosen as best examples of their category rather than the physiologically central color.

Dani is a language that has two colors, light-warm (covering white, red, yellow, and orange) and dark-cool (covering black, blue, green, and purple). Speakers of Dani generally chose central red, central white, or central yellow as the best examples of the warm category and central blue, central black, or central green as best examples of the cool category. A given speaker might choose different central colors as best examples on different trials.

There is also considerable evidence on how the color word system evolves over time—usually when its community encounters other languages. Figure 8.1 outlines the development as speakers of a language (like Dani) that has only two color words come to express further distinctions. Systematically, when a third word is added, it distinguishes white from warm; a fourth term will separate black from cool, and so on. Since this progression appears to hold very widely, it is further evidence that human color terms are anything but arbitrary. Eleanor Rosch tried to teach Dani speakers two types of color systems, one based on the English system and one random system in which the color terms didn't necessarily include central colors. The Dani speakers easily learned the English system, but couldn't learn the random system. Why is this?

The focal colors are determined by the properties of the color pathways in the visual system (Dowling 2000). Color is largely determined by cones in the retina and subsequent cortical processing. Three kinds of retinal cone cells respond preferentially to long, medium, and short wavelengths of light. People who have only two types of cones are called color-blind. Further along the color pathway are neurons with center–surround

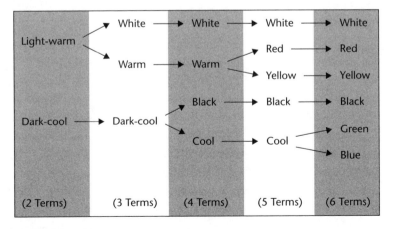

Figure 8.1
The development of color terms in the world's languages. (Source: Palmer, S. *Vision Science: From Photons to Phenomenology.* MIT Press, 1999, figure 3.4.1)

receptive fields. These cells respond maximally to configurations of one color in the center and a contrasting color surrounding, such as a red center and a green surround. Our perception of color is based on the relative strengths of the signals from different cells sensing light from each point in space. A strong signal from a red center–green surround cell is perceived as red. If you look hard at something that is bright green and quickly shift to something white, there will be a pale pink tinge to the new object.

Why is this interesting? It shows that there are human universals of color; color isn't arbitrary. In addition, it shows that color is not out there in the world. Colors are not individual wavelengths or collections of adjacent wavelengths. The color we perceive depends on the interaction between the illumination, a reflecting object, the reflections of nearby objects, and the detailed structure of our eyes and brains. We see in chapter 15 that a person's concepts and language can affect how he or she perceives color.

A child learning her native language has the task of figuring out how her community labels phenomena, such as colors, that she is experiencing. We need to understand in detail how our brains are able to do this. The next chapter summarizes how the relevant facts about the brain can be captured in computational models and used in theories of language learning. The following chapters present some of the fascinating results of studies about how children learn their first words.

In previous chapters, we saw how mental activities such as recognizing words could be described in neural terms. People are generally comfortable with the idea that words or concepts and the connections among them are entities in the mind. It also seems reasonable, in an informal way, to associate each mental concept with some neural structure and imagine conceptual links being captured as active neural connections. As we saw in chapter 7, we can explain various kinds of simple mental functions, such as priming or reminding, as direct consequences of spreading activation at the neural level. That is, *mental connections are active neural connections*. But there is a lot more to language and thought than simple spreading activation. We need to spell out how these more complex mental functions can also be realized as active neural connections.

Even to begin to explain the intricate processes of language learning and use requires a way of describing language and thought processes. A long and distinguished tradition, going back at least to the Greeks, has tried to define some formal "laws of thought" characterizing meaning and reasoning. Attempts to define exact grammatical rules for language go back to Sanskrit scholars of many centuries ago. The current work of many linguists is concerned with trying to describe the form and meaning of language in strict mathematical formalisms, deliberately avoiding any connection to human bodies or experience. Another group, the cognitive linguists, studies how language interacts with other mental functions, but they have lacked formal notations for expressing their insights.

Recent developments have suggested the possibility of finding a means of scientific expression rich enough to express the links of language to embodied cognition and also sufficiently rigorous to support simulation and direct experimental testing. The scientific notation that I adopt here is neurally inspired and based on the abstract model of neural computation presented in this chapter. The resulting methodology for describing language is discussed in chapters 21 through 24 and is the core of our treatment of grammar.

Even if we have a good way of describing the complexities of grammar, how could we explain language use in terms of neural structures and activity? The key insight is that, for many purposes, the brain can be viewed as an *information processing system*. All of the brain's intricate circuitry and exquisite processes of development and learning evolved to enable people to extract information from the environment and use it to achieve their goals.

Chapter 2 presented a general discussion of the information processing perspective on the functioning of animals. I will now explain some of the detailed mechanisms for describing neural computation that cognitive scientists have developed. The goal of their effort has been to establish a precise scientific methodology for specifying how the functioning of neural structures supports various behaviors. A theory of neural information processing is just what we need to build a bridge between brain and mind.

Any such theory will need to provide a neural account of three crucial information processing functions:

1. How are words and concepts represented in the brain?
2. How do these representations cooperate in mental activity?
3. How does the brain learn language?

There are no definitive answers to any of these questions, but enough is known to seriously constrain theories of language and thought. Notice that even the framing of question 2 assumes that any answers must explicitly involve the massive parallel character of our neural architecture.

Some insightful work was done on neural computation in the nineteenth century. The two greatest psychologists of the time, Sigmund Freud and William James, clearly understood that mental functions could be described as neural operations. It is no coincidence that they both started as biologists. Figure 9.1 is a mental connection diagram taken from Freud's early *Project for a Scientific Psychology* (Freud 1895/1950), of which he wrote, "The intention is to furnish a psychology that shall be a natural science; that is, to represent psychical processes as quantitatively determinate states of specifiable material processes, thus making those processes perspicacious

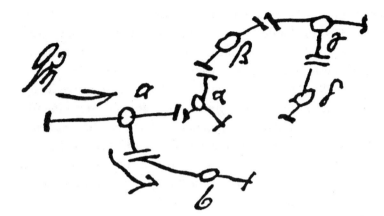

Figure 9.1
Freud's 1895 connectionist model.

and free from contradiction." Freud later abandoned this project, and it remained largely unknown until fairly recently.

William James's 1892 text, *Psychology: Briefer Course*, contains several of the key ideas of neural computation and learning: "The amount of activity at any point in the brain-cortex is the sum of the tendencies of all other points to discharge into it. . . ." The same section also anticipates Hebb's (see chapter 6) learning rule: "When two elementary brain processes have been active together or in immediate succession, one of them on recurring, tends to propagate its excitement into the other."

Neural Computation at Mid-Century

The idea of neural computation as a theory of mental activity was largely dormant for a half-century, until the 1940s. We have already met Donald Hebb who, in addition to his rule of coincidence learning, pioneered in thinking about the group behavior of assemblies of neurons. Working at about the same time, Warren McCulloch and Walter Pitts were more concerned with design of particular neural circuits, and this began the close cooperation with computer science and engineering that remains a major feature of current work on modeling neural computation.

The advent of electronic computers, starting in the 1950s, had a profound impact on how scientists thought about the information processing in the brain. Some of the basic ideas of electronic computers and programming, described in chapter 2, were immediately put to use in trying to model intelligence—but in two quite different ways. For most computer scientists, the goal was producing intelligent *behavior* and the structure of the brain was considered too complex and too mysterious to worry about. They focused instead on rules and representations that described mental functions in conventional computer programming terms. This *functional* approach to producing machines with humanlike abilities became the field of artificial intelligence, which continues to play a major role in cognitive theories and many practical applications such as expert systems for planning and decision making.

But the availability of powerful computers also enabled a radically different approach to building intelligent systems. Some scientists of the 1950s, most famously Frank Rosenblatt, sought to exploit the *learning* abilities of the brain by modeling collections of neurons to yield smart machines. The idea was to build (or simulate on an ordinary computer) a system that had a large number of neuronlike computational units, each randomly connected to some others. This research focused on discovering and testing training mechanisms that would enable such systems to learn from experience. We saw in chapter 6 that Hebb's coincidence learning rule does not enable a system to learn from its mistakes, so new ideas were needed.

Following what was already known about nature, all the learning rules in computational models focus on changing *the strength of connections* between (model) neurons. Ideally, one would like a rule that weakened connections that caused the system to make an error. But even in the simplified computer models for recognizing printed letters, thousands of neural connections participate in each decision, and there is no obvious way to know which were most responsible for the mistake.

Rosenblatt and others developed formal versions of an intuitively obvious idea. When the model network guessed wrong, all of the connections to the wrong guess were weakened by a small amount and the connections to the right answer were made a bit stronger. For certain simple networks, Rosenblatt proved that such rules would *learn to solve any problem that was in their range*. This caused great excitement for a while, until it was shown that many natural tasks could not be learned by rules of this kind. For example, such networks can not compute whether two inputs have the same value (both are 0 or both are 1).

The following two decades again saw relatively little interest in neural computation, until the arrival of the so-called new connectionists around 1980. This latest round of biological intelligence modeling has gone well beyond previous attempts and provides the technical foundation for the rest of this book.

Neural Computation and Connectionist Models

All scientific work is based on simplification, and many scientific break-throughs rely on finding a simpler way to view some complex phenomenon. But even our brief tour of neural structure and modification presents a picture of baffling complexity. How could all these facts about the brain and its operation help us understand how it learns and processes language? What we need for a neural theory of language is a way to abstract away from the biochemical details of brain function while preserving the information processing properties of neural systems that are essential for modeling human language and thought. This was also the goal of Freud, James, McCulloch, Hebb, Rosenblatt, and others, but our current theories of neural computation required major advances in both biology and computation to be developed and exploited for modeling intelligence.

We have already used some of the basic principles of neural computation informally in earlier chapters. If you recall the knee-jerk reflex of figure 5.1, the discussion was based on a simplified story of neural activity as a numerical quantity that could have positive or negative weighted connections to the receiving neuron, promoting or inhibiting its firing. At a more cognitive level, the discussion of priming effects in naming words (see figure 7.2) was also in terms of numerical quantities of "activity" spreading among connected concepts.

Contemporary neural computation modeling techniques allow both of these domains (biological and psychological) to be expressed in the same formalism. They also enable us to describe theories of how complex cognitive operations can be carried out at the neural level. This is clearly a cornerstone of any attempt to scientifically bridge mind and brain.

One of the beauties of the theory of neural computation is its simplicity. We saw in chapter 4 that a neuron transmits signals as individual "spikes" that depend in complex ways on the internal state of the neuron and its combined input. But the receiving units use only the number of spikes per second, or signal frequency. So in the computational theory, neural signaling is captured as a single numerical value, corresponding to this spiking frequency. Neurons are modeled as simple computational *units*, each of which combines incoming numerical signal values and computes the appropriate output signal strength. The output signal is then transmitted to all of its downstream neighbors, and the process continues.

In the most common models, each unit computes its output signal based on the weighted sum of its inputs. In such models, neural learning is represented as changing the weight on the incoming connections to each model neuron. The details can get complicated, but the basic theory needs no additional assumptions beyond weighted combinations of numerical signals. Such models are simple enough for people to understand and simulate on computers, but they are also enough like real neural functioning to yield scientific insights. It is possible, but usually not necessary, to extend the models to capture additional details of neural behavior.

We can already see that these neural computation models have several crucial properties needed to explain how the brain computes the mind (see table 3.1). The most important and striking feature is massive parallelism: all of the units in the model (like those in the brain) can be computing at the same time. This contrasts starkly with a conventional computer, which has a single central processing unit. In human brains, it is this massive parallelism that allows our relatively slow neurons to respond to visual input fast enough for our species to survive in tropical or urban jungles. In simulations, the numerically valued signals and weights allow the models to make graded judgments, not just yes/no decisions, again like the brain. The very wide connectivity, with each unit connected to thousands of others, permits our models to be sensitive to many contextual factors, as we know any system that understands language must be.

Representation: Holograms and Grandmother Cells

The mechanisms of neural computation are quite general; in fact they could be used as a universal programming language, as described in chapter 2. The many research groups working in this field agree on the basic principles of neural computation, but differ widely on how they use the general ideas to model and theorize about neural and mental processing.

One central question is, How many neurons are there in the basic computational or conceptual unit? Our discussion of the brain–world model was expressed in terms of a specific unit for each function. If we think of each unit as a single neuron, this would be an extreme "grandmother cell" theory, in honor of the one cell that would fire whenever you saw your grandmother. At the other extreme would be the holographic theory in which the core concept of your grandmother would be spread over millions of cells that also represented apple pie, the American way, and all the other concepts you know. No one knows exactly how concepts are represented in the brain, but it is clear that neither extreme theory can be right. I will give an idea of why this is so.

The simplest form of the grandmother cell theory makes no sense; any neuron has meaning only in terms of its connection patterns in a circuit. A possible, but also provably false, variant is that everything you know about your grandmother is linked to a single cell that is active if and only if your grandmother comes to mind. There aren't enough cells in the brain to dedicate one to every possible concept. Furthermore, such a coding system would be crippled by damage to a single key cell and would also have no way of representing graded concepts.

Spreading all the concepts over all your linking cells is equally implausible. If it takes a particular pattern over all the neurons to represent your grandmother, what would represent your whole extended family? If thinking about one thing activates all your concept neurons, how would you think about two things? Also, if a concept requires a pattern of millions of neurons, how could the brain express relations among concepts such as "a rose is a *type* of flower," as illustrated in figure 7.2. Despite heroic efforts, no one has shown how to model even the most basic operations of logic and reasoning with holographic representations.

In fact, there is compelling evidence that the neurons in the brain have specific, but overlapping functions. In our world–brain simulation of previous chapters, several people in China would have overlapping responsibilities for responding to various combinations of visual features. This has the obvious advantage of error tolerance—if some neurons die (which they do) the system can still function adequately. This overlapping function arrangement also has computational advantages. By pooling the activity of several neurons, the brain is able to judge differences finer than could be detected by individual cells in the retina.

Excluding the extreme hologram and grandmother cell theories still leaves a wide range of possibilities for how many neurons capture a concept and how much the same neuron is used to model many disparate concepts. I lean toward the low end, with each concept being represented as the activity of a *focal cluster* of 10 to 100 neurons connected to other such clusters. The details don't matter, but it is important to have explicit representations of concepts and the relations among them. For simplicity, we will use diagrams with a single node for each concept, but this should be read as shorthand for the small group representation.

Spatial and Other Maps

Neural representation is also characterized by dozens of systematic *maps*— collections of linked neurons with related functionality. We have talked several times about *spatial* maps. Starting with the retina, the neurons of the visual system are laid out in the brain in maps, according to the position in space that excites them. Other brain areas are laid out in systematic maps based on other properties; for example, the auditory cortex has maps organized by tone. Sensory and motor cortices have maps based on the body part involved. This is particularly striking in figure 7.2, showing that video sequences depicting various motor activities differentially activated different parts of the motor map.

Neural maps also play an important role in theories and models of brain function. Some explicit computations in visual maps form a central part of Regier's model of word learning (see chapter 12). More generally, there is reason to believe that spatial maps are the key to understanding how the brain's widespread activity is coordinated. We are situated and act in physical space. Any mechanism linking our perceptions to actions must include an encoding of *where* to act, and neuroscientists are learning how the brain does this. At a more speculative level, some leading theories of memory for events suggests that the hippocampal region of the brain uses *spatial setting* as the organizing principle in remembering episodes. That is, we organize our memories of events based on where they happened (Nadel et al. 2000).

But these maps are all relatively static structures and change very little in normal life. We also need to know how the brain represents and uses new ideas, like all the great ones you are getting from reading this book.

The discussion here focuses on how entities and relationships are represented and learned; more complex forms of knowledge will come up in later chapters.

Relations: Triangle Nodes

In particular, our models make extensive use of the idea of specific neural realization of concepts and their relations, such as those in figure 7.2. In the discussion in chapter 7, we considered the little triangles connecting concepts as just a convenient notation. In fact, the triangles represent an important theoretical stance on the structure of knowledge in neural computation models. If concepts are represented compactly, the connections between them can also be captured by small groups of links, which is what triangle nodes are intended to convey. Triangle nodes also depict a "2/3" activation rule that has proven to be very useful in neural computation. A triangle node is the graphical representation of a small network linking (the clusters for) three concepts, with the property that strong activity in any two of the concepts activates all three. We can see how this works and why it is useful with the help of figure 9.2.

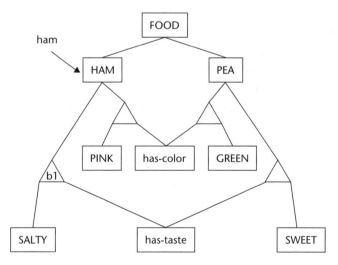

Figure 9.2
Model of knowledge represented with triangle nodes.

Figure 9.2 depicts a tiny fragment of what someone might know about food, in the triangle node format. All theories of the mind assume that there is some capability for representing *roles* (e.g., has-taste) and *fillers* (e.g., salty). Triangle nodes depict a neurally plausible way that roles and fillers might appear in the brain, and we use this theory extensively in this book. For example, the leftmost triangle node represents the belief that ham tends to taste salty. Since activating two inputs of a triangle node leads to the activation of the third input, our little system can answer such questions as "What do you think is the taste of ham?" Activating "taste" and "ham" would activate the (neural cluster of the) leftmost triangle node, leading to the answer "salty."

The same circuit can function in another, more interesting, mode. Because of the 2/3 property, activation of "taste" and "salty" (by direct tasting, a story, etc.) would tend to activate "ham" along with all other salty foods. Now if "color" and "pink" were also activated at the same time, "ham" would be double activated, but not sardines. That is, the network of figure 9.2 is also able to activate the food that is the best match to some set of active properties. Knowledge networks that carry out multiple tasks are important in our story, as are the idea of networks that find the best match to a collection of features. These neural computation properties go far toward explaining the basic nature of human concepts and language. But the main attraction of neural computation theories is the ability of these models to learn from experience.

Learning is the hallmark of intelligence, and even quite simple animals adapt to their environment. A key issue for any learning system, animal or machine, is the *correlation* problem. Suppose you move to a new job and want to be liked by your new coworkers. It might not be at all easy to figure out which of your actions are well received and under what circumstances. In general, real-world situations have many aspects and a large part of learning is deducing which features and actions are important for (corre-late with) good and bad outcomes. Both the animal and computer learn-ing systems I will be describing are able to extract correlations from ongoing experience.

Learning with Neural Computation

It is somewhat surprising that a massively parallel system can learn at all, since there is no central controller to decide what should be learned. Under the right conditions, independent local adaptation by each unit in a large system can lead to learning in the system as a whole. By looking at neural learning in several ways, we should be able to get a feel for the mechanism and for how it shapes language and thought.

We already know that *weights* (defining the strength of connection) linking one unit to another are the only thing in the model that can change, so learning must happen there. Going back to the underlying neurobiology discussed in chapters 4, 5, and 6, we recall that there are positive and negative synaptic connections between neurons. These biological synapses have differing strength depending on their size and the type and concentration of transmitting and receiving molecules. In *connectionist* models, modifiable connection weights model this varying strength of synaptic connections.

Supervised Learning

We saw in chapter 6 that synapses are formed and expanded in response to neural activity. This is the key to the first and simplest kind of learning we will study, called *Hebbian* learning after Donald Hebb. Much of neural development and some learning can be modeled as coincidence or Hebbian learning. But there is a problem with the Hebb rule for general learning—it has no information on the outcome of any action. This "neurons that fire together, wire together" principle has no way to correct an existing connection that consistently leads to disaster; some kind of feedback is needed. This was recognized in the 1950s, and the resulting *adaptive control theory* has been important in engineering and modeling ever since.

The most efficient learning could take place if each unit had a teacher who could (magically) tell it, at each time step, what signal it should have sent. An idealized learning rule could then exploit this detailed feedback to make weight changes to make the unit perform better in the future.

Although it is an idealization, this *supervised learning* plays an important role in neural computation. The basic rule is for each unit (model neuron) to change each of its incoming weights in the direction that would make its output value closer to the desired value, supplied as part of supervised training. So, when the output was too high, each unit should slightly decrease the weight on all input lines that just sent it high signals and slightly increase the weights on lines that sent it low signals. This ideal of direct supervision can be realized in very simple situations in which the output is directly linked to the training signals. In this case, the supervised learning rule is guaranteed to find a good set of connection weights if there is one. This is essentially the Rosenblatt result, which (in the 1950s) triggered the hope that we could easily build machines that could learn as well as people do.

This seemed too good to be true, and it was. The learning guarantee holds only for networks with a single layer of units (figure 9.3), and many calculations cannot be realized with such simple structures. The real brain has very complex circuits with important calculations many steps removed from any direct connection to the world and thus must be modeled by circuits with multiple layers. We still do not have mathematical learning rules for circuits as complex as the brain, but around 1980, several people realized that supervised learning could be extended to neural models with several layers of units, provided the structure was not too complicated and supervised training was available. These supervised learning techniques are now in widespread commercial use for applications from currency speculation to speech recognition.

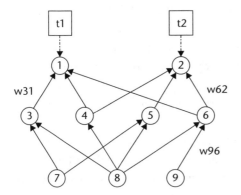

Figure 9.3
Layered PDP connectionist network. Circles depict nodes and solid arrows are forward connections. The boxes depict training inputs, see text.

Backpropagation and PDP Learning Models

The same ideas of supervised learning in layered neural networks are being applied in many areas of cognitive science, including models of language learning and use. In fact, this style of *connectionist modeling* is the most widely known, and the whole range of neural computation is sometimes identified with this one subtype. For clarity, we refer to cognitive models based on gradual weight change in layered networks as *PDP connectionism*, after the Parallel Distributed Processing group, originally at UCSD, that produced much of the basic methodology behind this approach. As we saw earlier, the problem with the learning rules of the 1950s is that is that they worked only for weights that connected (model) neurons directly to known desired outputs. The challenge of extending this to multilayer networks was met around 1980, using mathematical techniques that were already known in control theory, but it was some years before the relationship between the two fields was understood.

Using figure 9.3, we can understand the basic idea behind training multilayer networks. The figure shows only some of the connections; in the usual case each unit in one layer would be connected with every unit in the layer above. This figure has three layers of units, with connections (solid arrows) going exclusively from lower to higher layers. Each unit computes its output signal as a function of the weighted sum of its inputs. The weight connecting unit 3 to unit 1 is named w31, and so on. Units 1 and 2 are output units and capture the results of the network's activity. Inputs to the network would come to units 7, 8, and 9.

As a simple example, imagine that we were trying to train the network to recognize whether words of English could be nouns (unit 1 should be active), verbs (unit 2 should be active), or both. If we used the spelling of the words as inputs, we would need additional units in the bottom layer for all the letters, but that is easy enough. The big problem is that the spelling of an English word is a weak clue about its part of speech. So, although this is usually not stressed, the learning performance of a multilayer network depends crucially on the features used as input. No one seems to have tried our noun–verb task, and it is not obvious what input features of individual English words might work for it. There are programs that learn to do well at this task by looking at the surrounding context.

In any case, during the learning process, each of the output units gets training feedback, shown here as dashed arrows, from external sources t1 and t2. As in the earlier Rosenblatt systems, the idea is to change connection weights to bring the output of unit 1 closer to the answer t1, and so on. For each output unit (here units 1 and 2), we compute its *error* as the difference between what it computed and what it should have computed. For example, for the word "rose" both units 1 and 2 should have high output because "rose" can be both a noun and a verb. The weights on connections to the output unit are then modified by some small amount. The change must be small because weight modification is done for each training example, often millions of them.

Suppose the current example data caused unit 1 to produce a result smaller than its target, t1; the error would then be negative. Learning should involve increasing the input weights to t1 (e.g., w31). This is done for all weights unless the output of the previous level (e.g., unit 3) was zero in this example. This is because multiplying a zero output by any weight has no effect. The exact size of the change is a function of the error, the value computed by unit 3, and the current weight linking w31 to unit 1. A similar weight change operation can be done for all the links connecting the top two layers (w62, etc.). Given enough training data, this process often leads to network weights that compute outputs close to the desired results.

But what about a unit (like unit 8 in figure 9.3) that is deeper in the network and not directly connected to a training signal? This is where the clever idea comes in. If we are a bit careful with our mathematics, we can define an error score for units, like unit 5, that do not get direct feedback. We start, as before, with the fact that some units do get direct error feedback. If the network is strictly in layers, some units will be in the next-to-the top layer (here units 3–6). We can assign each of these units an error score equal to a weighted average of the error score of all of its downstream neighbors, each of which does have a direct value. For example, the error score for unit 5 is a combination of the error of unit 1 multiplied by the weight w51 and the error of unit 2 multiplied by the weight w52. Once we have a net error for an interior unit like unit 5, the same learning rule as before can be applied to *its* incoming weights—w85, and so on.

Again, the rule is to change each weight by a small amount in the direction that will reduce the overall network error on the current example.

Since errors are passed backwards along each weighted connection, the learning technique is usually called *error backpropagation*. For units that (like unit 8) are two steps from direct feedback, the error score is a weighted average of the error scores of its recipients, and thus an average of averages. This calculation becomes unreliable after a few steps, so almost all PDP networks have four or fewer layers. Practical applications, like speech processing, often involve networks with thousands of units and millions of connections. The training process for such networks can require weeks of computer time.

Some of the discussions of neural computation in this book, particularly in chapters 12 and 22, invoke these PDP backpropagation learning techniques and strictly layered networks. But neither the architecture nor the learning techniques are biologically plausible. Everyone knows that real neural circuits have feedback loops and the PDP computations also require unrealistic training signals and accuracy. Cognitive researchers use these techniques effectively to study what can be accomplished by pure learning methods using overly simple initial networks. For the detailed modeling that is our goal, another learning rule is more important.

Recruitment Learning

All of the rules discussed so far learn by making small changes in connection weights, typically taking thousands of training steps to converge to a desired outcome. Much of human learning is like this, particularly for skills such as a tennis backhand stroke or a child learning to pronounce the sounds of her native language. But there is also a lot of one-trial learning in language. For example, you probably didn't know that I was born in Pittsburgh, but now you do. The technical question is how this kind of immediate fact learning could be done by a neural system, using the only available mechanism for permanent learning—changes in connection weights. As we saw in chapter 6, human learning involves at least two shorter-term electrical and chemical memory mechanisms, but we can ignore them for now. What we need is a way to incorporate new information into a structured knowledge base like that depicted in figure 9.2.

The proposed mechanism for doing this, *recruitment learning*, will play a central role in the remainder of this book. Returning again to our world–brain simulation, let's think about linking up some piece of new knowledge such as the wife of George Lakoff. We could imagine that the workers of Switzerland, for example, were connected in both directions to various units representing different *men's names* (maybe in Italy) and units representing *women's names* (in France). There aren't enough workers in Switzerland (or neurons in the brain) to dedicate one unit to each possible pairing of a man with a woman. But suppose that each Swiss worker was connected randomly to a thousand French (women's name) units and a thousand Italian (men's name) units. Under realistic assumptions, a few Swiss units will happen to be linked to both the "George Lakoff" units in Italy and the "Kathleen Frumkin " units in France. What we would like to do is *recruit* these linking units to represent our new fact (Feldman 1982).

Here is how recruitment learning can quickly learn a single new fact: First, imagine a broadcast throughout Switzerland saying that a new pairing is being learned. All Swiss units that are not yet representing other links are put on alert. The two elements of our new fact (man, woman) are then highly activated. Each is randomly connected to some thousand Swiss linking units, but the odds are high that only a few Swiss units are connected to both "George Lakoff" and "Kathleen Frumkin." Now each Swiss unit worker looks at the total signal to its unit. If the total signal is very high, the worker knows his or her unit is connected to both inputs and can be recruited to link George with his wife. In the extreme case, the worker could set the weights on his currently active links to the maximum value and reduce all other weights to zero. At this point, activating the units that represent either marriage partner will tend to activate the other partner, because they are now connected by our newly recruited Swiss units.

This is the essence of recruitment learning, in which an important fact leads to selecting a previous uncommitted set of units to remember what should be linked together. Still in the imagined world–brain model, we must add one further complication to our description of recruitment learning. As we saw in figures 7.2 and 9.3, it is not enough to just link two related concepts; we also need to know *how* they are related. George Lakoff is linked to many women besides Kathleen—his mother, his ex-wife, his students, and others. So the recruitment learning model needs to be expanded to include another unit, representing the kind of relationship involved. In this version, potential triangle nodes (like those of figures 7.2 and 9.2) are also connected to *relationship-type* units (say in Austria, in our world–brain simulation). When a new fact is to be learned, the three components of the fact (e.g., wife of George Lakoff is Kathleen Frumkin) are activated. Potential Swiss triangle nodes that happen to be well connected to all three active units can be recruited to be the kind of triangle nodes depicted in figures 7.2 and 9.2.

Essentially the same recruitment mechanism could be used to provide one solution to the *binding* problem raised earlier in this book. The general problem is that thinking about anything (e.g., a trip) activates many separate circuits in the brain, all of which must work together without a central controller to keep track of everything. In addition, the trip planning networks must have changeable roles (e.g., destination) and *fillers* (e.g., Helsinki, store, bookcase) as discussed previously for the taste of ham. In each specific case, the destination role could be temporarily bound to Helsinki, for example, by the activation of triangle nodes in the recruitment procedure.

In later chapters, we will also be concerned with binding fillers to roles in motor actions, such as picking up objects of different shape; for example, the pick-up action schema will have an *object* as a parameter. One possible solution to the binding problem involves coordination through timing (Shastri 2002). If all the neurons involved in a coherent thought had synchronized patterns of activity, they could work cooperatively without interference from other networks that were active at different times. In the world–brain model, we could imagine different groups of Austrian–Italian–Swiss–French linking units working on different days of the week, and thus not interfering with each other. Of course, any neural version of this story would need to have much shorter (millisecond) time periods, but experimental results suggest some coordinated firing cycles among neural circuits. Whatever the mechanism, some plausible binding theory is necessary for a neural theory of language.

Several of the computational models we will discuss later rely on both triangle nodes and binding for roles, along with recruitment learning to build them. There is no direct evidence in the brain for the recruitment model or indeed for any other theory of concept learning, but all of the basic mechanisms are known to be neurally plausible. The story of rapid recruitment is consistent with the standard models of binding for episodic memories involving the hippocampal area, as described in chapter 6.

This is a case in which theory is ahead of experiment and suggests possibilities to test. The rest of this book does not depend on the details of the particular recruitment model, but does presume that there is some way of directly learning conceptual knowledge as neural structure. As we have discussed, there is considerable evidence that conceptual structure is directly captured in neural structure. Recruitment learning is a plausible model of how this might come about.

This story of the neural computation formalism and its role in bridging brain and mind completes the first stage of our journey of discovery. We have seen that much of language and thought is based on our direct experience, expressed as neural activity. The remarkable new insights from biologists into the chemistry and physiology of neural development and functioning provide a strong foundation for linking neural states with mental states. In some simple cases, like mental priming, the relation between neural and mental activation can be quite direct. For higher thought and language, we need to describe more elaborate processes. The scientific language of neural computation provides a proven way of expressing biologically plausible theories of mental function.

But, as always in science, the devil is in the details. The chapters of the next parts (part IV and V) study how individual concepts and words are learned and used by the embodied mind. We examine a wide range of linguistic and psychological evidence and review detailed neural computation models of how the brain might produce these well-known behaviors. In part VI, after working through concrete linguistic expressions we will look at abstract and metaphorical language. Part VII shows how the ideas of embodied language can be realized in a computer program that understands the meaning of news stories, including those that employ metaphor extensively. Finally, parts VIII and IX address the questions of how meaning structures are combined using grammar and how this complex process is learned. There is still a lot of ground to cover, but the ideas and tools we have developed in this chapter provide the basis for the remaining journey.

IV Learning Concrete Words

We now know that infants start to learn their native language several weeks before birth. I mentioned this surprising result in the discussion of neural development (chapter 6), and it may well have struck you as implausible. How could the baby learn anything about language in the womb, and how could psychologists prove that it did so?

Even the youngest children get bored and psychologists have two main ways of measuring boredom versus interest. When an infant's interest is aroused, she will suck more vigorously on a pacifier. Also babies will look longer at and play more with things that interest them. Using these kinds of measurements, psychologists have learned that infants have considerable neural abilities very early in life. The finding that is most relevant to us is that children, essentially from birth, have a preference for the sounds of their mother's language. In retrospect, the neural learning story of chapter 6, tells us why this should be so. Recall that neural wiring is partially specified by chemical markers, but the final tuning depends on experience. A baby in the womb receives the sounds of the mother's voice and we should not be surprised that the wiring of the auditory system uses this input in its development. The tuning of the auditory system continues after birth. We know that adults cannot fully learn to pronounce exotic language sounds, like the tones of languages such as Chinese. Even in the first year, the auditory system looses some of its flexibility.

Of course, a child needs to know a lot more about her language than the sounds it uses. Language has a wide range of social and emotional dimensions in addition to its function of conveying factual information. Much of our concern will be with various aspects of language learning and use and how they depend on the properties of the brain. In this chapter we focus on how children come to learn their first words. The central idea is simple—*the child's early words name her experiences and are used to communicate with caregivers.*

Communication is crucial for a social species like ours and particularly for human infants who are dependent on others for years. Not only can caregivers understand the cries, postures, and facial expressions of children but infants can, from birth, imitate adult expressions and thus establish an emotional bond. Our best evidence suggests that no other animal has the same ability to imitate, and it is a remarkable feat of neural computation (Meltzoff & Prinz 2002).

Somehow, infants are born with neural connections that map a complex visual image (mother's expression) onto commands to the baby's facial muscles that produce a comparable expression. It was thought that only a fixed set of expressions could be imitated; this could be realized by a few reflexes like the knee jerk. But children a few months old can imitate a very wide range of novel actions by adults or other children. For example, days after a single observation of someone doing a unique action with some novel toy (e.g., touching it with one ear), children will imitate the action the first time they are given that toy (Meltzoff & Prinz 2002).

No one knows exactly how imitation works in infants, but some recent neuroscience research in monkeys and human adults provides important cues.

As we saw in chapter 1, neurons (called mirror neurons) in the monkey's brain respond equally to the monkey performing an action, such as biting, and observing another primate doing the same action. It is not acceptable to record from individual neurons in people, but it is possible to observe areas of the human brain that show similar mirroring behavior. For example, a person watching a film of someone chewing exhibits activation in areas of the brain involved in controlling the chewing muscles. A brain circuit that responds to both observing and performing the same action would be a plausible basis for imitation.

In addition to imitation, several other forms of parent–child communication also develop well before language. These include shared gaze, greetings, and pointing. One interesting example is the child's raising of both arms to indicate a desire to be lifted up. As we will see later in this chapter, some of the child's earliest words are verbal equivalents of these well-established communication actions.

When children do start to learn language, they first learn to *recognize* words (as well as emotional tone, etc.) and only later *produce* words or the signs of sign language. There is no good way to tell exactly what an infant understands, so almost all of the research has been about what words children produce. As an important first step in producing language, the child must learn to produce the sounds of her language, which she already can recognize. These efforts are known as *babbling* and similar practice takes place in the hand movements of children learning signed languages. From a neural perspective, the long struggle to master sound production seems to be quite well modeled by the supervised skill learning methods described in chapter 9. In this case, the supervisory feedback on how good something sounds can come from the child's recently acquired mastery of the sounds of her language.

Once the child can produce enough of the basic phonemes of her language, the production of words starts and there is no looking back. The generally accepted estimate is that a child learns an average of ten new words a day between the ages of 2 and 12 years. At the beginning, the learning is slower, more like ten words per week. There are several remarkable things to discuss about the learning of single words before we move on to more complex language (P. Bloom 2002).

For one thing, the child (and adults) can often learn a new word from a single example. Called *fast-mapping*, this places severe constraints on theories of language learning. It extends beyond language, allowing infants to learn, from a single presentation, the appropriate action for a novel toy (such as touching it with the forehead). We can compare the fast-mapping requirement with various neural learning mechanisms discussed in chapter 9. It turns out that only one technique—recruitment learning—meets the fast-mapping requirement. Recall that this involves "recruiting" from a pool of randomly connected units, those units that happen to form a strongly linked path between the two concepts being learned.

This contrasts sharply with learning how to produce the sounds of one's native language, which is much better modeled by the gradual weight change of supervised incremental learning. It is no surprise that different aspects of language learning involve different kinds of computation. We now know that, in general, learning skills (e.g., pronunciation) and learning facts (e.g., word meanings) use largely independent brain mechanisms that are quite different in character.

Another fundamental question in word learning can be called the labeling problem—how does the child know what is being labeled by some new word that she hears? This is often called Quine's problem, after the philosopher W.V.O. Quine, who posed it for the case of an adult trying to learn a totally unknown language. If the learner sees a rabbit hopping near a tree and hears some new word, how could she know whether the word referred to the rabbit, a part of the rabbit, an action, the tree, or something else? This is a real problem for children learning language, and a good deal is now known about how they deal with it.

When children are explicitly being taught a new word, adults provide several kinds of clues including emphasizing the new word and pointing to or gazing at the object being named. This helps quite a bit, but children also use some strategies of their own. The child already has a rich base of experience in the world and assumes that new words label some aspect of that experience. On hearing a new word associated with an object, children assume that the word names the whole object and not a part or a property of the object. They also tend to assume that the object is being described as a basic level category, as discussed in chapter 8. For example, they will guess that the new toy is being labeled as a truck and not a vehicle or a Ford pickup. All of this was quite well understood by Saint Augustine (Augustine 1992):

When [my elders] named any thing, and as they spoke turned towards it, I saw and remembered that they called what they would point out by the name they uttered. And that they meant this thing and no other was plain from the motion of their body; the natural language, as it were, of all nations, expressed by the countenances, glances of the eye, gestures of the limbs, and tones of the voice, indicating the affections of the mind as it pursues, possesses, rejects, or shuns. And thus by constantly hearing words, as they occurred in various sentences, I collected gradually for what they stood; and having broken my mouth to these signs, I thereby gave utterance to my will.

But children also need to learn words for parts and properties of objects. The key to doing this is another child learning strategy called the mutual-exclusion principle. The child tends to assume that there is only one name for each thing, and so other words associated with that thing must be describing some part or feature of it, not just providing an alternative name for the same thing. So, if the child knows the word dog, she assumes that "black dog" and "paw" are not just synonyms for dog.

None of these strategies is perfect, and children do make mistakes in word learning. As we will discuss later in this chapter, when children move beyond single words and start to learn grammar, strong additional rules help determine the meaning of a novel word or phrase.

There is an even more basic problem in learning how words refer to things in the external world, which is usually ignored, but is important for our neural understanding of language. If, as our theory suggests, the child's experience is the product of her neural and hormonal activity, why should she believe in entities in the external world? A simple and traditional, but inadequate, answer is that the world is inherently made up of fixed entities and our brains evolved to recognize and deal with these entities, like the amoeba's food-detector molecules evolved. But, as we saw in chapter 8, humans categorize experience in various ways according to their situation and needs.

One part of an adequate explanation for our belief in an external world involves this general human tendency to categorize inputs. As adults, we don't often need to deal with wholly new situations, but you can remember or imagine traveling to a culture that you know nothing about. Children distinguish early between entities that are able to act on their own (agents) and passive entities (objects), and we would certainly use this distinction in this situation as novices in a new culture. What we would do is try to find cues about what objects might have properties (*affordances*) that could be useful to us and how we might understand and influence the behavior of agents. There is good evidence that children do something like this, both before and during language learning.

Another part of the story of how children learn about the world is suggested by recent findings on causal modeling. The details aren't important here, but the central idea is that it is very effective to model the world as having causal structure and that both children and adults do assume that events have causes.

These results suggest that children need to postulate external entities to act as the bearers of causation. That is, we assume that our experiences are caused by agents and objects in the world and seek to learn what causes our experiences. The scenarios we construct, postulating entities in the external world, can be used to simulate possible effects of our own actions and are crucial for planning. Much of the child's early play seems to be directed at understanding the effects of her actions.

The child's search for causal explanations is not always productive; some putative explanations turn out to be superstitions. But, in general, thinking in terms of causes provides a basis for reasoning and acting in the world, which inherently requires us to postulate the existence of entities in the world. Notice that this reverses the old view that says the world is predivided into entities and we must learn to recognize this eternal structure. The key idea is that our minds partition the world into entities in a way that enables us to make predictions about what we experience. This has profound implications for how language is learned and some of these will be important in later chapters.

I have been talking about word learning as the child labeling her direct experience, but have not yet said enough about that experience. For example, pushing something, being pushed yourself, and watching some pushing that doesn't involve you directly are quite different experiences. We refer to these as three different *perspectives* on experience: the *agent*, the *undergoer*, and the *observer* perspective, respectively. Even as adults, the experience we associate with a word and thus its meaning differs depending on our age, gender, profession, and so on. People who only watch a sport event or artistic performance cannot fully understand participants' conversation about the activity. As we discuss in chapter 18, all languages have grammatical constructions to specify which perspective is intended.

We will see that children learn some of their first words from each of these three perspectives. No research seems to have been done on how or when children learn to automatically extend a new word to all three perspectives, although the mirror neuron system discussed earlier provides some clues about how this might work.

With all this background, we can look at the words children do learn early and see how well our preliminary neural story covers the data. Table 10.1 presents the words learned by most of the 2-year-olds in a preschool center studied by the developmental linguist Lois Bloom (L. Bloom 1993). The left side of the table presents the nouns, which comprise about half of the set of early words. Notice that these nouns can be divided into object categories with fundamental functions for the child: the first column involves eating, the second column toys, and the fourth column people. The third column has one word each for clothing (shoe), body parts (eye), and the room (door).

The nouns (except mommy and daddy) all name basic level categories, as predicted by theory. Notice that most of the nouns are experienced from both the agent and observer perspectives—the child interacts with them and also observes them from afar. Some words, such as "shoe" and "spoon," are first learned from the undergoer perspective—they are involved in something that is done to the child. It isn't at all difficult to imagine children learning these words through the kind of direct instruction scenario St. Augustine talked about. In general, although a great deal of research has been dedicated to noun learning, the results do little to distinguish one theory of language acquisition from another.

The words in the right half of table 10.1 are much more interesting. The first column to the right contains four words for common sounds. Children need to learn the difference between "cow' and "moo," but parents and teachers provide lots of cues including using a very different pronunciation of the words for sounds. The second column to the right contains four words (oh, uhoh, whee, yum) for expressing the child's emotional state. Again, it is not hard to imagine how children learn these by noticing how they feel when these words are said. Of course, it is a bit more complicated; "yum" is associated with food and "uhoh" involves an unexpected problem.

The column on the far right has words that label previously learned nonverbal acts of communication (yes, no, hi, bye, more, no more). These can be quite complex, but the preverbal gestures already have the same

Table 10.1
Words learned by most 2-year-olds in a play school (Bloom 1993)

Food	Toys	Misc.	People	Sound	Emotion	Action	Prepositions	Demonstratives	Social
	cow								
apple	ball								yes
juice	bead		girl				down		no more
bottle	truck		baby	woof	yum	go	up	this	more
spoon	hammer	shoe	daddy	moo	whee	get	out	there	bye
banana	box	eye	mommy	choo-choo	uhoh	sit	in	here	hi
cookie	horse	door	boy	boom	oh	open	on	that	no

complexity. Notice that these words explicitly involve acts of communication with another person. As we will discuss later, this seems to require that the child have causal simulation models that involve other people.

The second column from the right contains four words (this, that, here, there) that can be viewed as verbal equivalents of pointing or shared gaze communication. These again entail the existence of another person and an expectation of changing that person's behavior through an act of speech. Given the appropriate modeling and preverbal communication abilities, it is not difficult to craft a plausible neural story about how these words might be learned by being paired with the underlying gesture. The number word "two" was also spoken frequently; children at this age tend to know that the word has something to do with number, but not exactly what that is.

But the middle two columns on the right are much more complex to understand and model. How could children learn words for actions (go, get, sit, open) or spatial relation words (in, on, up, down, out)? It is probably true that, for many young children, "up" is the verbal equivalent of the raised arms gesture we discussed earlier and "down" a general request to be taken out of a highchair, for instance. If so, these words could also be learned as labels for earlier communication gestures. But the other examples present genuinely new and challenging issues for any theory of how children learn the meaning of words.

There is no simple way to model how children could learn either action verbs or spatial relation words. Much of this section of the book is concerned with demonstrating how the neural theory of language explains the learning of this kind of complex concept. Considerable evidence indicates our understanding of spatial relations is based on a relatively small number of quite general concepts such as support, containment, and so on. Chapter 11 describes these primitives and their use in language as well as some additional primary mental frames that seem to underlie our thought and language. Chapter 16 suggests how abstract concepts arise from experience with these embodied basic ones. With this cognitive linguistic background, we are ready, in chapter 12, to study the first detailed computational model of how children learn the meaning of complex relational words such as "in" and "on" for a wide range of different languages.

The meanings of verbs of action, such as "go" or "sit," are even more complex. We can visualize a noun like "ball" as a picture and imagine there is some comparable representation in the brain. For a spatial relation word such as "on" we can visualize a canonical case—a pencil on a desk. But for an action word such as "go," there is no static picture that captures its meaning. We seem to need some little cartoon or film clip to visualize the meaning. In chapter 13, we describe a neural model of how the brain could represent actions in a way that would allow us to learn and use verbs. Then, in chapter 14, this neural theory of action is used in a detailed computer model of how children learn words of hand action such as "shove" and "grasp." This model has been quite successful and suggests a general theory of how children could learn individual words of all kinds from labeled experience.

Syntactic Cues to Possible Word Meanings

Children do not need to learn all words in isolation. In addition to the cues provided by parents through intonation, gesture, and so forth, human languages have grammatical rules that can help greatly. I describe in detail how children learn grammar in chapters 21 through 25, but now we can look a bit at what is called syntactic bootstrapping—using grammar to help in word learning. Table 10.2 (from Lois Bloom) shows some of the basic clues from grammar in English.

Table 10.2
Grammatical clues to English word types

Syntactic Cue	Usual Type of Meaning	Examples
"This is a *fep* / the *fep*."	Individual member of a category	Cat, forest
"These are *feps*."	Multiple members of a category	*Cats, forests*
"This is *fep*."	Specific individual	Fido, John
"This is some *fep*."	Nonindividuated stuff	Water, sand
"John *feps*."	Action with one participant	Sleeps, stands
John *feps* Bill."	Action with two participants	Hits, kisses
"This thing is *feppy*."	Property	Big, good
"This dog is *fep* the table."	Spatial relationship	On, near

But, of course, children need to learn more than the kind of word involved; they also need to know the specific meaning, like the difference between "in" and "on." This is the heart of the problem of learning word meanings and has proven quite hard to understand or model. In fact, it was the attempts to model detailed word learning by our research group that led to the neural theory of language that is the focus of this book.

We saw in chapter 8 how, in all languages, the words for basic color terms are grounded in the neural representation of colors. This is the simplest case of what I believe to be the general embodied nature of meaning. Words for describing spatial relations such as "in" and "on" also appear to be based on underlying neural circuitry, but the story—the subject of chapter 12—is more complex. Before examining this detailed modeling study, we need to learn more about conceptual systems in general, and particularly about the representation of space in languages around the world.

The child's first words are labels for his or her experience, but not all experiences can be described with a single word. Actions such as "grasp" or spatial relations such as "support" inherently have multiple participants, or roles. Grasping requires roles for at least the grasper and the thing being grasped. We saw in chapter 5 that coordinated motor activities such as grasping are called *motor schemas*. The same term, schemas, is used to describe relational information as in the concept of "support." Many of these cognitive structures are universal across all languages and cultures, and I refer to all of these as *conceptual schemas* or sometimes just *schemas*.

The embodied theory of meaning suggests that the child needs to have conceptual structures for understanding experiences before the words for labeling them can make sense. For example, every language has a notion of physical support, with roles for the supporter and the supported. The support schema is central to the literal meaning of the English word "on" and to related literal and metaphorical meanings in other languages.

Other coherent collections of experience are particular to some culture, and following convention I refer to these as *frames*. Typically, a cultural frame such as the baseball frame will involve several basic conceptual schemas such as run, grasp, contact, and goal. Notice that a single word, like "shortstop," can *evoke* the baseball frame, with its many roles, actions, and relations. In this chapter, I discuss both schemas and frames and also introduce notation for computationally modeling their roles.

Color and the words that describe it are a particularly simple case of universal language tendencies. When cognitive scientists look for phenomena that are "universal," they cannot look at every language in the world, so they study several languages from different language families. If they find the same phenomenon in these unrelated languages, it is likely to be universal. Cognitive scientists have extensively explored the idea of conceptual schemas (like support) as universal, bodily based representations of experience.

Proposed universal schemas, such as *support*, arise from our common genetic heritage and shared developmental experiences. Every child learns how to perceive and understand quite a lot about his or her body and environment before learning language. No one knows how many universal schemas there might be, but the best estimates are in the range of a few hundred. We will look carefully at a few schemas that are particularly well studied and seem to be important in language and thought.

For now, I focus on static schemas representing fixed relationships between things, such as the supporter and the object that is supported. In chapter 13, we extend the discussion to include actions, events, and other changes over time. In chapter 15 and 16, we examine how universal schemas and cultural frames form the metaphorical basis for abstract thought and language. Schemas will continue to play a central role throughout our discussion.

One of the most thoroughly worked-out classes of schemas involves the conceptualization of physical space and its use in organizing other domains.

The first major insight came from Len Talmy, in the summer of 1975. Talmy, looking at a wide variety of languages, had a deep insight. Language constructions that describe space can be broken down into primitive spatial relations, where each language uses the same primitives, but puts them together in different ways. The central sense of English *on*, for example, uses the conceptual primitives above, contact, and support. Not all languages have a complex concept corresponding to *on*, but they all have ways of expressing above, contact, and support. Talmy also noticed that primitive image-schemas fall into three types:

Topological (where relative nearness is preserved under shape change) A container (that is, a bounded region of space) is one example, and a path is another. If you change their size and twist them around, they remain bounded regions and paths. Contact is also topological.

Orientational (defined relative to bodily orientations) "In front of" is an example.

Some schemas are also oriented around external features such as gravity or the horizon.

Force-dynamic (making use of some kind of force) "Against" is an example.

In addition, each primary image-schema comes with what Talmy calls a *trajector* and a *landmark*. For example, in *The car is in the garage*, the garage is the landmark, relative to which the car (the trajector) is located. What is important for our purposes is that all of these are embodied, with orientations such as *in front of* defined relative to beings with fronts, and force-dynamic schemas defined relative to how muscles and sensors operate.

These structures have been extensively studied by cognitive scientists under the name *image schemas*. In English, spatial relation words include above, below, through, under, and around. Are these expressed the same way in other languages? No, they are very different, even in languages similar to English, such as German or Dutch. In some languages, the entire system is different. For example, in the Mexican language Mixtec, the system of spatial relations is based on bodily projections, so "The cat is sitting under the tree" would be expressed as "The cat is sitting the tree's foot." We have similar expressions in English, but in Mixtec all spatial relations are described in this bodily projection fashion.

While the concepts that are given names vary, a universal set of image schemas do seem to support spatial relation terms in all languages. Some of these schemas are directly related to our sensing of the physical world, for example, up/down, which is based on gravity. The English word *above* is based on this schema. Many image schemas are expressed in terms of a reference object (*landmark*) and a usually smaller object (*trajector*) that is moving or located with respect to the landmark. Other related schemas include physical contact and support. The most basic meaning of the English *on* involves all three of these schemas—the pen (trajector) is above the table (landmark), it is in contact with it, and is supported by it. In German, this concept is labeled *auf* and another word, *an*, is used to describe situations such as a picture on a wall, where only contact and support are involved. Dutch has three terms covering roughly the same semantic territory.

The English word *in* labels a more complicated situation. There is a schematic *container* or bounded region in space composed of a boundary, interior, and exterior. There also must be a landmark located in the interior of the container and a trajector that is at least partly within the container region. Some uses of *in* also entail a force-dynamic schema in which the container exerts force on the material located in the interior. For instance, the bottle keeps the water in it from spilling out. Watching a toddler at play should convince anyone that children teach themselves about fundamental schemas like support and containers well before they learn the words for labeling them.

A rich semantics of spatial relations is covered by the English words *in*, *on*, *above*, and *around*. Other languages name regions of this semantic space quite differently. For example, Spanish *en* is used much more widely than English *in* and *sobre* much more narrowly than *on*. The important point about these examples is that around the world the image schemas are the same, but they are organized in different ways. For instance, the container and support schemas are found in language after language, but are combined with other schemas differently in various vocabularies.

Another important universal image schema is the source/path/goal/ or SPG schema. In its concrete embodied form, the SPG involves moving from a source, along a path, to a goal. For a young child, uses of the SPG schema include putting something in her mouth, moving herself, or inducing her parent to move her or some desired object. Image schemas come with inference rules. For example, the SPG schema entails the rule that if you travel from point A to point C, you have reached all the points on the path between A and C as well. As we will see in chapter 16, metaphorical projections of these schematic inference rules are the basis for much of our abstract and technical reasoning.

Magnitude is important for certain kinds of reasoning about space, but some spatial relations terms, including many prepositions, are independent of magnitude. They are topological. Knowledge of the world sometimes adds to our understanding of terms, such as "to." For instance, "going to Thailand" and "going to a neighbor's house" suggest different distances and forms of travel, but that kind of reasoning is based on real-world knowledge, not on the spatial relations schema evoked by "to." For many other concepts, magnitude is of the essence. In fact, there seem to be general universal schemas for *scales* that appear in myriad literal and metaphorical uses. All of these schemas are part of our neural wiring, but to talk scientifically about them and their properties, we need some technical terminology.

The Computational Level of Description

We have been talking about schemas in ordinary language, but we know that they are really embodied structures in our brains. Neuroscientists studying the neural basis of verbal behavior must make computational models that are significantly less detailed than the real network of neurons. The elaborate neural structure is not known and, even if it were, we would not be able to model and understand a system with millions of interacting units. I have talked (see chapter 9) about connectionist network models as a crucial link between brain and behavior. Some simple schemas (e.g., contact) can be described as connectionist models, and we will see some examples in the next chapter. But for complex schemas and frames such as baseball, to keep the complexity manageable we need one more level of modeling, the *computational* level.

Table 11.1 presents the four levels of description that I use in the rest of this book. Of course, the goal is to describe how the top level, language and thought, can be realized by the neural systems at the bottom level.

This follows the standard practice in neuroscience of introducing simplified computational models to help describe and understand complex systems. The key, as in all scientific modeling, is to suppress some detail while preserving the crucial features that help explain the phenomena under investigation. The mechanisms at the computational level 2 form a bridge between levels 1 and 3 and must do two linking jobs at once: the modeling of cognitive and linguistic behavior at level 1 and the representation of computational function in the connectionist structures at level 3. This is the key link in the chain from language to the brain.

The example shown at level 1 in table 11.1 is Spanish for "Ham tastes salty." As we will soon see, property descriptions like this are very common

Table 11.1
Four levels of description

Level	Example
1. Language and thought	El jamón prueba salado.
2. Computational models	Table 11.2
3. Connectionist networks	Figure 9.2
4. Neural systems	Figure 5.1

in computational level modeling. Figure 9.2 depicts this same fact in terms of triangle nodes, which are a way of graphically presenting connectionist models of neural-like computation. No one knows exactly how such facts are actually represented in the brain, but it is presumably with neural circuits, something akin to that in figure 5.1.

We will introduce the computational level using the example of feature structures. The general idea of entities having *features* (or roles or properties) is universal in science and everyday language use, and it plays an important role in the theory of knowledge. There is convincing evidence that people organize their perceptions and actions in terms of features and values.

Table 11.2 presents four distinct kinds of semantic feature structures. First notice that all four columns of table 11.2 have the same form—two entities each with a list of feature names and a value or type of value for each, like color ~ pink. The left column of table 11.2 presents data that might be contained in a university payroll system.

As we saw with colors, the neural circuitry supporting a concept is active and is connected with circuitry that supports other mental activity. There aren't any isolated concepts in the brain. But it wouldn't be helpful to write down all these interlinked circuits, even if we could. So, following standard practice, I will describe schemas using isolated symbolic descriptions, with the understanding that the text is a shorthand for the neural

Table 11.2
Feature structures in four domains

Feldman	Ham	Container	Push
dept ~ Comp	color ~ pink	inside ~ region	schema ~ slide
salary ~ 10000	taste ~ salty	outside ~ region	posture ~ palm
start ~ 1/1/1988		boundary ~ curve	duration ~ ANY
			direction ~ away
Lakoff	Pea	Commercial event	Stroll
dept ~ Ling	color ~ green	buyer ~ person	schema ~ walk
salary ~ 11000	taste ~ sweet	seller ~ person	speed ~ slow
start ~ 9/1/1968		cost ~ money	direction ~ ANY
		goods ~ thing	

connections. The second column of table 11.2 contains an alternative way of expressing the information about some features of foods that was presented as a connectionist model in figure 9.2. When cognitive scientists write out the text form of a schema or frame, they use notation such as that in the table. They are trying to produce some description of neural structure that can be used for reasoning about and designing experiments.

The third column shows how both image schemas and cultural frames can also be described in terms of features and value types. The general *container* schema can be described by features for exterior, interior, and so on along with the types of entity required for each. A particular instance of the container schema such as your house would have specific values for each feature. This kind of description also works well for the cultural frames discussed later in this chapter. The lower example in the third column shows how some of our knowledge of commercial transactions can also be represented in terms of features and values.

The right-hand column, which also has similar form, describes some of the features and values associated with basic actions, here strolling or sliding an object on a table. These descriptions of dynamic schemas are discussed in chapter 13, and they play a central role in the learning of words about action, as we will see in chapter 14.

For both practical and pedagogical reasons, our computational level models are based on formalisms and techniques that are well established in computer and cognitive sciences. Using standard computational ideas makes it easier to communicate with colleagues pursuing different approaches and often makes it possible to exploit existing results and sometimes actual computer code for parts of a model, as I will soon show.

There are also dangers in using conventional formalisms and methods. None of the traditional techniques were developed for linking brain activity to behavior and they all are inadequate if used only in the conventional way. In addition, the standard notation might be taken as the whole theory, ignoring the underlying bridge to the brain. Computer scientists and engineers building applied AI systems use some of the same computational techniques in their programs. But the goals of engineering systems and those of neural models are quite different.

For embodied cognitive science, any computational level formalisms must be effectively reducible to the connectionist level and thus to brain mechanisms. Computational level descriptions may fail to capture several key neural properties, including massive parallelism, robustness, spreading activation, context sensitivity, and adaptation and learning. As in all science, the trick is to have levels of description that are mutually consistent, with each facilitating different kinds of reasoning.

The fact that all of these situations, and many more, can be partially described in terms of features and values suggests that some similar mechanism might well be an important part of our ability to think and use language. I use variants of this notation in several examples throughout this book. The following definition from embodied construction grammar (discussed in chapter 23) is one convenient way of describing feature structures and schemas:

schema: Container
  roles
    inside: Region
    outside: Region
    boundary: Curve

Feature structures, as depicted in the left column of table 11.2, are typical computational level mechanisms that are widely used in programming electronic computers. These routine database applications have both similarities and differences with neural information processing. In both cases, the information is organized as features and values associated with each entity. In a payroll program, each feature has a precise value that is set by an administrator, and these data are used only when the payroll program is called on to compute something about a particular person. The computational mechanisms are quite different for neural systems or their connectionist models, as we described in chapter 9. In a connectionist or neural system, features will have graded values: ham is not nearly as salty as pretzels. Also, neural systems are richly connected and continuously active; no central program "accesses" the value of a feature—the action resides in the knowledge itself.

So, even though the second column of table 11.2 has a similar form to the database features, the computational implications are quite different. For us, the feature structure formalism is a convenient means of expressing the triangle node diagrams like those of figure 9.2. This is what I mean by the statement that a computational level mechanism is reducible to the connectionist level. For some purposes, we can focus on just the names of the features and their values, and not worry about the neural processing details. At other times, we will need to invoke neural and connectionist principles to explain why various aspects of language work the way they do. For example, one thought will often remind you of other related thoughts. The notation in table 11.2 does not capture this spreading activation nature of neural networks, and engineers have been unable to replicate it in computer systems.

I will also use another formalism that lies between the fixed values of a database and the spreading activation of neural and connectionist systems—probabilistic models. In this version of table 11.2, we would allow a feature to be described as having several possible values with different probabilities. For example, the direction associated with push is usually away, but we can also talk about pushing something to the left or right. So the possible values for the direction feature of push could be given as [away (.8), left(.1), right (.1)], where as always, the probabilities must add up to 1.0. I use these probabilistic feature values in chapter 14 to discuss a model for learning in which features and values determine the meaning of various action words. In later chapters we also use inferences among probability values—for example, computing the probability that recession will lead to increased unemployment.

Both the simplified versions and the full connectionist interpretation will be needed in discussing how feature structures interact with the schemas used to describe motor control, as suggested by the right-hand column of table 11.2. In a general way, we can see that pushing an object lying on a table can be viewed as a slide action away from the body, with a force of any magnitude. By way of contrast, "shove" can be used for a wide range of directions, but does imply a high degree of force. In chapter 14, we will see the crucial part these feature characterizations of actions play in learning simple verbs.

Image schemas play two important roles in what follows. First, we use the ideas around image schemas as a basis for the first demonstration of a connectionist model of language learning in children. In the next chapter, I describe a program by Terry Regier that is able to learn words describing spatial relations across a wide range of languages. More generally, image schemas play a central role in metaphorical mappings of abstract language to direct embodied experience, as is discussed in chapter 16.

Image schemas are conceptual primitives, but they also have internal structure. A container schema has features or *roles* for a boundary, an interior, a portal, and the exterior. A spatial relation word, such as *in*, evokes an instance of the container schema and this brings along all of its roles. So when we hear a phrase, like "in the bottle," it is natural to associate the parts of the bottle with the roles of the container schema. This idea of evoking structural roles becomes even more important in the next section, where we discuss cultural *frames*, which usually have many more roles than primitive schemas.

But schemas, like neurons, never work in isolation. Thought and language are the result of complex interactions among schemas; recall that schemas are just our way of writing down basic neural structures. We need notation to describe how multiple schemas are linked in representing the meaning of a word, phrase, or story. Consider the English word *into*, which combines *in* and *to* in the following way: *In* is defined relative to a container schema (a bounded region of space); it locates an object in the interior of container. *To* is defined relative to a source-path-goal schema, and locates an entity on a path with a goal. *Into* combines both the container and source-path-goal (SPG) schemas, so that the goal is in the interior of the container and the source is outside the container.

There is a standard way to diagram these schema relations, which we use in later, more complicated cases. We use multislot boxes, as in table 11.2, to represent the features of each schema. The conceptual links between schemas are depicted as double-headed arrows, as we can see from the rendition of *into* in figure 11.1. The arrows depict graphically the facts that

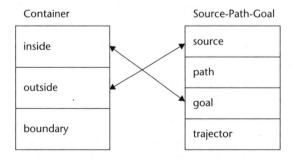

Figure 11.1
Into binds *inside* to *goal*.

the exterior of the container is the source and the interior the goal of the SPG schema for *into*.

Related concepts have similar diagrams. English *out of* would have a link between the exterior of the container and the goal of the SPG schema. And *through* specifies that both the source and goal of the SPG link to the exterior of the container and the path of the SPG link to the interior of the container.

Cultural Frames

Image schemas are used to describe basic and universal packages of human knowledge. There are obviously also many packages of knowledge that are specific to a given culture, profession, or other entity. In the mid-1970s, Charles Fillmore (Fillmore 1989) observed that to really understand the relationships between related words, you had to understand the structure underlying the conceptual setting, which he called *a frame*. For instance, to understand the relationships between words such as "buy" and "sell" you have to understand the commercial event frame. In any frame, there are participants. In the commercial event frame, the main participants are "buyer" and "seller." Other entities are "money" and "goods." Some frames also have scenarios, which have multiple states. In the commercial event frame, the progression is as follows:

The initial state:
  Buyer has money and wants goods.
  Seller has goods and wants money.

The middle state is an exchange.
  The Buyer gives money to the Seller.
  The Seller gives goods to the Buyer.

In the final state:
  The Buyer has goods.
  The Seller has money.

The concepts in the frame, such as "have" and "want," are simpler than "buy" and "sell" and could be primitive conceptual schemas of the sort discussed previously.

You can also make inferences given the structure. For instance, if you say "John bought a book from Mary," you can infer that John owns the book now and Mary had more money afterwards. The idea is that words such as *buy* and *sell* derive their meanings from frames—from the overall structure of related frames. The frames integrate all the entities and also define semantic roles of the participants and entities, such as agent, patient, and source. In the phrase, "John bought the book from Mary," John is the agent; Mary is the source; the book is the patient.

Frames are important to our story in two ways. From the embodied perspective, we experience the world in coherent scenarios, and it makes sense that we should organize our knowledge this way. As we will see, words can be best understood as calling into mind (evoking) a frame. Many words can evoke the commercial event frame, including ones that are not explicitly mentioned in its definition including price, cost, and bargain.

There is also a more technical way in which frames are important for our purposes. Frames encourage us to describe events as a sequence of situations, each of which is described by a collection of features (like buyer) and fillers (like John). Both the idea of sequences of actions and their representation in terms of features and values are used throughout this book.

We can also consider frames for basic actions such as walking or touching a nearby object. When you think about it, we know remarkably little about how our bodies and brain actually carry out these actions. We saw the same thing earlier in discussing color perception and vision in general—we have no way to consciously tap into the massive neural computations that we now know are responsible for our vision.

It is worth experiencing again this inaccessibility of detailed mechanism. Try to figure out what is happening as you reach to touch some nearby object. In fact, this action involves elaborate coordination of many muscle and control systems including shifting your body posture to balance the movement. Although you probably didn't think of this, the motion is accompanied by adjustments in the visual system that take into account your changed head position and gaze.

So a great deal of our bodily activity cannot be talked about directly in language or consciously thought about or modified. Of course, some features of our actions we can talk about and, it seems, these are the same features that we can consciously control. For example, in touching an object you can choose the body part that does the touching, the direction, speed, and force of your movement, and possibly a few other parameters.

Some indirectly relevant *parameters* include the properties of the target object and your reason for doing the touching. There are also some general control parameters that can accompany any action, for example, whether it is done once or repeatedly.

The limited accessibility of the details of actions raises an intriguing possibility: perhaps frames represent all we can say directly about bodily actions. This fits in beautifully with the embodied idea of word meaning this book explores. Each of us has rich experience with our bodily actions and perceptions, but we can say only a very restricted set of things about them. Since speakers and listeners share both the experience and the frame parameters, however, a word or expression can convey a great deal of meaning. The theory developed over the next few chapters relies heavily on the ideas that language primarily operates at the level of frame parameters and understanding involves imaginative simulation invoked by these frames.

This simple picture has two complications, and they are both important. While we have little direct control over the fine structure of a movement (say, touching), there are many indirect ways of modifying our actions that can be readily conveyed in language. So you could reach to touch an object as if you were a baby, very old, very tired, frightened, and so on. This kind of language use also has an obvious base in experience (and mirror neurons; see chapter 6). We discuss this in connection with metaphorical language, which plays a central role in the second half of this book.

The other complication with the idea of universal meaning frames is that human languages differ greatly in how they express things, including actions. As with words for spatial relations, different languages have quite distinct ways of talking about the same underlying actions. For example, Spanish has two words, *pulsar* and *presionar*, that capture different senses of the English *push*. The first of these would be used for pushing a button and the second for pushing a box.

The diversity of ways to describe actions across languages presents a challenge for frame semantics and, indeed, for any theory of language understanding. In fact, the packaging of information into frames can differ markedly among languages, requiring a more fundamental cross-linguistic level of representation. Image schemas, including the primitive motor schemas, are the cognitive scientist's means of describing these language-independent foundations of thought.

Image schemas and cultural frames figure prominently in the core semantics of human language. They form a crucial part of the computational level description of our neural circuitry for language and thought. We use them in the discussion of news story understanding in chapter 20 and they are central to the theory of language understanding and learning developed in chapters 21 through 25. In the next chapter, we will see a first instance of how image schemas can combine with connectionist modeling to support a detailed simulation of word learning.

We are finally in a position to see how all of the scientific findings summarized in the preceding chapters can be brought together to help explain how children could learn the words of their language. The core of this demonstration is a detailed computational model that learns how to label a visual scene with an appropriate spatial relation word. The same program learns words correctly for each of the several languages tested, although, as we saw in the previous chapter, spatial terms differ very widely across languages. The program incorporates many aspects of embodied language. It also illustrates how a neural theory can be applied to the specific task of learning words that describe spatial relationships.

We explored the idea of computational models in chapter 3, using weather prediction as the prototypical example. We saw how people can build a computer program incorporating an approximate version of the laws of physics as they apply to weather systems. After feeding the program measurements of various weather parameters, the computer is run and predictions about future weather are produced. The main limitations are the computing power and measurements involved—the science is not completely understood, but is developed enough to make quite good predictions given accurate data and enough computing time.

Chapter 2 also briefly discussed computational models in science, and we now consider these issues more carefully. The traditional methodology of science involves two techniques for understanding nature: theory and experiment. The conventional paradigm is that preliminary observations and experiments suggest a possible theory. For a theory to be considered scientific, it must explain existing data, but also must predict results for experiments that have not yet been done, and possibly suggest new experiments. This has meant that scientific theories in the physical sciences had to be expressed in very precise terms, usually in some mathematical form. The cycle is complete when the predictions of the theory are compared with the results of new experiments, often leading to a revised theory.

The growth of computational modeling has altered and significantly enhanced the options for gaining scientific understanding. Any scientific theory must be expressed in a technical language so that its consequences can be predicted and tested. Traditional theories formulated as mathematics are often too hard for people to evaluate, that is, to prove what the consequences of the theory would be in some untested situation. The wonderful property of computational models is that they can be *simulated* to yield predictions, rather like weather forecasts. Scientists in all fields now use computer models to explain and predict data in situations that are much too complex to be treated with traditional mathematical theories and the predictions computable from them by human proofs.

In contrast to weather prediction, the link between scientific computer models and measurable data is often indirect. This is also true when weather prediction is extended to climate modeling, where the whole point is to make predictions about probable future conditions long before any confirming data arrive. This modeling in advance of the data is especially necessary for theories in cognitive science, like those I will be describing.

As yet we have only limited knowledge of the neural circuitry that underlies the human ability to use language. Even if we could make detailed predictions about this circuitry, there are no available techniques for measuring human brain activity at a sufficiently fine-grained level to determine if the predictions are accurate. There is a wide range of relevant behavioral experiments, some of which were described in chapter 7, but these only link indirectly to neural theories of language. Studies of patients with brain injuries and, more recently brain imaging studies, supply some general ideas of how we process language. Taken as a whole, the available data can rule out many possible theories of language understanding, but cannot provide sufficient support for the correctness of any detailed theory. Although we know a great deal about the chemistry and biology of the brain and have considerable understanding of how language is learned and used, we have no verifiable theory of how the neural circuitry produces any particular language behavior. Too many alternative models would yield essentially the same results at the crude level of experiment available to us.

The problem of linking structure to behavior is characteristic of science in general. For example, astronomers know a great deal about stars and have elegant theories of the underlying physics, but they have not worked out the linking mechanisms. Similarly, biologists appreciate the laws of physics and have remarkable knowledge of protein structure and function, but very little is understood of how sequences of amino acids specified by DNA fold into their three-dimensional shapes. In all such cases, bridging theories are used to suggest how to link (fairly well) known structure to observed behavior.

Starting with this chapter, I will be presenting detailed computational models that attempt to link what is known about neural computation to the observed regularities of language use and learning. This is conventional science, but is somewhat controversial. Given the current impossibility of confirming detailed neural models of language understanding, many scientists believe (and say loudly) that it is premature to even think about the problem as a whole. It is better, they say, for each discipline to pursue its own questions by its own lights and let later generations worry about how it might all fit together. I have no objection to this trade unionism, but am myself driven to understand what I can about the neural basis of thought and language in my lifetime.

Given that one is committed to doing scientific work in an area in which the ultimate truth is beyond our reach, the obvious strategy is to search for partial truths (Greene 2000). As we mentioned, ample data are available to rule out many neural theories of language understanding. The question is, what kinds of theories *are not* ruled out by what is known about language at all the various levels from molecule to metaphor. Currently, the most effective way to evaluate the viability of a theory in this area is to construct it as a computational model and see how well the model satisfies all the known biological, behavioral, and computational constraints. Because there are so many converging constraints, this kind of *adequacy* test is the gold standard in cognitive science and the one used in this book.

Terry Regier's model of how children could learn the meaning of spatial relation terms is the first of these detailed models (Regier 1996). Like all of the models we will discuss, it starts with a task that is known to be relevant to the overall problem of explaining embodied language and that has not been achieved by any existing program or explained by any existing theory. A computational system is constructed (this usually takes several years) to model some key aspects of the task while being consistent with the general constraints from all the relevant science.

To the extent that the model, using neural theory of language (NTL) principles, satisfies all the requirements above it can be viewed as support for the idea of studying language from the embodied perspective. In Regier's case, and the others to follow, there is no other model of any kind that accomplishes the target task at all, much less under the plausibility requirements discussed earlier. In general, the NTL approach enables us to attack and solve important problems not currently treatable by any other methodology or theory. This should, at the least, make the methodology an interesting framework for thinking about language from molecule to metaphor.

Regier's Program for Learning Spatial Relation Terms

Regier built his program to emulate a child viewing a simple geometric scene and being told a word that describes something about that scene in her language. The bottom of figure 12.1 depicts a typical scene with a circle somewhat above a rectangle, labeled by the English word *above*. One object is designated as Landmark and another as Trajector; in this example the rectangle is designated as the Landmark (LM) and the circle the Trajector (TR). The same scene could also be labeled *below* with the TR and LM roles reversed.

In different training sessions, native speakers of various languages (e.g., Russian, Bengali, Chinese, English) provided as input to the system the spatial relations term for the situation depicted. In each training session, the job of the model is to learn the spatial conceptual system of the language and its spatial relations terms well enough that the program can give the correct names for novel spatial configurations presented to the computer.

The program incorporates several of the connectionist modeling techniques that were discussed in chapter 9. The top of figure 12.1 shows how training data supplied by a native speaker is fed (dashed lines) to a learning system. The learning system itself is a version of the error

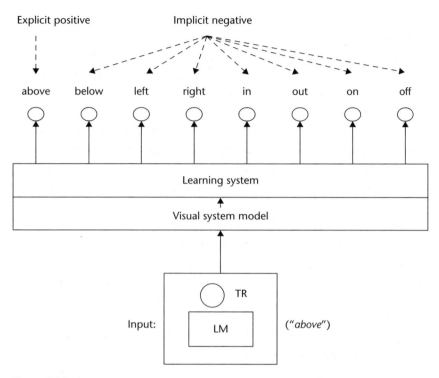

Figure 12.1
Overview of Regier's model for learning spatial relation words.

backpropagation network depicted in figure 9.3 and described in that section. The learning network was quite small; there was one unit for each possible spatial relation term (8 of them in figure 12.1) and about 10 units in the hidden middle layer from figure 9.3. Training times were also modest because of the small network and a clever and biologically motivated choice of the input features. The biologically based features also help fulfill another crucial requirement of the model—language independence.

The crucial requirement is that the same program should learn the words of whatever language it is taught, as a child would. As we saw in chapter 11, languages differ widely in how they describe spatial relations, so the program will fail if it tries to fit the words of all languages to the concepts that happen to have distinct words in English, because other languages might have more or fewer distinctly marked concepts. So the program needs to have a quite flexible way of dealing with the domain (here spatial relations).

Someone who believed in *tabula rasa* learning (pure nurture) might try to achieve the required behavior with a completely general program for machine learning, of which there are hundreds. There is no way to prove that this couldn't ever work, but Regier and others have tried this approach without success, and there are theoretical reasons to believe that existing pure statistical techniques will always fail. In short, if the program is not given enough definite structure, it will fail to learn at all, but if it is given culturally specific structure it will fail to learn languages that partition the world differently.

Regier's solution to this dilemma is important not only because it worked well, but also for what it suggests about how human language learning could develop. One of the key insights he exploited was that, while cultures differ, all people have essentially the same neural wiring and live on the same planet with its gravity, lighting, and so on. By building into his program a simple model of the visual system, he was able to introduce enough structure for the model to learn from examples, without introducing cultural bias that would cripple it.

We saw earlier with color terms that the focal colors in all languages have obvious links to the neurophysiology of color perception. Regier reasoned that there should also be universal primitives of spatial relation perception, but realized they would not be as simple as in the case of color. His technical challenge became understanding which properties of visual scenes are used in describing spatial relations in the world's languages.

Regier had done research in computer vision and also studied the cognitive science of image schemas, which we discussed in the last chapter. Previous cognitive linguistic studies had established that two distinct classes of visual features were important—quantitative geometric features (e.g., angles) and qualitative topological features such as contact. For example, one reason we see figure 12.1 as a good example of *above* is that an imaginary line connecting the centers of the LM and TR would be approximately vertical. If the circle were off to one side, we would be less inclined to describe it as *above* the rectangle. Native English speakers vary widely on this judgment; some people would label a scene with above if the circle were moved all the way to one side of the figure; others are much stricter about the vertical alignment requirement. Your friends will differ on this. If there was also contact between the circle and the rectangle, we would have a good example of English *on*.

Although all languages make use of the same visual primitives, these are combined in rather different ways. Rather than try to guess which combinations of features might be needed for each language, Regier combined his visual system model with a general supervised learning network, like the one of figure 9.3. Using constraints from both the biology and linguistics of spatial relations, he built a simple structured connectionist model of the visual computations that could support the learning needed for his task. The model used components known to be present in the human visual system, including center–surround cells, edge–sensitive cells, and systematic visual maps, all of which were discussed in chapter 5. He designed this model visual system to compute features that were known to be important in various languages including the image schematic notions of contact and containment, discussed in chapter 11. The visual system model also had connectionist networks for computing geometric relations such as the angle between center of the landmark and that of the trajector. The features computed by the model visual system were represented as activity in nodes of the neural network, and these were connected as inputs to the learning circuit.

Figure 12.1 gives an overview of Regier's computer program. Recall that the goal is to model how a child might learn to use the spatial relation words of her native language. The program is trained by being presented with a series of word-image pairs. The model assumes that the child has already learned which set of words is used for describing spatial relations and now needs to discover exactly what each word means. The simulation is also realistic in that the system, like a child, is not explicitly told when one of its answers is wrong. Later we will see some of the system's weaknesses as a model of child learning, but let's first look at what it can do and a bit about how it works.

The example shown in figure 12.1 shows a simple scene with a circle labeled TR above a rectangle labeled LM. The set of possible labels for this scene is shown as eight nodes (small ovals) at the top of the diagram. The model is trained for a given language in a series of episodes. At each step, a simple picture is presented as data to the program and, at the same time, the program is told which label goes with the scene. This instruction is done by an informant setting one of the eight top nodes to a positive value, while the other nodes are all set to zero. The program is given dozens of such training examples, each pairing a scene with a word. Then the program is tested on instances that are different from any it has seen.

The large box in the middle of figure 12.1 stands for a model neural network that links the visual image input to the various possible output node labels. Following the general model for simulated neural networks, the program works by activation spreading from the input image, through the network to the eight output units on top. The goal of learning is to train the connection weights between units in the network so that each input image strongly activates just the correct word node in the top layer of the figure. If the network has learned well, the correct top output node will become highly activated by a novel picture.

The training method that Regier used was discussed in chapter 9: the standard error backpropagation algorithm for using supervision to change the connection weights between units in a network. On each learning trial, the system is given an input image. Using the current values for the connection weights, the neural network spreads varying amounts of activation to the competing answer nodes representing the different possible labels for the given scene.

In backpropagation training, the system is directly provided with the desired answer, here an appropriate word for describing the scene. Without worrying about the computational details, we can see how the system can change weights to improve its labeling performance. Any weights that connect to the supplied correct answer will be made stronger and weights to alternative answers will be made weaker. Another presentation of exactly the same image will lead to higher activation of the correct label and lower activations of the erroneous competing word labels. It is not obvious that this procedure will improve performance on unseen examples, but it often does.

One trick that works well for this system, and probably for children, uses the idea that answer feedback differing from your current guess is an implicit negative, as shown on the top of the figure. When the system is told that a scene should be labeled *above*, it implicitly assumes that the other possible labels do not apply. This isn't always right, but it does serve as a valuable rule of thumb. For example, if the current weights in figure 12.1 made *left* the most active output and the training said the answer was *above*, then *left* is just wrong. But if the system's calculation yielded *out* as the most active, that is another perfectly good answer for this example. By making smaller learning changes for incorrect answers, the model allows for multiple correct labels for a given scene.

As we discussed in chapter 9, computational learning programs work because, in the long run, the right answers correlate with the relevant features more than with unrelated features that appear occasionally in the scene. There is good reason to believe that similar statistical principles are a crucial part of the mechanism for human learning of words and concepts. If you are in a foreign country and hear a certain word spoken whenever a trolley car goes by, it is a good guess that the word has something to do with trolleys. As we saw in chapter 8, children do (subconsciously, of course) use this kind of reasoning.

After completing his program, Regier tested it with a variety of situations and languages. The situation suggested by figure 12.1 is an experiment in which he trained the program on a set of examples including several variants on all eight spatial relations named at the top with a variety of object shapes and no explicit negatives. After the weights were trained, he tested the system using a novel landmark shape (a triangle) that the model had never seen in training. Essentially all of the test scenes were labeled correctly, and there were no gross errors.

The same program was tested (less extensively) by having scenes labeled with terms from Arabic, Bengali, Chinese, Mixtec (see chapter 11), and Russian, with largely similar results. Regier went on to extend the system to deal with scenarios in which simple objects moved and the motion was named. For example, the program learned quite well the difference between English *into*, *through*, and *around*. This involved an additional structured connectionist model of human motion perception followed by another supervised learning network, but the ideas are essentially the same as those we have discussed. No other program before or since has been able to model the learning of spatial relation terms across such a wide range of languages.

Regier's system for learning spatial relation words was an important first step in demonstrating the link between brain and language. A simple and biologically motivated computational model was able to learn spatial relation words of a wide range of languages from just labeled scenes. It did this without explicitly being told when it was wrong. The same system was extended to learn names for simple scenarios involving moving objects. As with any good theory, the model made a number of specific predictions about language learning, and these continue to be explored experimentally.

But the model also had a number of limitations, some of which turned out to be fundamental. Any pioneering effort makes certain simplifications to focus on the core problem—here, naming visual scenes. From the information processing perspective, children do several things with concepts that the program was not able to do. While it was great at *recognizing* a concept such as "left" in an image, it had no way to reason with the concept or use the concept in an action of its own such as moving its left hand or drawing a circle to the left of a square.

It wasn't just that the program lacked drawing ability, which would be easy to add. The pattern of connection weights that enabled it to recognize "left" simply isn't the right kind of information to control an action. From a linguistic perspective, the program could understand only the most literal and direct uses of words. And, of course, it could only deal with single words. Children learn spatial relation terms in a larger linguistic context, not as isolated words as the program does. A more realistic model of the child's learning of longer utterances is presented in chapter 25.

There were also limitations from the biological modeling perspective. Although the visual system model was neurologically plausible, learning words through supervised slow weight change is not realistic. Children learn words quickly, sometimes after a single example—weight change learning requires thousands of example runs. Also, no one considers the mathematical details of how weight-change learning is carried out by the backpropagation technique to be biologically plausible.

Much of the rest if this book lays out the tale of how these various limitations of the spatial-relation learning model were overcome. This required several new insights in cognitive science and computational modeling, which I will describe. But, at the end of the day (and of the book), many of Regier's ideas remain central to the bridge between brain and language.

Several of the limitations that we have been discussing arose from the use of supervised slow weight change (backpropagation) as the learning mechanism. This is a computational issue and addressing it requires computational solutions. One of these was described in chapter 9—*recruitment learning* is a faster and biologically more plausible model of neural adaptation than backpropagation. Other improvements have come from a variety of disciplines. As often happens in science, attacking a more difficult problem led to solutions that also overcome some of the Regier's model's limitations.

In this case, the more difficult problem was building a model of how children learn the words to describe *actions*, such as pushing a block. This was solved by David Bailey, as will be discussed soon. Bailey and his colleagues needed to develop additional computational mechanisms for biologically plausible models of action. The work also involved formalizing the cognitive science idea of frames. Computational models of frames and executing schemas are described in the next chapter and later applied to the task of building models of how children learn words for actions, again across languages.

V Learning Words for Actions

In this chapter, we explore how children learn words for describing actions, such as walking or pushing. We saw in chapter 10 that action words are among the first a child learns. Nervous systems evolved for sensing and action; language is a very recent extra. We start with two simple facts: (1) kids are very good at carrying out many actions before they learn the words for them and (2) an action unfolds through time, so the child has some unconscious neural plan for the actions she or he performs. The question for this chapter is how children, around the age of 2, learn how their own actions are described in their native language.

We begin by asking what the child's internal neural circuitry for actions might be like and how it could be modeled. For reflexes, such as the knee-jerk reflex described in chapter 5, the circuitry is extremely well understood and can be described, at a moderate level of detail, using diagrams such as the one in figure 5.1. This depicts the neural circuits as abstract computational units and shows which connections have excitatory and inhibitory effects, without specifying details such as the strength of various connections. The other important insight is that all motor control networks in the body involve feedback from sensory neurons in circuits that run through the spinal cord and various substructures of the brain.

The control circuits for nonreflex actions, like walking or pushing, are somewhat similar to that in figure 5.1, but they have multiple levels of control circuits. In fact, what we call the knee-jerk reflex is one component of the full control circuit for standing and walking. This reflex causes one leg to support more of our weight when the other leg slips. Computational modeling of complex motor behaviors such as walking requires the mathematics of *control theory*. We will not need this level of detail, but the executing schemas introduced later in this chapter are motivated by the key ideas of control loops and feedback.

The complete circuitry for walking has not been worked out, but what is known would already make any diagram in the style of figure 5.1 much too complex to be very useful. What scientists often do is to make more abstract and schematic representations of motor control such as the gait control model shown in figure 13.1. This depicts the control circuitry for two gaits of the cat. In the top half of figure 13.1, we see an image of the cat trotting. We can observe that in trotting, the left hind leg (LH) and the right front leg (RF) contact the ground at the same time, followed by the LF and RH legs simultaneously supporting the animal, in a repeating pattern.

This contrasts with the depiction of pacing (ordinary walking) in the lower half of the figure. Here, the LH and LF make simultaneous contact followed by the RH and RF coinciding, again, in a repeating pattern. The cat's fastest gait, the gallop, has the two hind legs making contact together,

Behavior   Model

"Trot"

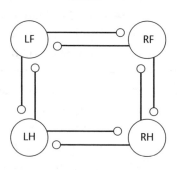

"Pace"

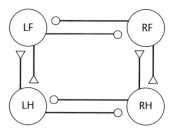

Figure 13.1
Computational models of gaits of the cat.

then the two front legs, and so on. One important finding for our purposes is that the cat's brain signals which gait to use by encoding the value of a single *parameter*, the desired speed. The decision of which gait to use is made by lower motor circuits.

This idea of characterizing actions by their parameters plays a central role in our models of language learning. Consider what you know about your own gaits (walking, skipping, etc.). People have no direct knowledge of what muscles and firing patterns are involved in walking, but can think and talk about a few parameters such as the speed, direction, and assertiveness of the motion.

Let's now look at the circuit diagrams on the right side of figure 13.1. These employ the usual convention that a link with a circular tip is inhibitory, so that activation of that link tends to turn off activity in the receiving unit. The models proposed in the figure suggest that trotting can be characterized as mutual inhibition between the activation circuitry for all the adjacent limbs. The proposed model suggests that pacing differs from trotting in that the limbs on each side have mutually positive connections, and thus tend to extend at the same time. We need not be concerned with the accuracy of this model, but should focus on the way it allows us to make precise predictions. In practice such models are evaluated by computational simulation, neurologic experiments, or both.

What matters to us most about figure 13.1, is the general idea of abstract neural models of motor control systems. The units and connections in the figure are not intended to depict neurons, but rather to model the behavior of the whole system. Another crucial fact about the figure is that it depicts what we will call an *executing schema*. The diagrams can be viewed as simple routines for controlling the cat's gaits and simulated to show how they work. They are sufficiently detailed to serve as programs for controlling robots, and similar notations are being used for such purposes.

Our theory of language learning and use relies heavily on this idea of executing schemas, and most of this chapter is concerned with spelling these schemas out. The theory also involves parameter (feature) values, like the desired speed of the cat's locomotion. The general story of feature values as computational level representation of neural parameters (see table 11.2) applies here as well. Describing motor activity in terms of features and values is an important simplification of the underlying connectionist models and neural circuitry.

More complex actions, such as human manipulations, will require several parameters and more elaborate executing schemas. These parameters play a central role in the theory of how children learn words to describe their actions. Consider the word "grasp." Everyone will agree that the meaning of the word involves the motor action of grasping in some way. The embodied neural approach to language suggests that the complex neural circuitry that supports grasping *is* the core meaning of the word. I choose this particular example because we know a great deal about the intricate distributed neural circuitry involved in grasping by monkeys and humans.

The action of *grasping* has both a motor component (what you do in grasping) and various perceptual components (what it looks like for someone to grasp and what a graspable object looks like). Other modalities are involved as well, such as the sensory component (what it feels like to grasp something or to be grasped yourself). And all voluntary actions have an associated goal and plan. Both the meaning of a word and the behavior it defines are context dependent—you grasp differently for different objects and purposes.

This embodied theory also suggests that the meaning of a noun (e.g., chair) involves how humans relate to it. We are willing to label all sorts of objects as chairs if people use them for sitting. Linguistic evidence also supports this idea that the meaning of a noun depends on the uses of the underlying thing. Many languages around the world, including Assamese, Bantu, Chinese, Navajo, Swahili, and Thai, often require adding a grammatical *classifier* to a noun. Such languages might have a classifier for "long-thin-thing," for example. In Chinese "one person" is: "yi ge ren" ("one CLF person"), where CLF stands for the classifier "ge," meaning single entity. Interestingly, nouns classified similarly must name the same category of thing, although the rules for what counts as "the same category" develop in some subtle ways. George Lakoff's (1987) book *Women, Fire, and Dangerous Things* is replete with such extended category examples.

Independent of any linguistic evidence, extensive brain imaging data now supports the idea of embodied language. More generally, there is increasing evidence for the common neural circuitry for actions and action words. Rizzolatti and coworkers (2001), over the last 20 years, have shown that the frontal area of both monkey and human brains contain neurons that integrate motor, visual, and proprioceptive modalities for the purpose of controlling actions in space and perceiving the area of space reachable by body parts. More recently, they have shown that these areas integrate not only visual but also auditory information about the location of objects within nearby space. These so-called *mirror neurons* and circuits show the same activity when the subject sees an action as when she or he does the action (Buccino et al. 2001).

Mirror neurons in monkeys and people suggest an overlap of the underlying brain circuits for the execution of actions and the perception of the same action. This is a plausible neural basis for the fact that an action word, such as *grasp*, denotes grasping, being grasped, or observing grasping. Several studies using different experimental methodologies and techniques have demonstrated the existence in humans of a mirror system, which responds similarly to action observation and execution of the same action.

The brain areas involved in spatial and motor behaviors, rather than having separate and independent functions, are neurally integrated not only to control action, but also to serve the function of constructing an integrated representation of (a) actions together with (b) objects acted on and (c) locations toward which actions are directed. This complex is what we take to be the substrate of the meaning of action words. If we accept this complex of neural circuits and behaviors as the core meaning of grasping, it remains to show how a word such as "grasp" gets associated with the embodied concept.

But there seems to be a fundamental complexity barrier. How could the meaning of an action *word* be the activity of a vast distributed *network* of neurons? The key to overcoming this difficulty in the models and, we believe also in the brain, is *parameterization*. A motor action such as grasping involves many coordinated neural firings, muscle contractions, and other elements, but we have no conscious awareness of these details. What we can be aware of (and talk about) are certain parameters of the action—force, direction, effector, posture, repetition, and so on.

The crucial hypothesis is that *languages label only the action properties of which we can be aware*. That is, a fixed set of experienced features determine the semantic space for any set of embodied concepts, such as motor actions. So, kids need to learn only which properties of their actions are crucial for their language.

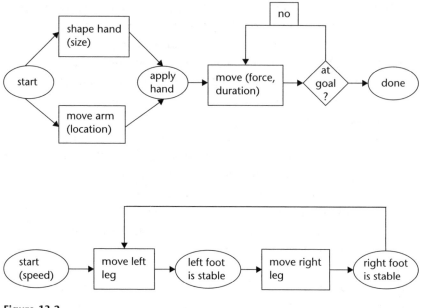

Figure 13.2
Schemas for push and walk.

We will be looking closely at feature representations of actions that a person might carry out with one hand on objects on a table. The top half of figure 13.2 presents a general schema for sliding an object across the table and is used in the next chapter as part of the model for learning the meanings of words such as "push" and "pull." As with the description of cat gaits, this schema is a breakdown of the overall action into subparts and the control links between them. This is at the computational level of description and, as such, is a shorthand for a more elaborate underlying connectionist model.

Let's follow the flow of control in the top of figure 13.2, starting from the left. If you reach to push a nearby object, notice that two things happen at the same time. Your hand attains the right shape for the target object while your arm is moving. This is modeled by the two arrows of control, one to the box labeled shape hand (size) and the other to move arm (location). When both of these actions are finished, the sliding can proceed and this is modeled by the arrows converging into the box labeled apply hand. Notice that the two initial actions both have parameters; preshaping depends on the size of the target object, and moving the arm obviously depends on the location of the target object.

The right part of the push schema is a control loop, more sophisticated than the knee-jerk circuit of figure 5.1. The basic idea is that the arm should continue moving until the goal is reached. The main action, move arm (direction, force), has as its parameters the desired direction of movement and the desired force. In this schema, the arm continues to move until it is explicitly stopped by an inhibitory feedback signal. So the parameters or features of this schema are location, size, direction, force, and goal.

Executing schemas such as those just described can characterize human motor actions quite well. In fact, such descriptions can be used to control the simulated android, *Jack* (Badler et al. 2002). *Jack* is a large, complex computer program that not only simulates muscle actions, but also computes the forces a human body would feel in acting or being acted on. Its programs are quite realistic in that a high-force push will cause the model shoulder to "lean in" as people do. *Jack* is used commercially to test how human bodies might fare in various work or danger situations, like a simulated car crash (Shi et al. 1999).

The engineers who built and market *Jack* use parameterized schemas like those of figure 13.2 to ease the task of programming *Jack* to simulate the actions required for some particular test. They hope eventually to use embodied semantic models, such as those described in this book, to command *Jack* directly in ordinary language. As we will see in the next chapter, *Jack* can also be used to demonstrate that a computational learning model has correctly learned the meaning of an English word such as "drop."

Let's also look at a simplified version of the executing schema for another common motor action, walking, which is shown on the bottom half of figure 13.2. Here just a single parameter, speed, controls the rate of moving one leg after the other. Walking, as opposed to running, is characterized by the right leg not moving until the left leg is felt to be stable. At a lower level of control, this involves the knee-jerk circuit of figure 5.1. We will look at a more complete schema for walking in chapter 17, in conjunction with the general discussion of repetitive actions. Walking is the base for many metaphors about progress of any sort and we use this metaphor extensively in chapter 20.

Executing schemas are central to the development of an embodied neural theory of language. While we have discussed the slide and walk schemas as controllers of motor activity, the same schemas can be used in several other ways. In our discussion of mirror neurons (chapter 5), we noted that some neurons (in monkeys) and neural systems (in people) show similar behavior when the animal sees the action or carries it out. We hypothesize that the schema representations of actions, as in figure 13.2, are also used to recognize the appropriate action when observed by the animal. No one has yet built a computer model that both executes and recognizes using the same schema, but some very successful models of action recognition use schemas quite like those presented here (Bregler 1997).

It is worth considering how these programs for visual recognition of human gaits do their magic. The central idea is *prediction.* Any animal or computer vision system needs to decide the best explanation for the flood of image data constantly coming in from its sensors. This is another instance of the general best-fit nature of neural computation. The problem becomes enormously easier if the system can predict the most likely possibilities. If you have no context, the next image you see might be of anything at all. In recognizing, for example, human gaits, we obviously can (and do) make quite detailed predictions of what we should see next—but how?

Action schemas like those of figure 13.2 provide an elegant answer. If the vision system has recognized someone walking to the left at 3 miles/hour, the action schema for walking can be used as a model to predict where various body parts should be going. The programs (and almost certainly our brains) actually do something a bit fancier. Starting off the recognition of a new action, the system cannot be sure which schemas and parameters fit best. The programs allow several alternative schemas to compete in trying to match the evolving input scene, and the model that makes the best predictions is the winner.

Computer models that use schemas for an action to recognize that action were developed before the discovery of mirror neurons, but fit beautifully with those findings. Using executing schemas for prediction and inference is a key feature of the language understanding theory we lay out later.

Another use of executing schemas, which is important for language and thought, is in imagination or simulation. There is very good evidence that people use much of the same neural circuitry while imagining an action as they do when it is really being carried out. Similarly, much of the brain that is active in perception is also active in visual imagination. Dreaming, even in animals, is also known to involve simulated action. There is a brain center that blocks dream activity from moving muscles, and failure of that center leads to dreams that are physically enacted, sometimes causing great trouble.

If a common executing schema underlies action, recognition of action, planning, and simulation, then many questions in language become less mysterious. Shared and parameterized neural circuitry for executing and describing actions provides a natural grounding for semantics. We can understand someone by imagining ourselves in their situation, and we apparently have evolved mechanisms that do this automatically. Imagination or simulation will play a key role in our theory of embodied language understanding, coming in chapter 20 and 24.

The remainder of this book relies heavily on the idea of executing schemas, each of which has a relatively small set of determining parameters or features. As a first example, the next chapter describes how a computer program based on these concepts is able to model how children learn action words across a broad range of languages.

We saw in chapter 10 that children first learn words that name their direct experience, including feelings, objects, properties, and actions. We all have strong intuitions about how to describe the properties of objects and can imagine how children learn to link the names of objects with their properties. The child's own actions are surely among its most salient experiences, so it is not surprising that some action words (verbs in English) are learned quite early. But we have much less intuition about how to describe actions and how children could learn to name them. The executing schema formalism described in the previous chapter provides a basis for describing actions and, in this chapter, is used in a model how children learn words for their own actions.

Our first model (chapter 12) of child word learning was Regier's program for learning spatial relation words in different languages. This system learned to label novel scenes with the correct word but had several limitations as a model of human language learning. For our purposes, the most important limitations of Regier's system were its very long training times and its inability to do anything with words except apply them as labels. When people learn the meaning of a word, they can also use it in reasoning and to request and carry out actions based on the meaning they have learned.

A few years after Regier completed his thesis, David Bailey set out to build a program that would overcome these difficulties and model child word learning in the challenging domain of actions. To limit the complexity of the task, Bailey restricted consideration to actions that could be carried out by one hand with objects on a table. The program is modeling a scenario in which a child is performing an action and hearing her parent's (one word) label. The child's (and program's) main task is solving the *correlation* problem—what features of the situation and of my actions is my parent talking about (Bailey 1997)?

To conduct experiments on this task, the system was programmed to have the simulated android *Jack* carry out various one-handed actions. For each example, a native speaker of the target language types a word that best describes that action in her or his language and this word is given to the program, thereby modeling the situation where the child hears the parent's label for an action. Using techniques that we will be discussing shortly, the program tries to solve the correlation problem and learn which executing schemas and features should be associated with each word.

Before looking at how the model works, let's think some more about its task. Even for actions involving only one hand, there are quite a lot of verbs in English including seize, snatch, grab, grasp, pick up, hold, grip, clutch, put, place, lay, drop, release, pull, push, shove, yank, slide, flick, tug, nudge, lift, raise, lower, lob, toss, fling, tap, rap, slap, press, poke, punch, rub, shake, pry, turn, flip, rotate, spin, twirl, squeeze, pinch, twist, bounce, stroke, wave, caress, stack, salute, and many, many more.

And that's only English. Other languages make distinctions that English does not. Moreover, each language has its own unique collection of linguistic gaps that reflect conceptual differences in the concepts named. Here are a few examples:

• In Tamil, *thallu* and *ilu* correspond to English *push* and *pull*, except that they denote a sudden action as opposed to a smooth continuous force. The continuous reading can be obtained by adding a directional suffix, but there is no word to indicate smooth pushing or pulling in an arbitrary direction.

• In Farsi, *zadan* refers to a large number of object manipulations involving quick motions. The prototypical *zadan* is a hitting action, though it can also mean to snatch (*ghaap zadan*) or to strum a guitar or play any other musical instrument.

• In Cantonese, *meet* covers both pinching and tearing. It connotes forceful manipulation using the two-finger posture, but is also acceptable for tearing larger items using two full grasps. Cantonese has no distinct word equivalent to *drop*; there is a word meaning *release*, but it applies whether or not the object is supported.

▪ In Spanish, there are two separate words for different senses of the English verb *push*. The word *pulsar* corresponds to pushing a button and *presionar* covers most of the other uses.

In general, different languages combine meanings in differing ways. Whenever there are multiple senses (meanings) for the same word, this creates serious learning problems for children and computers.

Like Regier, Bailey was faced with the problem of building a program that needed to incorporate the conceptual differences across languages to learn word meanings. Again, building in too many assumptions would preclude learning some languages, and leaving everything unspecified would give the program no chance at all of learning. It will come as no surprise that Bailey used the same strategy on what structure to build into the system—base it on the body and on neural control networks. Just as Regier employed a simple model of the visual system, Bailey's program is based on the executing schema formalism of motor actions described in chapter 13.

Figure 14.1 presents an overview of Bailey's model for learning words that describe one-handed actions. The first thing to notice is that there is an intermediate set of feature structures, shown as a large rectangle in the middle of the figure. As you may recall from the previous chapter, people do not have access to the elaborate neural networks that coordinate our actions. What we can consciously know about our own actions can be described by a relatively small number of features. This parameterization of action (also discussed in chapter 13) is one key to the success of the computer program. The particular features used in the program, and depicted in the middle of the figure, were chosen to fit the basic X-schemas and capture the properties known to be relevant to distinctions made in various languages.

Also, please notice that figure 14.1 shows arrows in both directions. The system not only learns to label actions with words, but it will also carry out requests expressed using the words it has learned. The two arrows on the right describe the labeling pathway; features are extracted from executing schemas (bottom right arrow) and these features are then used to decide which verb is the most appropriate label for the action. The arrows on the left depict the command pathway. A word that has been learned (e.g., shove) will activate a particular set of linking features and this will determine the particular action that is carried out.

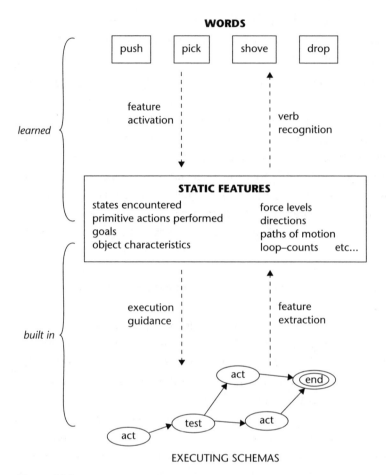

Figure 14.1
Overview of Bailey's model for learning action verbs.

The two downward arrows on the left capture an ability not present in Regier's model nor in any other system based on the supervised weight-change learning described in chapter 9--bidirectional learning. This pathway is used by the system to carry out actions that are requested using a verb that has been learned. For example, suppose that the program has learned (as it does) that the word *shove* involves using the slide-executing schema with high force and short duration. This information on which schema and parameter define the word *shove* would be stored as part of the word's definition. When asked to shove something, the system would activate the definition and select the appropriate schema and parameters from the large collection available in the middle of the figure. These can then be used to activate the appropriate schema (lower left arrow), here slide; this then leads to the simulated android *Jack* carrying out the requested shoving.

As we will see in later chapters, this ability to perform actions described by verbal input is the key to all language understanding. A system that can only label situations with an appropriate word has not come close to knowing the meaning of the word. The pathway on the left of figure 14.1—feature activation followed by execution guidance—underlies understanding of any language input. In the case shown here of simple verbs, the features in the middle of the figure need only specify which schema to execute and a few of its parameters, such as duration and posture.

According to the NTL, almost exactly the same thing happens when you hear a story about someone else carrying out an action like pushing. The only difference is that instead of acting yourself, you imagine (or simulate) someone else's action. This is what we call simulation semantics—you understand a story by simulating it. This is easy to believe for concrete language, but what about abstract stories like someone pushing for a promotion or ramming a legislative program through Congress? The NTL suggests that abstract meanings are understood by mapping them metaphorically to concrete image and action schemas such as those described in chapters 11 and 13. The metaphors and how they support language understanding in general are discussed in chapters 16 through 20. For now we focus on just the learning and understanding of concrete verbs of action.

As with Regier's model, Bailey trained and tested his program extensively in English and more sparsely in several other languages. In the main experiment, he presented the system with 165 labeled examples of actions corresponding to 15 English verbs and 18 word senses. Using learning techniques that I will describe shortly, the program was able to deduce the correct number of words and word senses. The system was then tested by asking it to label 37 novel actions according to the definitions it had learned. The performance was quite good; 80 percent of the scenes were given exactly the right label. Moreover, all of the errors involved overlapping concepts; for example, *move* for *push* or *jerk* for *lift*.

With no further training, the program was then tested for its ability to carry out the actions specified by the words it had learned. In these tests, the program was given a word that it had learned, and it generated parameters for the corresponding action. The execution plan was considered correct if the system assigned the original word to that action description. The results were quite similar; around 80 percent of the actions were optimal and the rest were near misses; of course, children make similar errors.

Bailey also tried some additional tests on English verb compounds such as *push left* or *pull up*. Some positive results were achieved, but it was recognized that real progress required a theory of grammar that was not then available. Chapters 21 through 25 discuss how models of word learning can be extended to cover complex patterns of words—grammar.

In addition to English words, Bailey tested his program on examples from Farsi, Hebrew, and Russian. The results for basic examples were good, but more complicated examples involve patterns within and across words, even more so than in English, and thus required a theory of grammar.

Let's now look into how Bailey's program works and what this can tell us about language and learning in people. The model improves on previous work in several ways. We know from the "fast mapping" results of chapter 10 that older children can learn words in a single episode. Bailey's program uses techniques with this one-shot learning property, which was missing from Regier's supervised learning model (chapter 12). The program requires only one presentation of each example because it uses a computational learning rule called model merging, which is the computational level version of recruitment learning (chapter 9) and is described below. Model merging, plus the use of the explicit features shown in the middle of figure 14.1, also provide the computational basis for the wider abilities depicted by the two upper arrows in that figure—learning to use words, not just treat them as labels.

We can see Bailey's model merging technique in action by following through the steps depicted in figure 14.2. In every case, the top row shows the names of features and the bottom row the given or predicted fillers for each feature. For example, the elbow motion feature could have as its values either extended or fixed.

On the left side of the figure are four episodes in which the program heard "push" in response to a variety of *Jack's* actions, and the right side depicts, at each step, the program's current guess about the word's meaning. On hearing push for the first time, the system's first model is (always) that the word meaning is close to what the robot just did. This is

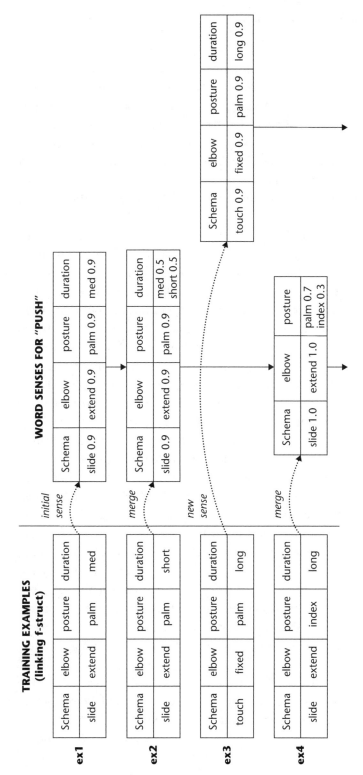

Figure 14.2
Four steps in the system's learning two senses of PUSH.

shown on the top right as a definition feature structure, which is the same as the action features except that each value is allowed certain fuzziness, shown as probability 0.9. Now suppose the system also hears the same word after doing a push of much shorter duration, as shown in the second row of the figure. The program revises its idea of the meaning of push to capture the fact that the duration seems equally likely to be either short or medium, as shown in the second row on the right. Technically, the program merges its original model of what push means with the information from the second example.

You can see how a program (or a neural system) that kept track of the various situations involving each word could come to learn the required correlations—the probability of various features' values being present in a scenario when each particular word is used. Looking back to Regier's system in chapter 12, we can view his program as using supervised learning techniques to learn connection weights that capture the correlation between visual scene features and the words used to label it.

But a major complication shows up in the third row of figure 14.2. The English word "push" is also used in situations that are fundamentally different from the standard one; here the features in example 3 represent the action of pushing against an unmoving object such as a wall. As we noted earlier, some languages such as Farsi use different words for these different actions, but English does not, and this is a problem for learning.

As figure 14.2 also shows, linguists refer to disparate meanings of a given word as different word senses. A crucial task for the child (and the program) is to decide whether or not to learn multiple senses for a given word. We will return to this question shortly. For the example shown, the program did decide to add a distinct word sense. The final example at the bottom of the figure differs somewhat from the standard "push," but not by too much for the basic definition to be modified to also include this example. Since the final example involves pushing with the index finger, the posture feature in the definition must be revised. Because two out of three examples involved the palm posture, the probabilities are set to approximate this data.

More interesting, the duration feature is now totally missing from the basic definition of push. Technically, a feature is removed from a definition when its values appear to be irrelevant. In this case, all three possible durations occur equally often in the basic push scenario so duration doesn't seem to matter. Of course, the situation has many other features, that are irrelevant to the use of the word "push." The color of the object, the time of day, the room we are in, and many other features need to be removed from the definition of push and these should, in principle, have been included in figure 14.2. But features that don't matter for one definition can be crucial for another; for example, the time of day is crucial in learning the names of meals.

Let's return to the problem of choosing the correct number of distinct senses for a word like "push." This is the most difficult technical problem in Bailey's system, and it is not important to explore the full details of how he and other computer scientists solve this kind of best-explanation problem. The techniques are quite close to those for choosing a best grammar, which we outline in chapter 22. But the general idea of *evaluating competing mental models* is important and well worth considering further.

We all frequently make internal mental models—of other people, of how things work, of routes to work. These internal models allow us to predict how we can get what we want. Choosing word senses is a special case of the general problem of deciding which situations to lump together in a single internal model. For example, you might decide that all professors are alike for your purposes and treat them all the same. Scientists developing theories about nature face the same problem—is it better to have one theory (model) of neurons, or should they be thought of as several different types?

You can see that the choice of how many models to use involves trade-offs. If you make too many distinct models, you might miss generalizations that can be crucial for dealing with new situations. On the other hand, if we lump too many situations into a single model, we lose the ability to make critical distinctions—if you are a student, it is not a great idea to treat all your professors the same way.

Bailey's program and many other machine learning systems use standard computational treatment of these model selection tradeoffs. The central idea is to use a measure of overall model goodness that is the sum of two terms. The first term is a measure of the complexity of the model itself, with simpler and more probable models being better. The second term evaluates how well each proposed model explains the data. In the case of learning action words, the program introduces a new word sense (see figure

14.2) when the extra complexity added to the vocabulary is more than balanced by each definition being a better fit to its subset of the scenarios.

This is as far as we need to go in our discussion of how children learn words that name their direct experience and how this can be modeled using an NTL. Of course, the child's experience of actions is much richer than the programs described here can model, but there does not seem to be any inherent barrier to more complete demonstrations.

In addition, many words, even for young children, do not directly label immediate experiences. Fairly early in life children start to use the same word in both concrete and metaphorical senses. One common example is when a parent says (with a pained tone) "Now, *see* what you've done." The child knows that she is supposed to learn (see) as well as perceive her transgression. In an NTL, abstract and metaphorical words derive their meanings from concrete words. Next, in chapters 15–17, we explore how this happens and some of the consequences for theories of language and thought.

VI   Abstract and Metaphorical Words

In previous chapters, we discovered how children learn to talk about their experience of spatial relations (chapter 12) and motor actions (chapter 14). For perception, action, emotions, and so on, human experience and the social relations shared by all people provide the basis for learning words. We explored in detail how children around the world learn their first words for colors, for naming things, for spatial relations, and for their own actions. The same basic labeling processes apply to many other aspects of direct experience, including the properties of objects and actions, personal desires, and family relations. The depth and breadth of the child's experience is remarkably rich and, as we will see, provides the source for all advanced concepts.

Of course, this universal shared experience of children is still only a small part of what comprises adult conceptual systems and language. The three chapters of this section outline a theory of how abstract, cultural, and technical words and concepts arise from the opulent substrate of direct experience. Neural embodiment remains central to the story—people, as neural systems, understand abstract ideas because these concepts are mapped to and activate brain circuits involved in embodied experience.

Let's start with a simple example of how children learn concrete words and concepts that go beyond their direct experience. Even the most fundamental embodied concepts fall into three distinct types. All of our examples so far have focused on only one of these—the *basic level* categories. Concepts at the basic level include car, green, cow, walk, screwdriver—categories of things that you know how to picture and interact with. Children learn these words first, but they soon move on to words that denote both more and less general types of categories. The more general *superordinate* categories corresponding to these examples would be vehicle, animal, colors, locomotion, and tool. Some more specific examples of each category at the *subordinate* level might be Camry car, turquoise, Guernsey cow, saunter, and Phillips #1 screwdriver.

Cognitive scientists, starting in the 1960s, have shown that concepts at the three levels are treated rather differently in language and thought. Eleanor Rosch, among others, demonstrated that basic-level categories have cognitive properties quite dissimilar from those of superordinate categories (Rosch 1973). The basic categories are defined by our capacities for motor movement, mental imagery, and gestalt perception (seeing things as meaningful wholes). Compare *chair* and *furniture*. You can get a mental image of a chair, but not of a general piece of furniture (as opposed to a chair, bed, table, or couch). You have motor schemas for interacting with chairs, but none for interacting with general pieces of furniture. Our concept of a chair has to do, after all, with our ability to sit, which has everything to do with our bodies. It is a fundamentally embodied concept. In short, the basic level is the highest level at which shared mental imagery, motor schemas, and gestalt perception characterize the entire category. Higher, superordinate, categories such as furniture do have some commonality, but it is more abstract.

The basic category level is associated with human interactions, but not all individuals or cultures experience the world the same way. For many city dwellers, *tree* is a basic level category—we interact the same way with all trees. But for a professional gardener, tree is definitely a superordinate category; all trees have important common properties, but the gardener's daily interactions with various kinds of trees are very different. One of the most compelling findings in this field is that each person's performance on psychological tests such as those of chapter 7 is consistent with his or her own category structure. You can learn much about how people categorize the world from their performance on such tests.

Of the many findings on levels of categories, the one that most interests us is that children, apparently everywhere, first learn words for concepts at the basic level. This makes sense because the basic-level concepts are those that arise in direct experience, as we have seen. There is no mystery about how children move on to learn names for more specific (subordinate) concepts as these become important to them. Caregivers point out and name specific instances that are important to the group and culture.

What is not so obvious is how children can go beyond direct experience and learn words for such superordinate concepts as furniture, vehicle, tool, and animal.

From the information processing perspective, there are very good reasons for working with concepts, like animal, at the superordinate level. We know a lot about the properties of animals in general, and it is inefficient to store each of these features separately for each class of animals. Even worse, there would be no way to know that some new animal you just learned about shares these general animal properties. In the case of super-ordinate concepts, there is therefore considerable evidence that people do go beyond direct experience, organizing their knowledge into more general categories and relationships. A few special superordinate category distinc-tions, for example, things that can and cannot act on their own, seem to be part of our biological heritage, but children still learn the words for them rather late.

From our embodied perspective, predicting that children will also find it natural to learn labels for this kind of superordinate knowledge is no problem. Recall from chapter 10 that children tend to assume a new word is not just a synonym for a word they already know. On hearing a super-ordinate category name such as *animal* associated with different specific animals, the child could make a good guess that the new word refers to some class that includes these specific cases. In fact, the process works in both directions—learning superordinate words also helps children organize their knowledge. Again, the particular superordinate category names pre-sented to children will be a function of their physical and social environ-ment. In any case, hearing all sorts of different-looking animals referred to as dogs definitely helps the child structure his or her world.

This interplay between direct experience and language-driven learning is the primary basis for the transmission of culture to children. As a child learns to deal with the world, family and community point out and label features of the physical and social environment they consider important. This inevitably controls the way the child perceives the world and orga-nizes knowledge and behavior—it determines the child's *conceptual system*. One of the most heated controversies involving the brain and language is whether the language (English, etc.) a person speaks limits what he or she can think about—often called *linguistic determinism*.

All Those Eskimo Words for Snow

Benjamin Lee Whorf and his teacher, Edward Sapir, in the first half of the twentieth century formulated the traditional basis of linguistic determinism in what is known as the "Sapir-Whorf Hypothesis."

Whorf proposed that "We cut nature up, organize it into concepts, and ascribe significances as we do, largely because we are parties to an agreement to organize it in this way—an agreement that holds throughout our speech community and is codified in the patterns of our language" (Whorf 1940; in Whorf & Carroll 1956, pp. 213–214).

And, in the words of Sapir: "Human beings . . . are very much at the mercy of the particular language which has become the medium of expression for their society. . . . The fact of the matter is that the 'real world' is to a large extent unconsciously built up on the *language* [my emphasis] habits of the group" (Sapir 1929; Mandelbaum 1958, p. 162).

The idea that language determines thought reached the mainstream perception through the popular concept that Eskimos had an enormous number of words for snow, because it was so important to them. The facts in this specific case aren't very important, but let's look at them. It is a bit complicated because there are several Eskimo languages and they all have grammar rules that use compound words for what would be a phrase or sentence in English (German does this to a much lesser extent than Eskimo). But there really are significantly more distinct words relating to snow in Eskimo languages. For example, a dictionary of West Greenlandic has at least 49 distinct snow entries, including basic words for such things as *nutarniq*, meaning "new ice formed in a crack in old ice." None of this is at all surprising from our perspective of language as labeling human experience. In fact, the existence of specialized vocabulary is no longer the core of the linguistic determinism controversy.

Several versions of the Sapir-Whorf hypothesis state that language controls thought, some of which are clearly wrong. For example, it is not true that people whose language lacks some grammatical feature, such as spatial relation words, cannot think about those features. They just express them differently, as we saw in the case of Mixtec in chapter 11. That discussion of Regier's program also described an embodied neural model of how children can learn the conceptual systems for space used by their culture, along with how it is expressed in their language.

But it is also clearly true that one cannot talk about (or think about) slam dunks, stock options, or the Internet in Mixtec or in most of the world's thousands of other languages. Thinking about a complex technical or cultural domain requires an extensive vocabulary and conceptual system, and there is usually not enough of a language community to build such a base. Similarly, English has no words for most of the plants named by Brent Berlin's native informants. Why would there be? The Tibetan language has distinct terms for several stages of meditation that most of us can't contemplate at all.

Recall that in chapter 8, we discussed universal conceptual schemas that are part of all human experience and introduced the contrasting idea of cultural frames. A cultural frame is a collection of words, concepts, and relationships characterizing some domain of human experience that is not universal, such as baseball, biophysics, meditation, or the Eskimo hunting culture. Although this is currently not provable, the embodied theory of language suggests that all *universal* conceptual schemas are expressible in any language, but many cultural frames will not be directly expressible in most languages.

So, we know that individuals' culture and conceptual systems, expressed through their *vocabulary*, do have a huge effect on the way they interact with each other and the world. Do any additional effects come from the rules of the native language itself—its *grammar*? Grammar generally refers to the rules of composition of a language, distinct from the meaning of individual words. We will be talking a lot about grammar in the last quarter of the book, but we won't need all that detail in discussing the (grammar) version of the Sapir-Whorf hypothesis, which is concerned with linguistic form. This is the core of the current controversy, mostly because it is part of a larger language war (see chapter 22) over the separation of grammar from meaning; that is, the autonomy of syntax.

The core unresolved issue is this: does the grammar of language that a person speaks affect the way she or he thinks. Grammatical influences were very important to Whorf. One of his core examples was the Hopi language, which uses verbal prefixes that distinguish different kinds of motion such as waving, spinning, flapping, and turning. Whorf wrote that "The Hopi aspectual-contrast which we have observed, being obligatory upon their verb forms, practically forces the Hopi to notice and observe vibratory phenomena, and furthermore encourages them to find names for and to classify such phenomena."

The general idea is that, if the grammar of a language requires a certain distinction to be expressed, speakers of that language will tend to be more attentive to that distinction. The interesting cases involve universal schemas of experience such as space, time, and color. We already know that specific cultural frames and their linguistic expression will cause people to notice and think about different aspects of a situation.

It is quite difficult to assess how grammar affects thought, because it is hard to test a person's thinking without using language. Difficult, but not impossible. A number of results from various labs now show language-related differences on some tasks. All of these results are tendencies—no absolute differences are known to arise from variations in the grammatical form of one's language. However, we now know that the language people speak does have a measurable effect on how they think.

Paul Kay and William Kempton (1984) carried out one of the most direct experiments relating language to judgment as an extension of their work on color terms, discussed in chapter 8. They tested, on a color-matching task, English speakers and speakers of Tarahumara, a Mexican language that has a single word covering the English colors green and blue. Subjects were each shown three color chips from a narrow range of blue-green and were asked which of the three differed most from the other two. As predicted, English speakers systematically identified as similar two chips that are given the same English name while Tarahumara speakers had no such bias, presumably because their language does not make this distinction. More recently, Kay and colleagues have shown that English speakers will fail to show linguistic bias if there is an interfering language task.

Steven Levinson and colleagues attained some fascinating Whorfian results on spatial cognition. There is another Mexican language, Tzeltal, in which the dominant way of representing spatial relations is *absolute*, as in the English cardinal directions N, E, W, S. Tzeltal speakers normally refer to the relation between objects, even indoors, in terms of being uphill or downhill from one another. When given a comparison task about which of two arrows was the same as the one they saw before from another angle, Tzeltal speakers overwhelmingly chose the one pointing in the same absolute direction. By contrast, speakers of English can be made to choose either absolute or relative (left, right) directions, depending on the task context. Levinson has gone on to show that speakers of languages that rely on absolute coordinates do notice and remember absolute spatial relations much better than speakers of English or Dutch (Levinson 2003).

John Lucy and his colleagues have worked extensively with speakers of another Mexican language, Yucatec Maya. Yucatec differs from English in that nouns for discrete objects like a banana refer primarily to the material involved and are further differentiated by a classifier term. Yucatec thus has phrases about bananas that are equivalent to one long-thin banana (fruit), one load banana (bunch), one plant banana (tree). When subjects are asked to sort objects into groups or decide which two of three objects are most similar, Yucatec speakers are much more likely to use the underlying material rather than shape or function, which are preferred by English speakers. So, the grammatical system based on materials and not shapes has Yucatec speakers focus more on the composition of an object than on its shape (Lucy 2004).

Time is another fundamental experience that can be conceptualized differently. We are used to thinking of time on a horizontal axis, but Mandarin Chinese also employs *vertical* scales. In a series of experiments, Lera Boroditsky showed that this distinction can result in measurable differences in reaction times. For example, bilingual Mandarin speakers identified that March comes before April faster just after viewing a vertical list of digits, even when the instructions were in English. English speakers do not initially show this priming effect, but will do so if they are explicitly taught to think of time vertically.

In another set of experiments, Boroditsky tested how well people could remember pairs of words such as (apple ~ Patricia). Subjects were native speakers of Spanish and German; both languages mark nouns for grammatical gender, but sometimes differently. Although the test was conducted in English, subjects were better at remembering pairs when the gender in their native language was the same as that of the paired word. Since apple is masculine (der Apfel) in German and feminine (la manzana) in Spanish, Spanish subjects are significantly more likely to remember apple ~ Patricia than are German subjects (Boroditsky et al. 2003). This is another indication of some measurable connection between grammatical form and cognitive behavior.

Dan Slobin (Slobin 2003) has explored the Whorfian idea systematically in "Thinking for Speaking." In a wide range of studies, Slobin showed that there are indeed differences in what people tend to notice and remember, depending on what distinctions are required by the grammar of the language used, even for bilinguals. Much of this work focuses on how people describe motion events in languages with differing grammatical structure. The key distinction is between languages similar to English (Slavic, Germanic, etc.) that code the manner of motion in specific verbs and others such as the Romance languages, Semitic, and Japanese that use an auxiliary phrase. For example, we would normally say in English

The dog ran/walked/dashed/ into the house.

In romance languages such as Spanish, this would be expressed as

The dog entered the house, running/walking.

In addition, verb-rich languages such as English have rather more words describing specific actions (leap, bound, jump, skip, etc.), which we will call *manner verbs*, after Slobin.

Slobin and his colleagues have studied the extent to which the grammatical style of a subject's language affects how he or she describes a scenario and what the person remembers about it. In one study of spontaneous conversation, speakers of verb-rich English used 34 different manner verbs while speakers of Spanish and Turkish used only the equivalent of *walk*. In studies of spoken event descriptions by children and also in famous novels, users of verb-rich languages used about twice as many manner verbs as those from the other language type. Slobin also suggests that speakers of verb-rich languages report imaging activities as continuous while speakers of sparse-verb languages tend to envision events as a series of separate frames.

The psychologist Richard Nisbett (Nisbett 2003) has assembled wide-ranging evidence suggesting a significant difference in cognitive style between northern Europeans (and especially Americans) and Asians, including cultures of West Asia (the Middle East). Americans and Europeans tend to classify objects into unchanging context-independent categories (as described earlier in this chapter) and are more likely to use logical reasoning and seek absolute answers. The Asian tendency is to focus more on situated, relational, and modifiable categories, empirical reasonableness, and graded answers. He notes that several grammatical distinctions between East Asian and European languages are consistent with these differences in cognitive style. Asian languages are more prone to omit nouns when they can be understood from context. There are no general abstraction rules such as the English "-ness" that allow us to make adjectives into nouns, as in selfishness. These language distinctions interact with variations in childrearing and other practices that constitute the distinct cognitive style.

These neo-Whorfian studies are rather new and require further confirmation, but grammatical form clearly has some measurable effects on cognition. All of this makes perfect sense from the perspective of this book. The brain is a massively interconnected system, and spreading activation is its basic mode of operation. Many, many influences shape the way a person thinks and interacts with the world. It would be very strange, indeed, if no regularities of grammar were among the factors affecting thought. If the grammatical feminine gender is often associated with real-world femininity, we should fully expect some priming of female names from feminine grammatical marking. All of these results are surprising only against a theoretical background that requires grammar to be a formal system separate from thought. We will come back to theories of grammar in chapter 21; for now we look more deeply at conceptual systems and their relation to language.

There are some grammatical distinctions that can bolster fundamental societal mores. In all languages, there are ways of expressing varying degrees of respect for other people, for what is being discussed, and so on. But there are a number of languages in which the grammatical form used in every utterance must explicitly encode the social relation between the speaker and hearer. Here, the social system, the conceptual system, and the rules of grammar reinforce one another so strongly that it makes no sense to try to say which is influencing the other.

A most striking example of a language in which social relations are encoded in grammar is Javanese. There are three main dialects of Javanese, each with its own stratification along social lines. The peasant dialect has three strata, the urbanite dialect has five, and the upper-class dialect has another five levels. The language rules apparently correspond closely to the general rules of social behavior, serving to encode and reinforce them. Observers agree that any fundamental change in the class structure would need to be accompanied by a corresponding change in language usage. As Stephen Levinson puts it, "Clearly, any language that forces a language-specific coding of events causes people to remember the relevant parameters at the time at which the events are experienced." The fact that one's language requires certain distinctions influences, but does not determine, how one perceives and remembers events in the world.

Abstract and Cultural Concepts

More generally, there is always a rich interaction between culture, conceptual systems, and the language used to talk about them. As we have seen, it is relatively unusual to have important conceptual differences encoded in grammar; most concepts are coded by vocabulary. The grammar of languages changes rather slowly, but all languages can easily incorporate new words for things, actions, properties, and so on. In earlier chapters, we suggested how an embodied mind could learn words for immediate experience. Earlier in this chapter, this capacity was extended to encompass learning of *superordinate* categories over such direct experiences.

But all of this covers only what we have been calling primary conceptual schemas. How do people learn the concepts and language covering rich array of cultural frames such as baseball, marriage, and politics? In particular, what does the embodied NTL have to say about learning and using the language of cultural discourse?

The answer is *metaphor*. Metaphor in general refers to understanding one domain in terms of another, as discussed in chapter 1 (Lakoff & Johnson, 2003). The NTL approach suggests that all of our cultural frames derive their meanings from metaphorical mappings to the embodied experience represented in primary conceptual schemas. The next few chapters elaborate on the related ideas of meaning as metaphor and simulation, culminating (chapter 20) in a demonstration of the theory in a program for understanding news stories through metaphorical simulation.

But before getting into the full development, it is worth looking at the metaphorical structure of one particular conceptual domain—our ways of thinking and talking about language and thought itself. This is more than just a random example; much of the language used throughout this book is inevitably based on conventional metaphors for thought and language. T.S. Eliot's Sweeney Agonistes famously said "*I gotta use words when I talk to you.*" Well, you gotta use metaphors when you talk about technical and abstract domains, including language.

Conceptual Models of Communicating and Thinking

Michael Reddy in 1977 and George Lakoff in 1978 discovered one of the most basic concepts in cognitive science, changing how we think about the mind. Reddy, in his classic paper on the *conduit metaphor* (Reddy 1979), suggested that the concept of communicating is best seen as metaphorical. Reddy's original description of the conduit metaphor is a good example of how conceptual systems derive their meaning from embodied schemas. The *mapping* looks like this:

Ideas are objects
Phrases are containers (for idea-objects)
Communicating is sending (idea-objects in phrase-containers)

In this conceptual system, communicators put idea-objects into phrase-containers and attempt to "get the idea across" to their interlocutor. Communication is successful if the interlocutor "gets" what they say. The metaphor has further details. Idea-objects don't fit into arbitrary word-containers; there are right and wrong words for an idea, and it is up to the speaker to put his or her ideas *in* the right words. In most cases, "the meaning is in the words." But when a speaker communicates insincerely, the words may be "hollow" or "empty." A speaker who is trying *not* to communicate directly can "hide her meaning" in "dense" paragraphs. Reddy lists some 140 such common, everyday expressions for this one conceptual metaphor.

Eve Sweetser observed that the conduit metaphor is a special case of a much more general and elaborate metaphor system—the mind-as-body system. The general mapping is as follows:

The mind is a body
Thinking is physical functioning
Ideas are entities (relative to which the body functions)

This general metaphor has four special cases of physical functioning: manipulating objects, perceiving, moving, and eating.

The conduit metaphor is a special case of thinking as manipulating objects. This metaphor includes the conception of understanding as grasping, teaching as providing students with ideas and includes such expressions as "tossing ideas around," "playing with ideas," and shaping a theory.

Under the mapping Thinking is perceiving, we have examples such as knowing is seeing, coming to know is observing, understanding is seeing clearly, communicating is showing, and so on. This metaphor is used in expressions like "shedding light on the subject," "being enlightened," "pointing out a fact," "a clear presentation," "a murky paragraph," and so on.

Another mapping is Thinking is moving, in which one can "lead someone step by step through an argument," "follow an argument" or "get lost," "talk in circles," "go directly to the point," "reach conclusions," "skip steps in an argument," or "zoom through a lecture."

A nice one is Thinking is eating, in which ideas are food, communicating is feeding, accepting is swallowing, understanding is digesting, and so on. This metaphor gives rise to such expressions as "spoon-feeding your students," "regurgitating information on the exam," "letting ideas simmer for a while," and so on. French, as you might expect, has a very elaborate version of this metaphor. A typical expression is "aux petites onions" (with little onions), which means a particularly exquisite idea.

These examples are all clearly metaphorical. They are systematic. They involve applying the reasoning of the embodied (*source*) domains to the abstract (*target*) domain. They define a large proportion of our modes of comprehension of what ideas, thought, understanding, and communication are. Try having a conversation about thinking, communicating, and understanding for 10 minutes without using any of these metaphors or any of the reasoning that arises from their use. You probably won't notice unless you pay close attention, but you will be using some of these metaphors.

Three other important metaphors for ideas are the following:

Thought is language. Examples include "Do I have to spell it out for you?"; "Let me make a mental note of that"; "She's an open book to me"; "I can read her mind"; "The argument is abbreviated"; "He's reading between the lines"; "That's Greek to me."

Thought is mathematical calculation. Expressions include "It doesn't add up"; "What does it all add up to?"; "What's the bottom line?"; "Give me an accounting of what went on"; and "We won't count that."

The mind is a machine. Expressions include "I'm feeling a little rusty today"; "The wheels are really turning now"; "He's cranking out ideas"; and "He had a breakdown."

Each of these metaphors for mind conceptualizes ideas in a somewhat different way, with different inferences. Yet they define the normal way we think and talk about ideas and the mind. Since a lot of this book is about language and thought, it uses such metaphors extensively. This is the standard way in which people try to understand new ideas in terms of familiar ones.

Cognitive scientists have studied many additional examples of complex conceptual systems, some of which are described in the next chapter. Diverse cultures, professions, and age groups, conceptualize a domain in different ways, and this has a profound influence on how people act. But the evidence suggests that all abstract conceptualizations share one character—they are mappings from embodied experience. In the next chapter, we explain how these metaphorical mappings are learned and how they dominate much of our reasoning.

In the last chapter we saw some of the incredible richness of human conceptual systems and the language used to describe them. Is there any way to explain how children learn the vast range of interlinked concepts that constitute their culture? The answer is both extremely simple and quite profound. There is now very strong evidence that essentially all of our cultural, abstract, and theoretical concepts derive their meanings by mapping, through *metaphor*, to the embodied experiential concepts we explored in earlier chapters.

In a general way, the embodied basis for abstract meanings can be seen as inevitable. A child starts life with certain basic abilities and builds on these through experience. Everything the child learns must be based on what she or he already understands. We know that prior conceptual knowledge has a strong influence even on what people will notice in a given situation. Someone who understands baseball will observe many subtleties of the game that a novice would not. All cultural knowledge must therefore arise from embodied experience.

But the data support a much more specific theory relating abstract concepts to experience. Elaborate systems of structural mappings link all domains of knowledge to the primitive schemas that I described in chapters 11 and 13. Much of the reasoning we use in thinking about complex and abstract subjects derives from our basic embodied knowledge of actions, goals, forces, and so on. We can learn to memorize disembodied facts such as "Silesia produces flax" without knowing anything about Silesia or flax, but it is unnatural.

In the introductory chapter, I talked about the metaphor "spinning your wheels" as a general way of describing futility in any goal-oriented activity. In this chapter, we will see how this is one special case of a pervasive family of metaphors about goals (called the *event structure metaphor*) that has been found in every language that has been studied. We will also consider in some detail how the abstract notion of *causality* can arise from embodied concepts, particularly physical force. Much of the discussion follows George Lakoff's lecture notes for our joint Berkeley class.

Primary Metaphor

A general theory elaborated by Joseph Grady in 1996 suggests that the metaphor system is grounded in the body in terms of "primary metaphors." In each primary metaphor, such as affection is warmth, an experience brings together a subjective judgment (here, affection) and a sensory-motor occurrence (temperature). For this metaphor, such an experience might be cuddling by a parent. Such correlations often show up in language, in which affection is described in terms of warmth. Here is a sample of the primary metaphors Grady studied:

Affection is warmth
Subjective   Affection
Sensory-motor   Temperature
Example   They greeted me warmly.
Experience   Feeling warm while being held affectionately.

Intimacy is closeness
Subjective experience   Intimacy
Sensory-motor experience   Being physically close
Example   We've been close for years, but we're beginning to drift apart.
Experience   Being physically close to people you are intimate with.

Important is big
Subjective   Importance
Sensory-motor   Size
Example   Tomorrow is a big day.
Experience   As a child, important things in your environment are often big, for example, parents.

Happy is up
Subjective   Happiness
Sensory-motor   Bodily orientation

Example I'm feeling up today.
Experience Feeling happy and energetic and taking an upright posture.

Bad is stinky
Subjective Evaluation
Sensory-motor Smell
Example This movie stinks.
Experience Being repelled by foul-smelling objects, such as rotten food.

More is up
Subjective Quantity
Sensory-motor Vertical orientation
Example Prices are high.
Experience Observing rise and fall of levels of piles and fluids as more is added or subtracted.

Help is support
Subjective Assistance
Sensory-motor Physical support
Example Support your local charities.
Experience A child is often aided through physical support.

These primary metaphors allow one to express a private internal (subjective) experience in terms of a publicly available event; this is one crucial feature of metaphorical language. I will follow the standard terminology and call the sensory-motor activity the *source* domain and the subjective experience the *target* domain of the metaphor. Largely universal, primary metaphors provide the grounding for much of the metaphor system.

From our neural perspective, primary metaphors can be seen as a normal consequence of associative learning. Recall from earlier chapters one of the central facts about the brain: *neurons that fire together, wire together.* This was shown in chapter 6 to be the key to detailed brain development and is also the basis for both Hebbian and recruitment learning, described in chapter 9.

The influential British philosopher of language, I. A. Richards, expressed this idea of association nicely in 1936 when he described metaphor as "two thoughts of different things active together and supported by a single word or phrase whose meaning is a resultant of their interaction."

When subjective and sensory-motor experiences are brought together in an episode, both domains are coactive. This, according to association learning theory, causes the strengthening of connections between the neural circuits supporting the different modalities. The new, strengthened connections physically constitute the metaphorical mapping. It is important that the modalities remain distinct (it is still possible to experience one without the other) for example, warmth without affection.

Learning Primary Metaphors

In *Metaphors We Live By*, Lakoff and Mark Johnson hypothesized that certain very basic conceptual metaphors arose from correlations in everyday experience. The example they gave was More is up, with expressions such as: *The temperature is rising; Stock prices hit bottom; and Thefts have soared in London.* They suggested that the metaphor could arise from the regular correlation of quantity with verticality, as when one creates piles or pours liquid into a glass.

This hypothesis was confirmed in research on child language learning by Christopher Johnson (Johnson 1999). In a study of the acquisition of the Knowing is seeing metaphor, Johnson found that children first learn the literal sense of *see* as in *See doggie* and *See Daddy*. Then they learn cases Johnson referred to as *conflations*, in which the domains of seeing and knowing are coactive, that is, both are involved, as in sentences such as: *"See Daddy come in,"* or *"See what I spilled."* Finally, children learn pure metaphorical cases such as: *"See what I mean."* Johnson has argued that metaphor arises from such conflation, or neural coactivation, in everyday experience of the source and target domains of the metaphor. The cases he studied occurred before the age of 3 years.

Conceptual Metaphor and Abstract Concepts

Joe Grady has shown that complex metaphors are conceptual combinations of primary metaphors. Each primary metaphor is directly grounded in everyday experience linking our (often sensory-motor) experience to our subjective judgments. For example, the primary conceptual metaphor Affection is warmth arises because our earliest experiences with affection correlate with the physical experience of the warmth of being held closely.

Grady, like Johnson, discussed previously, argued that primary metaphors arise via conflation.

The primary metaphors appear to be learned mainly to help the child understand and express language about subjective experience. But they also provide a mechanism for conceptualizing and discussing the full range of cultural and abstract concepts needed in human society. The metaphor mechanism also interacts with our capacity for organizing experience into the *frames* discussed in chapter 11. Metaphors usually map between conceptual frames (e.g., journey and career) rather than just relating two isolated words.

A child's early experiences involve various entities that play fundamental semantic roles such as agent, goal, source, and time. There is evidence that basic grammatical forms are based on the structure of these primary experiences, and we will discuss this further in chapter 21. Structural elements such as "agent" are also mapped by metaphor from various target domains to the domain of direct experience. For example, in the case of Spinning your wheels, the metaphorical agent always maps to the driver of the car.

Metaphors are selective mappings: many things that we know about cars (steering wheels, fuel, speed limits) have no role in the Spinning your wheels metaphor, although they are used in other metaphors involving the car journey frame. Much of cognitive linguistics is concerned with exactly how this works. As an illustrative example, we will examine in some detail the abstract notion of *cause* and how it can be conceptualized in terms of primary metaphors and schemas.

Causes Are Forces

The first cognitively modern study of causation was Leonard Talmy's classic paper from the mid-1980s, "Force Dynamics in Language and Thought," which showed that causation is metaphorically based on our embodied use of force in everyday life (Talmy 1988). Causes are forces is a primary metaphor, learned automatically and subconsciously in early childhood. It lies at the center of an elaborate metaphor system for causation, described in meticulous detail in Lakoff and Johnson's *Philosophy in the Flesh* (1999). Let's start with a few representative sentences exemplifying causation. The words in bold express causation—of one sort or another.

The noise **gave** me a headache.

The aspirin **took** it away.

The democrats **blocked** the balanced budget amendment in the senate.

FDR's leadership **brought** the country out of the depression.

He **pulled** me out of my depression.

A settlement **emerged** from long discussions.

Difficulties began to **arise**.

The data **forced** me to change my theory.

They are trying to **produce** a new theory of physics.

All of these sentences express causation—but not the same concept of causation. Consider the verbs of forced motion, such as *bring, take, push, pull, propel, throw, send, carry, drive,* and so on. Using the metaphors Causes are forces, States are location, and Change is motion, these can all be used to express causation. But each verb has a different logic, and each carries over to metaphorical uses. When you *bring* something, it accompanies you; you are applying force and control the whole way. But when you *throw* something, you apply force to an object initially, and then it moves on its own. These literal logics are used metaphorically in causal sentences *"FDR brought the U.S. out of the Depression."* Here FDR exerted force and control over the whole period, and the verb *throw* cannot be substituted. Compare this with *"The rail strike threw France into a recession."*

When causation results in a change of structural form, we conceptualize it via causes are forces, where states are shapes. Examples include **reshaping** *the bureaucracy and* **reforming** *politics.* When causation results in a new entity, we use physical creation metaphors, such as ***forging*** *a new alliance,* or progeneration concepts, as in *"The Internet **gave birth to** a new era of commerce."*

The embodied inferences concerning literal force are preserved in the abstract domain of general causation. There are kinds of causation with different inference structures, all of which are preserved under the metaphors. We do not have a single concept of causation, but many, each with different inference structures. The central metaphor is Causes are forces. It combines with other metaphors to yield complex causation concepts. Causation is embodied, mapping back to the everyday experience of exerting force.

Complex metaphors (e.g., the event structure metaphor) could arise neurally because primary metaphors can be coactive. When this happens, con-

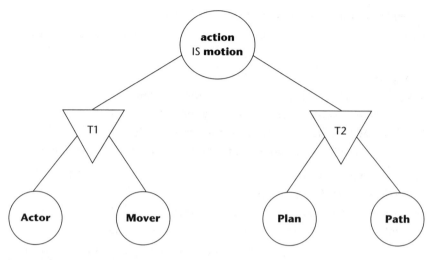

Figure 16.1
A triangle node model of metaphor activation.

nections between the coactive maps can give rise to circuits connecting the maps and allowing for their repeated coactivation, as in figure 16.1. This is a neural account of the basic metaphor phenomena, employing the general paradigm of recruitment learning (see chapter 9).

The Causes are forces metaphor combines with several other metaphors to produce a general mapping between physical journeys and any goal-oriented activity, however abstract. Some of the key primary metaphors involved are shown below. The resulting event structure metaphor appears in every language studied and is applied in a wide range of contexts.

States are locations
Subjective   A subjective state
Sensory-motor   Being in a bounded region of space
Example   I'm close to being in a depression and might go over the edge.
Experience   Experiencing a certain state as correlated with a certain location, for example, being cool under a tree, feeling secure in bed.

Action is motion
Subjective Experience   Action
Sensory-motor   Moving oneself through space

Example I'm moving right along on the project.
Experience One of our most common actions is moving ourselves through space.

Change is motion
Subjective experience Experiencing a change of state
Sensory-motor Moving oneself or being moved
Example My car has gone from bad to worse lately.
Experience Feeling the change in, for example, temperature as one moves.

Purposes are destinations
Subjective Achieving a purpose
Sensory-motor experience Reaching a destination
Example He'll ultimately be successful, but he isn't there yet.
Experience Achieving a purpose is correlated with reaching destinations, for example, if you want a drink, you have to go to the water cooler.

Causes are physical forces
Subjective Achieving result
Sensory-motor Exertion of force
Example They pushed the bill through Congress.
Experience Achieving results by exerting forces on physical objects to move or change them.

Difficulties are burdens
Subjective Difficulty
Sensory-motor Muscular exertion
Example She's weighed down by responsibilities.
Experience The discomfort or disabling effect of lifting or carrying heavy objects.

Linear scales are paths
Subjective Degree
Sensory-motor Motion
Example John's intelligence goes way beyond Bill's.
Experience Observing the amount of progress made by an object in motion.

The Event Structure Metaphor

The event structure metaphor combines several primary metaphors and organizes them in a complex way. It also relies on the common frame semantics of motion or journeys, which include the various source domain concepts such as locations, movements, paths, and forced movements. The mappings transfer the logic of this motion frame and apply it to the domain of events. Linguistic examples are given with the mappings below, but it is important to remember that the metaphor is not in the words—it is in the conceptual mappings. Particular linguistic examples may be ambiguous about which metaphor they are referring to, such as "move the meeting ahead" or "it's all downhill from here." The basic mappings in the event structure metaphor include the following:

Causes are forces.

States are locations (bounded regions in space).

Changes are movements (into or out of bounded regions).

Actions are self-propelled movements.

Purposes are destinations.

Means are paths (to destinations).

Difficulties are impediments to motion.

Expected progress is a travel schedule; a schedule is a virtual traveler, who reaches a prearranged destination at a prearranged time.

External events are large, moving objects.

Long-term, purposeful activities are journeys.

This mapping generalizes over an extremely wide range of expressions. For example, consider states and changes. We speak of being in or out of a state, of going into or out of it, of entering or leaving it, of getting to a state or emerging from it. This is a rich and complex metaphor whose parts interact in several ways. To get an idea of how it works, consider the submapping Difficulties are impediments to motion. In this metaphor, purposive action is self-propelled motion toward a destination. A difficulty is something that impedes motion toward such a destination. Metaphorical difficulties of this sort come in five types: blockages, features of the terrain, burdens, counterforces, and lack of an energy source. Here are examples of each:

Blockages   He got over his divorce. He's trying to get around the regulations. He went through the trial. We ran into a brick wall. We've got him boxed into a corner.

Features of the terrain   He's between a rock and a hard place. It's been uphill all the way. We've been bogged down. France slipped into recession.

Burdens   He's carrying quite a load. He's weighed down by a lot of assignments. He's been trying to shoulder all the responsibility. Get off my back!

Counterforces   Quit pushing me around. She's leading him around by the nose. She's holding him back.

Lack of an energy source   I'm out of gas. The economy is running out of steam.

Such examples provide overwhelming empirical support for the existence of the event structure metaphor. And the existence of that metaphor shows that some common abstract concepts—TIME, STATE, CHANGE, CAUSATION, ACTION, PURPOSE, and MEANS—are conceptualized via metaphor. Since such concepts are at the very center of our conceptual systems, the fact that they are conceptualized metaphorically shows that metaphorical mappings are linked to our core ideas. Metaphors are often organized in hierarchical structures, in which more specific mappings in the hierarchy inherit the structures of the more general mappings.

This inheritance hierarchy accounts for a range of generalizations. First are generalizations about words. Take the word "crossroads". Its central meaning is in the domain of space. But it can be used in a metaphorical sense to speak of any extended activity, of one's life, of a love relationship, or of a career. I'm at a crossroads on this project. I'm at a crossroads in life. We're at a crossroads in our relationship. Crossroads is extended lexically by the submetaphor of the event structure metaphor that Long-term purposeful activities are journeys; separate word senses are not needed.

Thus, the understanding of difficulties as impediments to travel occurs not only for events in general, but also in more specific cases, such as in a purposeful life, in economic progress, and in a career. The metaphor shows how the understanding of difficulties in life, love, economics, and careers is a consequence of such an understanding of difficulties of activities in general. The hierarchy also allows us to characterize words whose meanings are more restricted. Thus, climbing the ladder refers only to careers, not to love relationships or life in general. Such hierarchical organization is a very prominent feature of the metaphor system of English and other languages. Linguists have found that the metaphors higher up in the hierarchy tend to be more widespread than lower-level mappings. Thus, the event structure metaphor is very widespread (and may even be universal), while particular metaphors for life, love, and careers are much more restricted culturally.

Each conventional metaphor, that is, each mapping instance, is a fixed pattern of correspondences across conceptual domains. As such, each mapping defines an open-ended class of potential correspondences across inference patterns. When activated, a mapping may apply to a novel source domain knowledge structure and characterize a corresponding target domain knowledge structure. For example, if you hear someone talk about a "career detour," you might consider your own career somewhat differently.

Once a domain of knowledge becomes well known, it can itself serve as a source domain (basis) for understanding more novel concepts. We sometimes get metaphors mapping both ways, for example, between war and sports. These create no difficulty—the appropriate concepts in each domain are activated and inferences are drawn from the combined activation.

Metaphorical mappings should not be thought of as processes, or as algorithms that mechanically take source domain inputs and produce target domain outputs. Each mapping should be seen, instead, as a pattern of neural connections across domains that may or may not evoke a source domain knowledge structure. Words that are conventional in the source domain are not always conventional in the target domain. The source domain word may not have a conventional sense in the target domain, but can still be actively mapped in the case of novel metaphor. For example, the words "freeway" and "fast lane" are not conventionally used for love, but the meanings associated with them are mapped by the Love is a journey metaphor in such cases as "We're driving in the fast lane on the freeway of love."

In general, much of the power of metaphor comes from the ability to activate novel conceptual linkages. The remarkable fact is that we automatically carry over the crucial inferences from the source (embodied) domain to the usually more abstract target domain. Metaphorical mappings preserve the cognitive topology (that is, the frame and schema structure) of the source domain, in a way consistent with the inherent structure of the target domain. This is called the invariance principle.

The invariance principle specifies, for example, that for container schemas, interiors will be mapped onto interiors, exteriors onto exteriors, and boundaries onto boundaries; for path-schemas, sources will be mapped onto sources, goals onto goals, trajectories onto trajectories; and so on. As a consequence, the image-schematic structure of the target domain cannot be violated: one cannot find cases in which a source domain interior is mapped onto a target domain exterior, or a source domain exterior is mapped onto a target domain path. This simply does not happen. As we saw earlier, grammatical roles such as agent and patient are also always preserved.

This seems almost magical until we recall that our knowledge of abstract domains is *constructed* using these principles. We build our cultural frames by mapping them systematically to our experience. Because the principles of mapping are consistent, we know how to use the mappings in novel cases, like the previous freeway of love example.

The event structure metaphor is extremely rich. How can it be represented neurally and how would it arise? The theory of primary metaphors at the beginning of this chapter is an account of how the metaphors might originate. The claim is that the brain uses structures it has, such as the rich, detailed networks for sensory-motor concepts, and adapts them to other things, such as abstract concepts. Everything the mind does has to be done physically by the brain. Everything that is in the brain needs to be built in or learned.

We can also think about how metaphors would work in the neural processing of language. We know that metaphorical interpretations are often needed to understand a sentence. But how could the brain know which metaphor map to use before understanding what the sentence is about? This is another example of the kind of best-fit problem the brain evolved to solve. Figure 16.1 uses the triangle node mechanism (c.f. figure 9.2) to suggest how metaphor selection and sentence understanding work together. Recall that a triangle node is an abstract representation of a neural circuit that becomes active when two of the three clusters that are linked to it both become active. Figure 16.1 depicts a small part of a network that could both match and use the event structure metaphor. In a sentence such as "*France stumbled into recession,*" the word "*France*" activates the idea of actor and another word, "*stumbled,*" evokes the idea of walking and therefore a mover.

We can see from figure 16.1 that actor and mover are linked to the same triangle node—when both are active, the triangle node circuit T1 will become active. This, in turn, will spread activation to the top node of the figure, which represents the event structure metaphor as a whole. A sentence will always have other competing interpretations, but let's assume that the circuit of figure 16.1 is currently the most active and think about the effect this will have on the second triangle node, T2. Node T2 has one active input from above and there will also be activation on the Path unit, because it is associated with *stumble* as an interruption in walking. Now, since T2 has two active inputs, it will tend to activate its third neighbor, plan. We can interpret this as encoding the brain's knowledge that, under the event structure metaphor, a path is a plan. As before, the triangle node formulation models how the brain can bring together and exploit diverse pieces of knowledge.

If metaphorical mappings are embodied like this, we should be able to do psychological experiments on them. Ray Gibbs and his colleagues have done several revealing studies (Gibbs 1994). In one study, subjects were first asked to read little stories about anger, such as one in which someone returned John's car with new dents in it. They were then given the lexical decision task we described in chapter 7—decide as fast as possible whether some string of letters is an English word. They were given three different kinds of sentences as priming contexts:

(1)   He blew his stack (appropriate idiom).

(2)   He got very angry (literal).

(3)   He saw many dents (neutral control phrase).

The target strings were either metaphorically connected words like "*heat,*" unrelated words, or nonwords. When primed by sentence 1, subjects responded faster for heat, but not for unrelated words or nonwords, even though sentence 1 has no direct mention of anything involving heat. Neither literal sentences nor different metaphors for anger had this priming effect. Recall that priming is believed to work by spreading activation among related neural representations. The obvious explanation for the findings is that a metaphorical sentence like sentence 1 evokes the mapping from anger to heat and thus makes it faster for people to identify the string *heat* as an English word.

Let's suppose that abstract domains really do derive their meaning from metaphorical mappings, usually to domains of direct experience. Does this tell us anything about how people reason and comprehend language? Decidedly so—the next four chapters present a detailed and implemented model of story understanding that relies crucially on embodied semantics. The key idea is again *simulation*; we understand a story by imagining ourselves in it or observing it. By linking abstract language to embodied knowledge, we are able to tap into all of our rich experience of the world and social systems as the basis for inference. The process is not simple, but it does provide the only worked out theory of how people are able to understand stories containing novel ideas and language.

We are now ready to look in detail at language understanding from an embodied neural perspective. Let's proceed like linguists and examine a collection of related sentences (table 17.1, overleaf). Try to think about what it is like to comprehend each of the examples in the table. First, reflect back on the kind of café you brought into the story—is it in a city or town, does it serve coffee or liquor, is it upscale or seedy, and so on? None of the sentences suggest anything in particular about the café, but we need to fill in some details to imagine (simulate) the situations they describe—an essential part of understanding the discourse. In this chapter, we will explore the neural basis for mental simulation and a variety of ways in which simulation is used in language comprehension.

Each of the seven examples has a distinctly different meaning and linguists can explain how each meaning derives from the sentence structure. Example b suggests that Harry started near the café and definitely entered it. Example a ("*to*" instead of "*into*") suggests that Harry started rather far from the café and leaves open whether or not he entered it. In example c, where he walks into the wall, we get a different meaning of *into* and much richer inferences about his possible state before and after the event. Example d, with "*came*," places the speaker on the inside of the café; the first three are described from an exterior perspective.

The important point for us is that much of language can be seen as setting up the conditions for imagining the scene being portrayed. Examples e and f, with Harry *waltzing* or *stumbling*, obviously give extra detail on how he entered, but they also do a great deal more. Waltzing or stumbling evokes graphic suggestions of Harry's probable mental and physical state. By offering us more information on Harry, these sentences also invite us to simulate the scene from Harry's perspective; we can imagine being

Table 17.1
Seven sentences on the adventures of Harry

a. Harry walked to the café.

b. Harry walked into the café.

c. Harry walked into the café wall.

d. Harry came into the café.

e. Harry waltzed into the café.

f. Harry stumbled into the café.

g. Harry escorted Josh into the café.

Harry in this situation. The first four examples are detached and lead us naturally to imagine the scenario as an observer—we watch Harry do his thing. The final example, with Harry escorting Josh, is even richer in possibilities. We can also imagine or simulate this scene from the perspective of Josh, who is not the initiator of action in this scenario, but is being acted on. At least in my dialect, the last example has overtones of coercion, which it would lack if Josh had been Jane.

So, the process of understanding through embodied simulation inherently involves a choice of perspective. The three basic alternatives are *agent* (pushing), *experiencer* (being pushed), and *observer* (seeing third party pushing). We can use this insight and think back to the word learning programs discussed in earlier chapters. Regier's system for learning spatial relation words was done entirely in the observer perspective; it modeled a child looking at visual scenes. Bailey's program for learning verbs of hand action was done from the agent perspective—it models a child doing things and hearing verbal names for the actions. No one has built a program modeling the child as an experiencer, although that is clearly a lot of what happens. We did encounter early words learned from this experiencer perspective in chapter 10. For example, children often learn *"up"* in connection with someone lifting them up.

Evidence for Mental Simulation

The general idea of understanding as imagination or simulation seems plausible enough, but is it right? Is there evidence for this kind of mechanism in people? Are there alternative models of comprehension that might be better? There isn't space for complete answers to these questions, but I will outline the reasons for postulating that language understanding is best seen as simulation.

There is considerable evidence that much of the circuitry used in carrying out an action is also involved when people simulate their own actions or those of others. Some of this evidence comes from reaction time experiments, like those described in chapter 7. For example, if subjects are asked to *imagine* walking to targets at various distances, the elapsed times to the imagined goal are similar to those for actually walking. Another experiment exploited the fact that the right hand is controlled by the left side of the brain. Subjects were asked whether they would use an overhand or underhand grip to grasp a cylindrical object, presented briefly to either the left or right visual field. Although no motion was involved, the choice of a righthanded posture was much faster when the left side of the brain saw the picture. There are also various clinical reports that patients with specific motor deficits show similar problems in imagination tasks.

There are several reasons why this ability to simulate our actions is ecologically valuable. An obvious use of mental simulation is in planning—imagining how to do something before doing it, for example, gives us a better chance of getting the right tools. At a finer level of detail, much of our perception requires neural copies of current motor commands. For example, the vision system receives signals regarding ongoing eye movements, which it takes into account in processing image changes. It seems quite likely that these signals about planned actions could be used in simulating those actions. Simulation is also useful as a form of practice; some studies suggest that athletes can improve by imagining the desired performance.

Recent findings in brain imaging provide additional support for the plausibility of mental simulation. I talked earlier about mirror systems in monkeys and humans. These are neural networks that show essentially the same activity when the agent perceives an action as when she carries it out herself. The discovery of such circuitry provides a plausible neural mechanism for the machinery needed for mapping from observing an action to executing that same action yourself. There is also direct evidence of similar brain imaging patterns when subjects carry out real and imagined movements such as touching a finger to the thumb. More generally, a number of studies report increases in heart rate and other indicators of metabolism

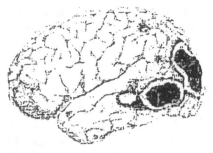

Blood flow changes while
SEEING WORDS

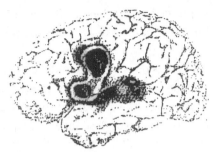

Blood flow changes while
SPEAKING WORDS
(read aloud BIKE: "Bike," subtracting off
response to reading silently)

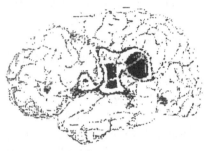

Blood flow changes while
HEARING WORDS

Blood flow changes while
GENERATING WORDS
("Ride" for BIKE, subtracting off response
to "Bike" above)

Figure 17.1
Blood flow while executing language tasks. (Source: Posner, M.I. and Raichle, M.E. *Images of Mind*. Scientific American Books, New York, 1994, p. 115)

for simulated action. Mirror circuitry could be used for linguistic as well as visual input and preliminary experimental results suggest that this does, indeed, happen.

There is very solid evidence that language tasks make heavy use of brain areas that support the appropriate activities. Consider the brain activity images in figure 17.1. This figure shows the pattern of blood flow, and thus neural activations, during four language-related tasks. In the upper left, the subject is reading words (e.g., *bike*) silently, and the greatest activity (dark areas) is in the posterior brain regions concerned with vision. On the upper right, the subject is speaking the word aloud. The figure shows the additional active brain regions, including those traditionally associated with speech. On the bottom left, we see which additional areas are operating when the subject is hearing the words. Finally, the image in the bottom right shows additional processing areas activated when the subject is asked to name an activity that would be appropriate for the printed word (e.g., *ride* for *bike*). These additional areas of high blood flow include prefrontal brain regions associated with planning and also parts of the brain that are used in carrying out the actions themselves.

So there is at least suggestive evidence that language understanding involves activation of neural mechanisms that would carry out the appropriate activities—that is, simulations. But this evidence is all very new; people have been studying language for thousands of years and have developed theories of understanding that are quite different from the simulation theory used in this book.

Understanding as Logical Inference

The conventional way to model language comprehension is to view it as a form of logical deduction. Sentences in language are mapped (using grammar) to propositions in mathematical logic, and then the rules of logic are used to draw inferences. The classical case, which really goes back to the Greeks, is

Socrates is a man. All men are mortal.

From this we should conclude that Socrates is mortal. The vast majority of scientists studying the semantics of language still pursue this approach, and they have made many important discoveries in both logic and linguistics.

But from what we have seen about how the brain and conceptual systems work, we should not expect classical logic to explain all the phenomena. It is hard to believe that we get frightened or excited in reading a story because of the logical deductions it gives rise to.

In fact, no one now claims that the formal approach is sufficient. A great deal of current work is focused on inference methods based on more quantitative and probabilistic reasoning. We obviously need more than formal logic to understand sentences like

Harry stumbled into the café.

Stumbling suggests some kind of physical problem, and we need to learn or imagine whether Harry was sick, or drunk, or just tripped on some obstacle. As we will see in chapters 19 and 20, this kind of probabilistic reasoning plays a central role in the simulation model.

Active Simulations

An adequate theory of understanding requires more than just describing in general how simulation can support comprehension and suggesting how it might arise in the brain. Our methodology is based on building detailed computational models that test whether the hypothesized neural mechanisms could produce the required behavior. In chapter 20, I describe Narayanan's program that uses simulation semantics to model the understanding of news stories. To build such models, we need to work out the details of how language gets mapped to simulation and how simulation yields understanding. The first part, mapping language input to a form suitable for simulation, is the role of *grammar* and will be discussed in detail in chapters 21 through 24. For now, we assume that this mapping can be done and concentrate on how appropriate simulations can yield understanding.

We saw the beginnings of the simulation story in figure 14.1, in connection with Bailey's model of learning words for hand actions. Recall that the middle of that figure depicted a large collection of features that were used in mapping from language (above) to action (below). For example, a word like "*shove*" activates the **slide** action schema along with features like force–high and duration–short. These feature connections were used in chapter 14 in the model of the child learning to carry out the actions named by words the child has learned. We then noted briefly that the same mechanism could be used to imagine carrying out the action.

This is the most basic notion in simulation semantics—the language processing and motor circuitry needed for carrying out a requested action is also employed in understanding that action through simulation. Recall that our computational model of an action is an executing schema, as depicted in figure 13.2. It is computationally quite straightforward to use these schemas for simulation. Rather than directly controlling the robot's effectors, we use the schema to make changes in an internal model. This is the computer equivalent of the mind's eye or imagination. In fact, we know that animal brains do a kind of simulation in dreaming.

The simulation of action schemas is the heart of the computational model, but we also need to represent the entities involved in a story and their relationships. We have already seen almost all the required machinery. Objects and situations are represented as frames (chapter 11). For example, you supplied a café frame to your interpretations of sentences a through g at the beginning of this chapter. Many of the inferences required for simulation semantics are present in the frames themselves. One particularly important class of semantic frames is the image schemas discussed in chapter 11. We also require fairly elaborate models of actions, as described in chapters 13 and 14 and further discussed in the chapter to follow. As I mentioned earlier, this ability to imagine our own and others' actions is the core of understanding.

When we envision Harry going to the café, we simulate the café as a destination, filling a role of a source-path-goal (SPG) image schema. In the cases in which he enters the café, we also envision the café as a container—with an interior, exterior, portal, and so forth. As we will see later, one main function of grammar is to link up the appropriate frames, image schemas, and active schemas for simulation. For example, when Harry walks into the café wall, the café is not being imagined as a container, but as a large solid object. This helps the grammar system realize that the required meaning of "*into*" is not the one that fits with containers, but the one involving *contact*, another primary image schema.

We now have some basic idea of the computational simulation of simple concrete language like the examples of this chapter. A grammar system (to be described in chapter 23) analyzes the utterance in context and produces a linked collection of frames and schemas that specify what actions took place and which actors and other entities were involved. We have seen simple examples of active schemas linked to agents and objects in earlier chapters.

The action schemas are carried out using a model instead of the real world; that is, they are simulated. For example, the hearer of our first example sentence (sentence a in table 17.1) would simulate (imagine) Harry walking. Finally, the results of the simulated execution are the inferences that result from the input sentence. The input sentence provides only part of the information for the simulation. The background, context, and goals of the understander determine exactly what will be simulated and at what level of detail, as we saw with the initial examples from table 17.1.

Our examples so far have been artificial; let's consider a sentence that has exactly the same form as sentence b (in table 17.1):

Osama bin Laden walked into the United Nations.

Anyone reading this in a news story in early 2006 would immediately want to know more. Was it really the head of al Quaeda? How did he get there? What was he planning to do? If no more information were immediately forthcoming, you would start to imagine possible scenarios, using your rich knowledge of the international situation. As you learned more, your simulation would be updated to reflect the additional information. It would be hard not to imagine possible outcomes; we naturally understand things by predicting their consequences.

Understanding This Book

As a reality check, we can attempt to imagine Harry trying to understand this book. It is easy enough to picture him sitting and reading in the cafe and also to empathize with his frustration. But suppose we want to simulate this situation in much greater detail and imagine what Harry's brain is doing as he reads. Several perspectives are available for this simulation. Using the world brain metaphor from chapter 5, you could imagine the billions of worker neurons collaborating to learn new connection weights that capture the ideas in each section of this book. You might want to simulate at a deeper level, and think about neural firings and chemical changes. Or you might choose to adopt the information processing perspective and consider what concepts, relations, and rules Harry is trying to learn. Ideally, you will be able to simulate at any of these levels and map from one to another.

Of course it's not Harry's brain, but your own, that you should simulate. The purpose of the first nine chapters was to provide ways of thinking scientifically about how your brain thinks. If you can imagine in detail how your brain is understanding this book, then you "get it." The rest of the discussion will be just filling in the details and suggesting some of the consequences. If not, I suggest that you bookmark this section and come back to it from time to time. Grasping the overall story does not require remembering all the details of the various discussions. I certainly could not reproduce them without looking back.

Understanding Metaphorical Language

The idea of understanding as simulation can also be carried over to metaphorical language (chapter 16) in general. Consider what happens when we take the seven examples from table 17.1 and examine how they look with the event structure metaphor, in which economic progress is mapped onto physical progress toward a goal. The sentences marked with # are of questionable acceptability.

All of these examples are based on the event structure metaphor, discussed in detail in the previous chapter, where goals (here economic ones) are thought of in terms of physical destinations. Not all of the sentences about Harry moving toward the café make sense with this metaphor, and it is interesting to see why not. The crucial insight is that a recession is a metaphorical hole (a subtype of container) in the event structure metaphor. Example a doesn't make sense because *to* requires its object to be a location. Similarly, example c fails because the café wall is a barrier and not a container, although there are also barrier economic metaphors such as "the economy is backed into a corner," or "ran into resistance." Example d seems odd for a different reason; it assumes a person who is already in the container is talking, which makes no sense here. We probably would accept a sentence such as: Germany encouraged France to

Table 17.2
Metaphorical counterparts of the examples from table 17.1

a. #France walked to recession.

b. France walked into recession.

c. #France walked into recession.   ~ barrier

d. #France came into recession.

e. France waltzed into recession.

f. France stumbled into recession.

g. France escorted Belgium into recession.

come into recession. The general point is that metaphorical language is accepted and understood when the mappings preserve the appropriate conceptual types.

Now let's look at the examples that do make sense in the metaphorical version. Examples b, e, and f all convey similar meanings—France (metaphorically a person) encountered an obstacle (recession ~ hole) in its economic progress. The difference lies in the concrete verb: walked/waltzed/stumbled convey the writer's view of the attitude of France while this was happening. Try substituting other verbs of human locomotion and see what each suggests about France's economic policies. The simulation theory suggests that in each case, you (subconsciously) imagine a person physically moving as described by each particular verb and then metaphorically map the features of the physical motion experience to economics. For example, if France *slid* into recession, it had no control over a relatively slow economic decline.

Finally, example g is probably entirely new to you. This is not a common usage in writing about economics. But you almost certainly came up with a natural interpretation, without conscious effort. We assume that France, as a larger country, would be able to bring Belgium along into recession. It would be much less natural in the other direction. Again, this can be seen as extension of the direct experience that an adult can escort a child, but not vice versa.

Of course all of these examples are quite simple, but the idea of inference as simulation carries over to much more complex cases. In the next chapter, we discuss simulations with multiple interacting events. Another classical problem in semantics involves scenarios with multiple times, places, and people.

Multiple Simulations—Mental Spaces

Simulation is a fine means of understanding discourse, but a single simulation will not always suffice. Let's consider a few more variations on our little scenario (table 17.3). In each of these cases, more than one simulation is required. In the first example, we are being invited to think about what happened last week in addition to the current discourse. Example b requires us to separate out what Josh believed from what actually happened. We can reason about Josh's inferences without confusing

Table 17.3
Some mental space examples

a. Harry walked to the café last week.

b. Josh believed that Harry walked to the café.

c. Harry told Josh that he walked to the café.

d. If Harry walked to the café, he will need a ride home.

e. In the movie, Harry walked to the café.

them with Harry's actions. All of these sentences require what are called *mental spaces*, following Gilles Fauconnier (Fauconnier & Turner 2003). In understanding a discourse, we (again unconsciously) build up and simulate different scenarios involving various people, places, times, and other factors mentioned in the story.

Example c requires us to think about at least three spaces: what really happened, what Harry told Josh, and what Josh believed. Example d is complicated in another way; we are asked to reason about two alternatives—one in which Harry walked and one in which he drove. Example e is typical of an additional rich class of mental space phenomena—depiction. We routinely understand quite complex discourses involving different media, people, times, places, and possibilities all mixed together.

People can do even more than this. We talked earlier about *conceptual blends*, combinations of concepts that derive special meaning from being united. Simple examples included red hair, which isn't anything like the prototypical red. Conceptual blending also occurs across mental spaces, often giving rise to very rich inferences. One famous example is the 1990 quote from then Texas Governor Ann Richards:

George Bush was born on third base and thinks he hit a triple.

This goes well beyond such standard baseball metaphors as "struck out" or "hit a home run." We are invited to think about the elder Bush's privileged upbringing and also about his mental attitude. It is hard to imagine any better way to convey this complex of ideas to an American audience. More generally, complex scenarios involving several mental spaces can be evoked even by quite simple statements such as "He lied." This entails that one person said to a second person something that the first person knew to be untrue.

It will come as no surprise that no one knows how mental spaces are realized in the brain. We do know that the hippocampal area is involved in spatial memory and therefore has some mechanisms for separating out scenarios by spatial location; this could be part of the mental space mechanism. There are also some intriguing recent results on different patterns of brain activity when imitating the actions of others versus seeing oneself imitated.

In chapter 20, we look in detail at how a computational model is able to understand news stories involving economic events like France slipping into recession. This obviously goes beyond the concrete sentences discussed in this chapter in that it requires the metaphorical mappings presented in chapter 16. It also requires the system to deal with richer action simulations involving ongoing actions such as "Harry is *walking* into the café," as described in the next chapter.

VII | Understanding Stories

The seven sample sentences discussed in the last chapter differed in many ways, but to simplify the discussion of simulation, they all used exactly the same grammatical form for the verb—*walked, came, waltzed, stumbled,* and *escorted* are all in the simple past tense. This suggests that the action involved was already complete and we need not simulate it in detail. Consider the different message conveyed if the verb in each example is changed to what is called the *progressive* (table 18.1, overleaf). Again, please reflect on what each example conveys.

Now we are placed into the middle of any ongoing action and expect to hear more about what happened in the process. For the most part, all the other semantic cues remain unchanged from the previous example. The one exception is sentence c′ in which the grammatical form requires us also to reconstrue an event (collision) usually envisioned as instantaneous and expand it into an ongoing process. You probably imagined example c′ as describing the time just before Harry made contact with the wall.

So, the grammatical form used in expressing a sentence tells the reader how to imagine or simulate the situation being described. The manner in which language specifies the fine structure of action, technically called linguistic *aspect*, plays a crucial role in our target task of understanding news stories. In this chapter, we explore how the active schemas (X-schemas) discussed earlier can provide the link that allows a program (and presumably our brains) to simulate what is expressed in language.

Linguistic aspect is expressed quite differently in various languages and covers a wide range of issues. For us, the most important distinction is between ongoing and completed actions. There is obviously a big difference between "France is falling into recession" and "France fell into

Table 18.1
Progressive variations on the examples of table 17.1

---

a'. Harry was walking to the café.

b'. Harry was walking into the café.

c'. Harry was walking into the café wall.

d'. Harry was coming into the café.

e'. Harry was waltzing into the café.

f'. Harry was stumbling into the café.

g'. Harry was escorting Josh into the café.

---

recession." For people, or a computer program, to simulate a story with ongoing action, there must be some way of imagining the action unfolding. The active schemas of chapter 13 are perfectly suited to model ongoing behavior and the fine-grained differences in linguistic descriptions of action needed for comprehension.

As always, we begin with the embodied reality—how does the brain control the fine structure of actions? Much of the answer has already been provided in earlier chapters. We know from the discussion of the knee-jerk reflex in chapter 5 that all of our motor activities have hierarchies of neural feedback networks. We saw how high-level control of these systems could be represented by executing schemas (X-schemas), starting with the gaits of the cat in figure 13.1. From figure 13.2 we then learned how human actions, such as **push** and **step**, could be described by executing schemas, with choices for parameters such as speed and duration. We know that children, well before they learn language, have the conceptual schemas for starting actions, continuing them, stopping actions, and so on. In chapter 14, we found out how these executing schemas were used to model children learning the action words of their language.

Figure 18.1 depicts an action schema for walking to the café/store. Following the general neural principle of hierarchical control, it uses the **step** schema of figure 13.2 as a component. Looking at figure 18.1, we see it is a cycle that uses the step schema as the (hexagonal) core of an ongoing process. This is just a way of capturing the idea that walking consists of the ongoing process of taking one step after another. Recall that the step schema itself will make use of more basic neural circuits, like the one involved in the knee-jerk reflex. The *parameters* in the lower left are just like the ones we have seen before for X-schemas. They code the limited range of variability that we can sense and talk about.

Figure 18.1 uses a more detailed description of executing schemas, which is necessary for fine-grained simulation and language understanding. The circles represent possible states of neural activity and the small vertical boxes depict transitions, representing neural connections. In this notation, a black dot inside a circle models activity of the named neural state. So at the upper left of figure 18.1, the two dotted circles model the situation in which the agent is upright and sees that the path ahead looks OK.

When the model is simulated, activity would then spread to the circle labeled *ready*. The other dotted circle in the figure is the one labeled *ongoing*. This encodes the idea that we should simulate the walking as an ongoing activity, as specified by the example sentences a' through g'. For sentences a through g of the previous chapter, which were in the simple past, the simulation would have the *done* circle marked, meaning that understanding does not require imagining the action in progress.

The test (at the top of figure 18.1) determines if the process is finished depending on external factors, here reaching the goal. If no ending condition is detected, the simulation will continue indefinitely. This is not realistic, and the full model includes the fact that you deplete your energy while walking. With a more fully elaborated rendition, X-schemas as in figure 18.1 can describe actions well enough to control robots and are used this way in some commercial systems.

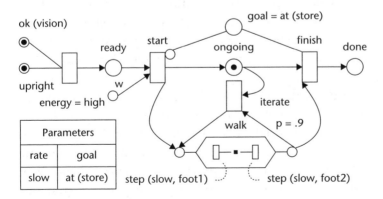

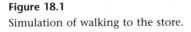

Figure 18.1
Simulation of walking to the store.

Another property of figure 18.1 that is much more interesting is its *generality*. We could replace the step schema (the hexagon on the bottom of the figure) with almost any other basic physical action and the resulting schema would describe a human motor activity. This is obvious for other repetitive behaviors such as typing or chewing. But the idea applies equally well to actions such as pushing—the ongoing process in pushing involves the continuous application of force.

Srinivas Narayanan, working with David Bailey on characterizing motor control schemas, made an interesting discovery that, in retrospect, should have been obvious (Narayanan 1997). He suggested that all higher-level motor schemas have the same basic control system structure:

- getting into a state of readiness
- the initial state
- the starting process
- the main process (either instantaneous or prolonged)
- an option to stop
- an option to resume
- an option to iterate or continue the main process
- a check to see if a goal has been met
- the finishing process
- the final state

First, you have to reach a state of readiness (e.g., you may have to reorient your body, stop doing something else, rest for a moment, etc.). Next, you have to do whatever is involved in starting the process (e.g., to lift a cup, you first have to reach for and grasp it). Then you begin the main process, and while you doing it, you have an option to stop; and if you do so, you may or may not resume. This *general controller* is pictured in figure 18.2.

The generalized controller X-schema discussed above captures important insights about actions. The key thing is the process. Essentially any physical activity (including static ones like *sleep*) can be described by an X-schema and embedded as the *process* node in figure 18.2. There are notions of being ready, canceling, starting, being ongoing, iterating or interrupting, suspending, resuming, and being done. Once we grasp this idea, it is easy to see that the general control also applies to abstract

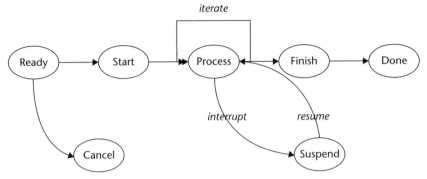

- Part of Conceptual Structure.
- Generalizes over actions and events.

Figure 18.2
The generalized controller X-schema.

actions—bidding, boycotting, and so on. This led to an even more remarkable finding: the dynamic neural control structure of figure 18.2 has exactly the organization needed for much of the semantics of linguistic *aspect*, the structure of events in general.

Some verbs (e.g., tap) are inherently repetitive and some (e.g., sneeze) are normally seen as happening only once. The inherent aspect of a verb can be captured by marking the appropriate node of the controller schema for the action denoted by the verb. Another dimension of linguistic aspect structure indicates granularity of control—encapsulated as a whole, spread over time, or broken down into various levels of detail. We saw this in the difference between imperfective (walking) and perfective (walked). All languages have words and grammatical aspect markings that label how we should simulate an action. Another distinction is between processes that specify completion (He read the book) and those that are neutral about completion (He was reading the book).

In English, we have phrases for all of the states and transitions in figure 18.2—the very words in the diagram. You can see how easy and natural it is to apply all of these to a sample sentence like our standbys. We say "Harry resumed his walk to the café," and so on. There are also some more subtle encodings. For example, the word *stumbling* from example f' conveys the complex idea of the interruption of an ongoing walking process—all in one word. We say that the word stumbling *evokes* an ongoing walk X-schema with the suspended state of its controller marked for simulation. If a more detailed simulation is required by the user's goals, the word stumble also encodes the manner in which a walk can be interrupted, compared with other interruptions such as slip, slide, and trip.

The inherent aspectual marking of a verb can be overridden depending on the surrounding linguistic context. For example, a verb like *jump*, which is normally interpreted as a single action, becomes iterative in a phrase such as *kept jumping*. We also saw this in example c', in which *"Harry was walking into the café wall"* caused us to override the inherent punctuate (point like) aspect of *walk into*. These meanings can be represented by various markings of the controller schema and by the simulation framework that results from hooking up different event controllers in various ways.

We have been discussing the controller schema and the related linguistic expressions as they apply to a person's own actions. By combining this idea with the simulation semantics story from the previous chapter, we can see how to model the understanding of action details. In accordance with our general theory of simulation, we assume that the controller schema (like any schema) can be used in both directing action and modeling the actions of others. This notion was already implicit in the example sentences at the beginning of the chapter. On hearing that Harry was walking into the café, we imagine an ongoing process and await further details concerning its unfolding.

Exactly the same reasoning carries over to the metaphorical actions that are needed in understanding news stories. When we hear that France was falling into recession, we imagine an ongoing process and await further details concerning its unfolding. Cognitive linguists have long noted that aspectual structure is preserved in metaphorical mappings. If the sentence says *falling into recession*, we are being told that the country is not yet in recession, but is heading toward it. This is a remarkable economy of language. All of the modeling, simulation, and inference capabilities we have for directly embodied stories get reused, through metaphor, in countless abstract and technical domains.

For Narayanan, it was no coincidence that motor control and linguistic aspect had the same computational structure. He hypothesized that conceptual aspect, which structures events of any kind, *is* neurally the same control system that governs bodily movements and perceptual recognition of those movements. This would be an instance of the historical property of unfolding neural systems at work: a system that evolved earlier for motor control is recruited to reason about events. Thus, we have an embodied neural explanation for the existence of aspect of the kind seen in all languages.

We now have almost all the mechanisms we need to model the understanding of news stories. Metaphorical mappings (chapter 17) take us from abstract domains like economics to embodied knowledge of health, walking, and other activities.

A phrase like "France stumbled" evokes a simulation of a metaphorical person encountering difficulty while moving along a path. The consequences of this embodied simulation are then projected back to the economic domain where they are treated as economic difficulties.

We have seen how some elements of an input sentence specify which actions need to be simulated and which parameters are needed for each. Other facets of the input sentence tell us which perspective to take on each action and whether its internal details are relevant for the current simulation. All of these factors taken together provide enough information for a person to imagine or a computer to simulate the story being told and to draw the appropriate inferences.

We are lacking just one major mechanism for the full understanding of news stories and other language input—implicit inferencing. When you hear a story or process other language input, your mind does a lot more than just comprehend what was said. Without conscious effort, you automatically encode the consequences of this new knowledge for other things that you believe.

From our earlier discussions of neural architecture and spreading activation in the mind, we know why we make these inferences—the brain is organized to adapt to new information. So, we need a biologically plausible way to add to our model of language understanding, this capability for implicit inferencing. The next chapter describes a computational mechanism, called probabilistic belief networks, that is the best current means of modeling human implicit inference.

Language understanding never occurs in a vacuum; in making sense of an utterance, we use both our general experience of the world and our beliefs about the current situation. The previous two chapters described how we can use our general knowledge of action and processes in comprehending language. This was the most complex and novel part of the embodied theory of understanding, but the programs that interpret news stories must also make inferences from descriptive (frame) knowledge, described in chapter 15.

As I discussed in the chapter on simulation (17), traditional theories of meaning have focused almost entirely on logical deduction as a model of understanding. Although much has been learned from this approach, it covers only a small fraction of the kinds of inferences people draw when understanding language. From our neural perspective, inference is better seen as a process of quantitatively combining evidence in context to derive the most likely conclusions. When you hear or read something new, your brain's spreading activation mechanisms automatically connect it to related information.

In this chapter, I describe a computational technique, *belief networks*, which models the *best-fit* character of neural inference and allows us to model a much wider range of language behavior. As before, I have chosen a computational formalism that is the best available approximation to the related neural mechanisms, here spreading activation. In the next chapter, I will combine these belief networks with the active schemas of chapters 17 and 18 in a computational model of how people understand the meaning of news stories about economics. That computer program also relies heavily on the metaphorical mappings described in chapter 16 and serves as a major milestone on our path from molecule to metaphor.

For our purposes, descriptive knowledge can be packaged in coherent frames (chapter 15) and represented computationally as feature structures (chapter 11), which correspond to the computational neural circuitry. As a first example, recall that figure 11.2 showed four different feature structures, including one that describes the color and taste of various foods. Let's look more closely at descriptive knowledge, using the food example.

In all of our representations, entities are described by a collection of *attributes*, each of which can have various possible *values*. For example, the attribute **taste** of foods might take on values including salty, sweet, sour, bitter, and rotten. Our knowledge of a fruit, say apples, includes the fact that apples sometimes taste sweet, sometimes sour, and sometimes rotten. Similarly, we know that apples come in several **colors** including green, yellow, brown, and red. There is compelling evidence that human knowledge goes beyond just listing the possible values for each attribute, also including estimates of the probability or likelihood for each value. Following the standard convention that the sum of probabilities for a set of choices adds up to 1.0, the beliefs about the likely colors of apples might be red (0.6), green (0.2), yellow (0.1), and brown (0.1). Similarly, a person's beliefs about the likely tastes of apples might be sweet (0.6), sour (0.3), and rotten (0.1).

But we know a lot more than this. We not only have estimates about both the color and taste of apples, we realize that these attributes are not independent. If we know the color of a particular apple, our guess about its likely taste is altered. This is what is known in the trade as a *conditional dependence* link and is the basis for the belief networks that we, and myriad others, use in computational models. People's beliefs are such that the probability of one property (say, ripeness) depends on the current value of some other property, here color. A belief network is a collection of such relations among the beliefs of some agent.

Computational methods for solving these large probabilistic networks are relatively new, having been introduced in the 1980s by Judea Pearl (Pearl 1993). If the probability of one feature value in the network is changed, a solution involves computing the most likely new value for all of the other beliefs. These solutions are important in many applications, and they also model how people can subconsciously work out the consequences of some new piece of information.

Applied belief networks are used in medical, financial, and engineering applications and can involve thousands of attributes and links. Various programs from the software monopoly employ belief networks to help guess what a user is trying to do and act accordingly. The main effort in such applications is often in developing programs that attempt to learn these giant belief networks from many, many examples. For example, numerous companies are attempting to find useful correlations in their accumulated business data using what is called data mining. In human brains, we assume that the neural connections capturing relations among features are modified based on experience in a somewhat similar way.

We will use belief networks to model how people reason about uncertain events, such as those encountered in economics and politics. We know that people do reason probabilistically, but they also do not always act in accord with the formal laws of probability. Daniel Kahneman won the 2002 Nobel Prize largely for his work with Amos Tversky explaining many of the limitations of human probabilistic reasoning. Some of the limitations are obvious, for example, the calculations might just be too complex. But some are much deeper, involving the way a question is stated, a preference for avoiding loss, and some basic misperceptions about large and small probabilities. So, belief networks only approximate the underlying evidential neural computation, but they are by far the best available model. It is interesting that so much of the theory of uncertainty was developed by Israelis—Pearl, Kahneman, and Tversky.

Belief Network Examples

Although I will not be presenting any detailed belief network calculations, it is worth seeing how they work in a simple case. Let's reduce our apple description to two colors: red, which occurs seven-tenths of the time, and green, which has 0.3 probability of occurring. We suppose that there are also just two tastes, sweet and sour, which occur with probabilities 0.6 and of 0.4, respectively. So 0.6 is just the chance of an apple being sweet, given no other information. But a smarter agent would have estimates on how color and taste are related for apples. The agent's beliefs about the conditional dependence of apple taste on color could be as shown in table 19.1. For example, the top left entry encodes the belief that a red apple is very likely (0.8) to taste sweet.

Table 19.1
Conditional dependence of apple taste on color

	Sweet	Sour
Red	0.8	0.2
Green	0.3	0.7

Here is how this information could be used in practice. An agent with the beliefs described above, when offered a totally unknown apple, would estimate there was a probability of 0.6 that it would be sweet. But if the agent knew that the available apple was green, he or she would guess that the probability of it tasting sweet was only 0.3, because of the beliefs recorded in table 19.1. The agent's belief about the taste of the apple can thus be *updated* using the additional information about its color. This process of probability updating is the fundamental operation in belief networks and is the basis for our model of story understanding. In processing a news story, the model will update its beliefs about the likely economic situation being described.

A full belief network discussion would be much more complex. Even for this tiny example, we know that the likely taste of a green apple depends on which variety of apple it is—a green Granny Smith is much more likely to be sweet than a green Macintosh. As is often the case, therefore, the likelihood of different apple tastes depends on two separate pieces of information, either or both of which may be known. The belief network formalism includes rules for making the best current estimate based on whatever information is available. In table 19.2, the combined information about color and variety allows the agent to make better estimates on the likely taste of an apple. But belief networks also support a much more difficult kind of inference—reasoning from observations to their most likely precursors, and this ability accounts for much of the attractiveness of the formalism. Staying with our example of apples, we can imagine someone tasting a sweet green apple and concluding that it probably is of some green variety such as Granny Smith.

This is boring, but here is an equivalent example that is probably of more personal interest. Suppose you come home and detect that your spouse (parent, roommate) is really upset. It might matter a lot to make a good

Table 19.2
Conditional dependence of apple taste on color and variety

	Sweet	Sour
Red Mac	0.8	0.2
Green Mac	0.1	0.9
Green Granny	0.5	0.5

estimate of whether this was the result of some action or inaction on your part or was due to forces beyond your control. Such cases with multiple causes also introduce the important notion of *explaining away*. If you know that your spouse had a bad day, that helps explain why he or she is distressed. If there is another reason for your spouse to be upset, you can be less worried about whether it was caused by something that you did or failed to do. In economic news stories, there are many examples where readers make inferences about likely causes of, for example, inflation, and assume that a known or highly probable cause makes it less likely that other possible causal events were responsible.

For belief networks with many elements, it becomes impractical to display all the conditional probability tables, and I will not use these tables directly in this book. What people do instead is to display, in various graphical forms, which elements depend on which others. The crucial assumption in these diagrams is that any elements not explicitly linked are assumed to not depend directly on one another and interact only in specific ways, such as the explaining away just discussed.

For example, suppose some other property of apples, say size, was believed to be independent of color and taste, but not of variety. Then the conditional dependence graph could be drawn as shown in figure 19.1. This shows that the values for size and color depend directly only on variety and the values of taste depend on color and variety, but not on size. The variety of apple depends on nothing in this belief set; it has no incoming arrows. Such graphical presentations are always shorthand for the detailed probability tables.

This kind of dependence diagram is used in all manner of applications of probabilistic reasoning and seems to be the clearest way to describe how different factors interact.

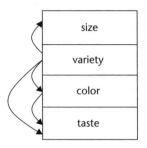

Figure 19.1
Conditional dependence among apple features depicted by arrows.

The preceding examples about fruits were just an introduction to the general ideas. We now look more carefully at the economic knowledge, encoded as belief networks, that is used in the models for understanding news stories about economics.

Some of the required background for the stories consists of facts that are not expected to change, such as that the United States is a market economy. A more interesting kind of information concerns the different kinds of economic systems that might be mentioned in the stories. The model has a four-level scale of increasingly outgoing trade policy: autarky, import substitution, free trade, and export push. It also characterizes economic policy in terms of trying to move along this scale. The two relevant policies are liberalization and protectionism.

The stories whose meaning we will model involve countries using various policies to attempt to achieve economic goals and also some unplanned economic events. Some typical examples are

France fell into a recession. Germany pulled it out.

The Indian government is taking bold new steps. It loosens its strangle hold on business, slashes tariffs, and removes roadblocks to international trade.

The U.S. economy is on the verge of falling back into recession after lurching forward on an anemic recovery.

Belief networks will be used to capture the story understanding agent's beliefs about the economics domain as well as some more general inferences about the aspectual structure of actions, as discussed in chapter 18. Figure 19.2 shows the elements used in the economics domain and their

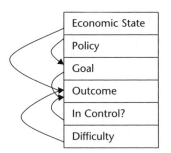

Figure 19.2
Conditional dependence among news story features depicted by arrows.

dependency relationships, following the same format as figure 19.1 did for the features of apples.

Figure 19.2 shows six elements in the agent's beliefs about economic policy and progress, namely:

Economic state Recession; low, medium, or high growth
Policy A nation's planned policy, for example, liberalization or protectionism
Goal Autarchy, import substitution, free trade, or export push
Outcome Success/failure
Difficulty Absent/present
In control Yes/no, is the agent in control of events

Recall that the model involves computing probability estimates for the various possible feature values based on the content of news stories. So the description of an economic situation will include the agent's estimates of how likely the country is to be in each possible economic state, which policy it is probably pursuing, and so on. Understanding a news story involves computing new values for some of these probabilities, based on the news.

Figure 19.2 also depicts the five dependency relationships (the arrows) that will be used. The goal of a policy depends on which policy it is. The probable outcome (success or failure) of a policy depends on the current economic state and the goal being sought. The outcome also depends on whether difficulties are present and whether or not a country is in control of events. This is obviously a simplified model, but it will suffice for a large number of news stories, as we will see in the next chapter.

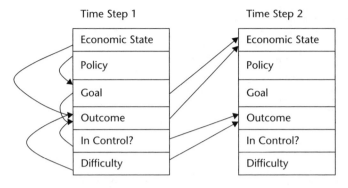

Figure 19.3
Dependence between economics features at two steps.

Temporal Belief Networks

So far, our discussion of beliefs and inference has been limited to a single point in time. But beliefs do change over time. In particular, the whole point of reading a news story is to update your beliefs, and any model must capture that fact. For this purpose, we need one final addition to our technical machinery—*temporal* belief networks.

The basic idea is simple, but has turned out to be quite powerful. We simply make a copy of a belief diagram (e.g., figure 19.1 or 19.2) for each point in time considered; usually three time steps are used. Figure 19.3 depicts two time steps for the belief system defined in figure 19.2. What gives this network its power are the links from elements in the first column (first time step) to elements in the second column. Each of these arrows specifies that the feature value at the head of the arrow (second time step) depends on the values at the tail of that arrow (at the first time step). In this case, the goal at time 1 impacts the economic state at time 2. The economic state at time 2 is also influenced by the success or failure outcome at time 1. And the outcome at time step 2 depends on difficulty at time 1 as well as whether the agent has control. I have omitted some dependency links from figure 19.3 to make it more readable. All of the links within each time step, shown in figure 19.2, are still present in the temporally extended belief networks. The full diagram would also include "persistence" links connecting each box at time step 1 to the box of the same name at time step 2; these encode the fact that probability values persist over time unless they are explicitly changed. The flow of inference uses links within each time step, as well as those across time steps, to compute the belief updates for each sentence in a news story.

As I mentioned earlier, the belief network mechanisms can use the information represented by these diagrams either to predict likely outcomes or to reason backwards to estimate the probable origin of a current economic situation. This capability will be needed to understand some of the example news stories considered in the next chapter. The details of this aren't important for us, but the general idea of making best estimates is at the core of neural computation, and we shouldn't be surprised that it plays a central role in understanding stories, even in a domain as abstract as economics.

This completes our discussion of knowledge representation and inference in probabilistic belief networks. In the next chapter, we bring this computational technique together with several other ideas from linguistics and from modeling in a demonstration system for understanding news stories in the domain of economics.

It is now time to redeem many of the promises made throughout this book. This chapter looks at how all of the ideas about embodied language developed so far can be brought together in a computer model that understands the meaning of news stories about economics and draws appropriate inferences. This task is a paradigm instance of adult language comprehension in a complex abstract domain. Here are some examples of the story fragments, all taken from the media, that were successfully processed by the model system:

France fell into a recession. It was pulled out by Germany.
The economy is moving at the pace of a Clinton jog.
The World Bank prescribed a structural adjustment program, bleeding developing countries.
The Indian government is taking bold new steps. It loosens its strangle-hold on business, slashes tariffs, and removes roadblocks to international trade.
Japan continues its long, painful slide into recession.
The U.S. economy is on the verge of falling back into recession after lurching forward on an anemic recovery.
A protectionist policy is the mistaken therapy of prescribing palliatives to the economy in response to painful change and perception of injury.

All of these stories involve metaphors described in chapter 16, and each uses the active schemas of chapter 17 to convey its meaning. Of course, understanding any of the stories also requires some knowledge of basic economics. The program I will now describe uses belief networks (as discussed in the previous chapter) to capture the required economics information and make appropriate inferences.

I will first describe how the computer model, developed by Srinivas Narayanan (Narayanan 1997), understands the meaning of these stories and then point out the significance of this result for our quest. All of the discussion in this chapter, like the rest of the book so far, sets aside the problem of grammatical analysis—how sentences like the examples above get analyzed into their structural components and relations. Grammar is discussed in detail in section VIII, after we learn more about what jobs grammar needs to do.

Consider what meanings you might derive from reading the first sentence of a news story that starts with the sentence:

France fell into a recession.

We will see what the program concluded from its preanalyzed version of the sentence, and you can then compare this with your understanding of the same story. Most people are surprised to learn how much goes into processing even a simple five-word sentence.

In building his story understanding program, Narayanan used the standard scientific technique of focusing on only a part of the overall task. Since he was not studying or modeling grammatical analysis, he built the system to use preanalyzed sentences, rather than raw text, as input. By using preanalyzed input, he eliminated the need for grammatical analysis, which is treated in a later chapter. From our earlier discussions, it will come as no surprise that the input format is a collection of feature~value pairs, like those described in chapter 11 and used in various ways thereafter. For example, the input features and values corresponding to the sentence

France fell into a recession.

would be as shown below:

Agent ~ France
Economic state ~ recession
Event ~ fall into
Aspect (event shape) ~ completed

The main outcome of running Narayanan's program is to add two assertions about the presumed situation after the simulation. These encode the state of the model's understanding after processing the features from the input sentence:

Current Economic state ~ recession
InControl (France, economic state) ~ false (0.9)

The first line indicates that, after the simulation, the program believes that France is in a recession. If the input had been Event ~ escape, we would expect a quite different conclusion and the program produces such a result. More interestingly, the second line adds new information, namely that the system believes with probability 0.9 that the agent (France) had very little control over the descent into recession. Recall our initial example about France waltzing into recession. The word "fell" used in the input sentence here has connotations of being accidental in the embodied domain, and these are mapped to the assertion that France's leaders had no control. This probably is close to your own conclusions from reading the sentence.

System Overview

An overview of Narayanan's model (figure 20.1) goes as follows: the pre-analyzed (parsed) sentence fills in some parameters and then appropriate metaphorical maps are activated. Using the features from the input and the mappings, the appropriate embodied X-schemas execute and, as a result, fill in other parameters. Those parameters are passed back to the economics domain via the metaphor maps. The belief net is then updated to accord with these transmitted values. Additional input information causes the system to repeat the cycle, and then the effects of that new information and the resulting inferences are represented in the belief net. So the process continues as long as new text keeps coming in. This models how we understand the meaning of a story as we are reading it.

We will examine some other examples of how Narayanan's program interprets the meaning of news stories, but it is also important to get a clearer picture of how the model carries out its task and what its architecture can tell us about language processing in our brains. Let's begin with an informal discussion of how it all works for the first example, and then look into the details.

Each of the four input features conveys something important. The program has some economic knowledge of different countries, so a story about France would be processed differently from one on India. The other explicitly economic fact is that the economic state under discussion is recession. The economic knowledge is conveyed to the temporal belief network (chapter 19), shown on the upper right in figure 20.1.

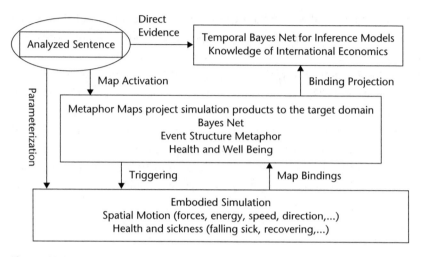

Figure 20.1
Overview of Narayanan's story understanding program.

The other two input features are not directly about economics at all. The event is *fall into*, a physical occurrence. And, as we saw in chapter 18, the simple past form "fell" (as opposed to "was falling") conveys the idea that the event can be viewed as completed and not worth simulating in detail. That is, this story is about the consequences of France falling, not about the process itself.

Using these four feature values, the program proceeds as follows. Since the input contains a physical action and an agent, which is a country, it tries to make these two fit together using the metaphor Country as agent. The program associates the word "recession" with a hole on the path of economic advancement, as specified by the event structure metaphor (chapter 16), which maps progress in any domain to physical motion toward a goal. This suggests to the program that the story should be simulated as a metaphorical agent (France) falling into a hole while on a path toward some unspecified physical goal. The program uses its metaphor maps to inform the embodied simulation at the bottom of figure 20.1 that a completed falling action needs to be simulated. Finally, since the event shape is marked *completed*, the system focuses on the consequences of the fall, ignoring any details of how or why it happened.

Purely at the level of human actions, we know that a fall causes someone to interrupt their progress toward their goal and possibly injures them as well. We don't know if the person was able to get out of the hole and haven't been told yet in the story. The system has similar inferences in its schema model, and the simulation of our sample story will trigger them.

The next step is the crucial one—the system maps the conclusions from its simulation back to the domain of economics. Since the traveler is assumed to still be in the hole, the Country is agent and Recession is hole metaphors, combined, yield the belief that economic state ~ recession, as discussed earlier. This is shown as the two upward-pointing arrows in the middle of figure 20.1. The metaphorical person (France) is assumed to still be in the metaphorical hole (recession). The system can also draw the somewhat more subtle conclusion that France was not in a recession before the time of the story. This comes from the fact that "fall" suggests a change of physical state and therefore, metaphorically, a change in economic state. Now, back in the belief network, additional inferences can be drawn. Since a physical fall suggests lack of agent control, the Country is agent metaphor suggests that (the government of) France probably had no control over the onset of recession.

Viewing all this at a more technical level, Narayanan's system has three interacting modules, each of which uses techniques that have been discussed in earlier chapters. Its knowledge of economics is represented by a temporal belief network, as described in the previous chapter. Its simulation model of embodied domains such as health and progress along a physical path uses executing schemas and the controller-based simulation framework, as were defined in chapter 13 and used in chapters 17 and 18. For modeling the detailed event shape of actions (aspect), the model uses the ideas of chapter 18 on encapsulated and ongoing views of events. We will now look at how all this mechanism works in understanding our example story.

The key to linking the abstract domain of economics with embodied simulations is, of course, metaphor. For this example, we need two specific metaphors: Country is agent and Recession is hole. These, as we have seen in chapter 16, are part of a large system of interacting metaphors.

How the System Processes the Example

We are now in a position to trace the flow of information as the model tries to understand the meaning of the example sentence. The first step is to establish initial values for the temporal belief net representing the economic situation. Then two things happen in parallel. The links in the economics model specify that some feature values should be projected forward in time; in this case, the economic state may change. At the same time, the system looks for metaphors that might be applicable, using the metaphor-matching algorithms discussed in chapter 16.

The easy metaphor map to recognize is Recession is hole. This is a conventional metaphor in economics and the system, like people, knows this. It is not as simple to decide that the Country as agent metaphor should apply, even if it is also conventional. The problem is that there are other metaphors, such as Country as patient, that are also common in news stories. Within its limited scope, the system knows that the verb *"fell"* applies to agents in the embodied physical motion domain and thus chooses the correct mapping. Once the metaphor mappings are chosen, these mappings establish the bidirectional link between the news domain (economics) and the embodied simulation, here of a person falling into a hole.

The next step is to carry out a simulation of the action underlying this particular story. As we saw in chapter 17, any simulation requires the specification of which action schemas, image schemas, parameters, and frames are involved. In Narayanan's system, the participants in the simulation come both directly from the features of the input (fall into, completed) and from the results of metaphorical maps (agent, hole).

Since the story used *"fell,"* the simulation is of a completed action and is not focused on any ongoing falling activity. One result of the simulation at the embodied level is that the agent is still very likely to be in the hole. Notice that if the story had used *"had fallen"* instead of *"fell,"* we would believe the agent was probably already out of the hole and we would hear more about that in the next sentence, and the program would do the same. Anyway, in this case the agent is still in the hole. Here is where the metaphor maps have there greatest payoff. Because the system has a bidirectional map, Recession is hole, it concludes that the agent (France) is still in recession. As we mentioned earlier, only some of the source domain concepts get mapped back to the economic domain—a person who fell might feel stupid, but that has no counterpart in economics.

The conclusion, that France had little control over its descent, arises in a similar fashion. Part of the system's knowledge of the word *"fall"* is that it suggests the agent involved did not take the action voluntarily and may even have been surprised by what happened. It also implies a rapid descent, although this wasn't brought out in the implementation. Again, the system exploits the bidirectionality of the metaphor Country is agent by mapping feature values from the embodied domain back to economics. Since the agent in the embodied model had no physical control, its metaphorical projection, France, is deemed to have no economic control. Technically this involves a submetaphor mapping Economic Control is physical control. As we saw in chapter 16, all our metaphors have this kind of elaborated structure.

Narayanan's model was able to draw appropriate inferences from a wide range of news stories in its domain, and we will examine some of these to get a feeling for the scope of the result. It is worth looking first at one more detailed example, which illustrates additional properties of the system. This fragment is from the *New York Times*, August 1995:

In 1991, India set out on a path of liberalization. The government started to loosen its strangle-hold on business and removed obstacles to international trade. Now the government is stumbling in implementing the liberalization plan.

This example has several interesting features aside from its massive use of metaphor. The basic metaphor is event structure, mapping an arbitrary goal to a travel destination. But the term *strangle-hold* introduces at least an additional health metaphor and potentially others such as control and injury. Notice also how the use of the term *strangle-hold* conveys an enormous amount about the political views of the writer.

But we are most interested in the analysis of the final sentence. Its mapping to feature structures is given below. The technically most important issue is the feature Event shape ~ ongoing, which means that the simulation needs to focus on an ongoing process, not one that is already over and can be viewed as finished, as in the previous example. Before going into the details, we can notice that the wording *"is stumbling"* leaves the reader expecting some further information about how it will all turn out.

The initial feature settings for this example are

Agent ~ India
Economic plan ~ liberalization
Event ~ stumble
Event shape ~ ongoing

The main metaphors involved are the usual Country is agent and event structure. As in the previous example, the program begins by looking for the best fitting metaphors and, at the same time, propagating beliefs that will not change over time. Here the agent and plan will not change. What the simulation does is add some conclusions about the likely outcome.

Goal ~ free trade

Event shape ~ suspended

Outcome ~ failure (0.6)

Of these conclusions, one follows directly from the system's knowledge of economics, namely, that the goal of a liberalization policy is free trade. The other two conclusions are the indirect results of a complex simulation in the embodied domain of progress along a path, as given by the event structure metaphor. This metaphor becomes active because the lexical items from both the embodied ("stumble") and economic ("liberalization plan") domain trigger it, as depicted in figure 16.1. The coactivation of the economics frame and the traveling frame activates the event structure metaphor, because Economic progress as travel is a known metaphor, and this includes "goals are destinations" as a part. As before, the Country is agent metaphor is conventional in stories about economics and matches easily.

Much of the richness of this example comes from the use of the word *"stumble"* in the discourse. For one thing, stumble indirectly indicates that the walk executing schema is involved, because stumbling is something that happens while one moves along a path. In addition, stumble suggests that the walking has been interrupted, and this has two implications. First, there must have been some ongoing process before the utterance. This means that the simulation must start with events that happened before the situation described by the input. Both the executing schema formalism and belief nets have the ability to reason *backwards in time* from events to possible causes, and that is needed here. In this case, the lexical entry "stumble" directly encodes the instruction to simulate an ongoing walk that is interrupted. More generally, the exact type of simulation will depend on the goals of the system—a program that was trying to figure out the political views of the author would model the same sentence rather differently.

Also, the use of the progressive form "is stumbling" means that the simulation leaves us in a state in which we envision the person still in the process of stumbling; we don't know whether he will recover or fall down. This is exactly what *stumbling* means, that someone was walking and that walk was suspended for some reason. In the model, inferences about aspect (action shape) map directly between the embodied and the abstract domains.

In the current model, the stumbling is assumed to be caused by an obstacle. Since Difficulties are obstacles is part of the event structure metaphor, this gets mapped back to the economics domain as the inference that India probably (0.7) encountered a difficulty in its liberalization effort. As before, the probabilities are set by the system designer or learned from examples.

The general idea is that metaphors enable the system to take a term like *stumble* in a sentence about the economics domain and map it to the concrete embodied domain. It then knows that *stumble* is an interrupted walk, from which it can infer in the embodied domain that the agent didn't reach his destination. When the metaphor that Goals are destinations is active, there is an inference back to the economics domain that the economic agent quite possibly (0.6) didn't achieve its economic goal. That inference may lead to other inferences in the economics domain, although none is shown in the example.

The next sentence in the story could cause you to revise these values. For instance, if the next sentence says that the Indian government is recovering, you will revise your prediction of failure. The task for the program is to have the feature values in the right state, so that new information has the correct effect on beliefs. If it gets no new information, the final state describes a 0.6 probability of failure. In general, the context of previous utterance, world state and discourse state as well as background knowledge, should be combined in a full system.

Notice that the final inferences cannot be drawn with only the event structure metaphor or only knowledge of economics. The system needs to understand what *stumble* could mean both within the field of economics and in the context of the story. So there are two inference structures. One is in the embodied domain, where active schema execution is used to draw inferences about what it means to *stumble*. The other is in the target domain (economics), where belief nets are used to model our knowledge about how government policies may affect economic growth. Both kinds of inference are necessary to understand statements about economics.

Let's look briefly at some of the other examples that the program processed successfully. Two of the examples rely on the Economic Health is physical health metaphor, with the submetaphor Policymaker is doctor:

The World Bank prescribed a structural adjustment program, bleeding developing countries.

A protectionist policy is the mistaken therapy of prescribing palliatives to the economy in response to painful change and perception of injury.

Both of these sentences employ the health metaphor more than once, both are about bad economic situations, and both evidently disagree with the policy that was "prescribed." The following two examples use both the event structure and health metaphors in a single sentence:

Japan continues its long, painful slide into recession.

The U.S. economy is on the verge of falling back into recession after lurching forward on an anemic recovery.

These are examples of the dreaded mixed metaphors that your grammar school teacher warned you about. In fact, it is very common and often effective to combine different metaphors to convey an idea. It is instructive to understand how the program deals with multiple source domains like health and a journey. The key is the belief network that yields the (probabilistic) inferences about the result of reading a story. Belief networks are explicitly designed to combine evidence from several bases—that is their raison d'etre. In the first example, both *painful* (from health) and *long slide* (from journey) add to the belief that the recession is a deep one. In the second example, both *lurch* and *anemic* suggest that the U.S. recovery was a weak one. The system could also deal with conflicting messages, but those are not common in news stories.

Recapping, the action of Narayanan's model goes as follows: the parsed story fills in some parameters and some metaphorical maps are activated. Using the features from the input and the mappings, the appropriate X-schemas execute and, as a result, fill in other parameters. Those parameter values are passed back to the economics domain via the metaphor maps. The belief net is then updated to accord with these transmitted values. Additional input information causes the system to repeat the cycle and the effects of that new information and the resulting inferences are represented in the belief net. So the process continues as long as new text keeps coming in. This models how we understand a story as we are reading it.

We can also relate the function of this particular program to the underlying neural theory of language. The belief networks model the spreading neural activation that is postulated to be the basis for mental operations. The metaphor maps embody the hypothesis that we understand abstract domains by relating them to direct experience. The matching of metaphors is assumed to follow the triangle node circuit in figure 16.1. And the executing schemas are operating models of physical actions that might use the circuitry of mirror neurons as discussed in the simulation chapter (chapter 17). In some ways, this completes the path from molecule to metaphor, promised in the book's title.

An obvious limitation of Narayanan's program is that it could not analyze input sentences on its own—he had to spoon feed it preanalyzed structures with the appropriate semantic relations. The rules that relate linguistic form to the underlying semantic relations constitute *grammar*. The next two chapters present an overview of grammar theories and some of the controversy that has arisen over whether human grammar is innate. Chapter 23 describes a new approach to grammar, embodied construction grammar (ECG), which is an outgrowth of the neural theory of language. Then, in chapter 24, we show how ECG can be used to derive the semantic relations needed for deep understanding models, like the one described in this chapter.

VIII | Combining Form and Meaning

21 Combining Forms—Grammar

The story understanding system of the previous chapter, and in fact everything up to this point in the book, has used the tacit assumption that *semantic relations* could be extracted from language input. I will now describe how these meaning relations are represented at various levels and across different types of languages, and how such semantic relations are derived from *linguistic forms*.

As I have discussed throughout the book, thinking about anything involves many areas of the brain and billions of active neurons. The fundamental problem of language is how to communicate this massively *parallel* mental activity in a *serial* stream of sound, gesture, or print. As Scott Delancey (1997) eloquently states it: *"In its communicative function, language is a set of tools with which we attempt to guide another mind to create within itself a mental representation that approximates one we have."* From our neural perspective, it would be more accurate to say *"evoke"* rather than *"create within itself,"* but the idea is the same. Such evocation requires, among other things, that the listener or reader share enough experience with the author. We have all heard discussions, using words that we know, which made no sense to us because the subject was outside our experience. I was raised in a rural Pennsylvania mill town and knew a lot about hunting—tromping through the winter woods with a shotgun. At a dinner party many years later, we were several minutes into a discussion before I realized that everyone else's experience of hunting involved horses, dogs, horns, and foxes.

Given some shared knowledge and experience, languages provide a range of mechanisms for helping guide another mind. A key assumption we have been using all along is that the meaning of language can be expressed by a discrete set of parameters and by semantic relations among entities and actions, as discussed in several chapters. The question is how these relations are encoded in the sequences of letters or sounds that constitute language form. Over the next few chapters, we will learn about the associations between linguistic form and meaning and how these associations can also be seen as manifestations of the basic neural best-match character of the brain. The discussion is largely at the computational level, but as always, this is an abstraction of postulated neural computation.

We start by focusing on written language, ignoring for now intonation and gesture, which are potent sources of meaning in spoken interactions. For all the complexity of written languages, there are only three distinct mechanisms for conveying a semantic relation, and all grammars use combinations of these: a word that conveys some meaning, word order, and some change in a base word such as an "-ed" ending for the past tense. As I mentioned, spoken language also involves intonation and gesture, but we'll skip these for now.

The most common means of representing a semantic relation in English is word order. We say "red fire engine" and "fire engine red" and know that the first phrase describes a vehicle whose color is mentioned and the second denotes a particular color. A number of semantic relations are expressed by special words like the spatial prepositions studied by Regier (chapter 12): *in, on, through,* and so on. There are also a fair number of words used to mark grammatical structure rather than any specific content. For example, the English infinitive is expressed in the form *to verb,* as in *to walk;* other languages express the infinitive as one word. The grammar school dictum that we should try to not split our infinitives arose because Latin uses a single-word infinitive, for example, *ambulare* (to walk). Other grammatical particles are used to help mark verb tenses such as *were, will,* and *have been,* and in many other functions including the spatial relations discussed in chapter 12.

Some semantic relations in English are coded by a systematic change in spelling and pronunciation as in the regular plural (car, cars) or in converting a verb to a noun (evoke, evocation). In chapter 22, we will see that one particular case, the English past tense, is at the center of a major controversy over the nature of language, its development, and its realization in the brain. Known as *morphology* (from the Greek "study of form"), this class of operations plays a much larger role in many languages than it does in English. Most linguists use English as a base language, and this helps explain why much less attention has been paid to morphology as a source of meaning than to words and word order.

Other languages routinely convey meaning by assembling and modifying meaning units into a single word. As a first example, consider Hebrew-based names such as those of my two sons, Benjamin and Michael:

ben	*yamin*		*mi*	*cha*	*el*
son	right hand		who	is like	God.

Modern Hebrew carries this idea much further, yielding words like

ve	*le*	*ke*	*she*	*ti*	*t*	*ragel*	*u*	$\rightarrow$	*ulixshtitraglu*
and	to	as	that	you will	(refl)	used	(pl)		

"when you(pl) will get accustomed"

where (refl) is a reflexive marker and (pl) is a plural marker. As always, some forms change pronunciation when they are combined into larger words.

Our discussion of the Eskimo words for snow (chapter 15) left out an important part of the story. Eskimo languages really do have more explicit words involving snow, but they also have a very rich morphology system that greatly extends what might be called a "word." One can, for example, tell about one man talking about another man as a single word: *tik-itqaarminaitnigaa*, meaning "He(1) said that he(2) would not be able to arrive first." So part of the argument about the number of "words" for snow in Eskimo languages confused conceptual issues with grammatical style. The Turkic languages have yet another way, distinct from the Eskimo or Semitic style, of combining meaning units into large words. It simply isn't possible in these languages to list all viable words in a dictionary. In fact, even in English we rely on some systematic morphological rules such as the one that takes us from the adjective *"happy"* to the adverb *"happily"* and the noun *"happiness."* This rule works for new words as well; if we accept *nerdy* as an adjective, we know the meaning of *nerdily* and *nerdiness*.

An adequate theory of grammar will need to incorporate all the different types of form-meaning mappings, including morphology, intonation, and gesture. I will sketch the outlines of how an integrated neurally based grammar might go in chapter 23. For the rest of this chapter and the next, we focus on the traditional restricted notion of grammar and syntax as based on function words and word order.

As we have seen, individual words can each have a wide range of related and unrelated meanings, and one necessary task for language comprehension is *disambiguation* of the intended meaning of each individual word in an utterance. But we are more concerned here with how meanings associated with different parts of an utterance are combined to yield a best interpretation of that utterance in the context of a discourse. This, in the broad sense, it what we mean by the rules of *grammar.*

Everyone learns rules of grammar in school, but these only talk about the *form* of language and supply only part of what is needed for analyzing sentences. The relation between linguistic form and meaning includes a lot more than the diagramming of sentences that we learned in elementary school, itself often called *grammar* school. Grammar provides the mechanisms that enable us to take a fixed set of (some 50,000) words and express an essentially boundless range of thoughts and emotions. Theories vary widely on how all this works, but anyone who thinks about language quickly realizes its amazing power of composition.

The nature of grammar rules is at the core of the most heated controversies about brain, mind, and language. We saw some of this in connection with the Whorf-Sapir hypothesis of linguistic determinism in chapter 15, and we will delve into the wider language wars in the next chapter. This chapter provides the background and terminology for the various discussions of linguistic form and meaning that dominate the remainder of this book. The discussion here is based on explicit formal grammar rules; the next chapter takes up the question of how these rules, or something equivalent, might be realized in the brain, or not.

To begin at the beginning, all languages have some *form rules* that operate independently of any relation to meaning. Anyone who has struggled to learn a foreign language knows full well that some sounds in English are simply not acceptable in other languages, and vice versa. Moving on to pairs of letters, several perfectly pronounceable pairs of English letters are not used in words. The easiest way to see this is to look at loan words (from another language) that are common in some English dialects and use letter combinations not found in native words. For example, the Yiddish word *"shtick"* was accepted by my spell-checker without complaint, but the combination of letters "sht" is just not part of English. Similarly, the combination "sri" is common in Indian names, but again is not a standard English sequence. Of course, people can understand heavy accents and other violations of the rules of a language, but they are recognized as such.

Some spelling rules result from pronunciation patterns, again independent of meaning. Although we are usually not aware of it, one of the basic rules of English grammar is that the singular determiner "a" becomes "an" whenever the following word starts with a vowel. There are also some rules of pure form in the grammar of combining words. It is not correct English to say "#Him Xed he," whatever action X might be. The # is the usual linguists' way of marking a questionably grammatical sentence.

Most grammar rules, however, do have an effect on meaning as well as on form. When we write "her novel," we are not only using the correct pronoun form but are also expressing a semantic relation between some female and some book, presumably both known from context. As you probably noticed, the actual idea conveyed might be that the female owns the book, wrote the book, or, in different contexts, quite a range of other things including editing, selling, or being the subject of the novel.

Although grammar rules of a language can be written down in many ways, we will follow the general practice of using a formal mathematical description. This has all the standard advantages of formalism in science—clarity, universality, and the ability to derive the consequences of rules. In addition, a formal description of grammar opens the possibility that computer programs could use the rules in systems for language understanding or other tasks. This works well for programming languages; in fact, all programs for translating computer programs to machine code rely on formal grammars specifying exactly what is a legal program. The value of formal grammar for natural languages is more controversial, but let's first establish the ground rules.

We start with a review of what many of us learned in grammar school—diagramming sentences. Figure 21.1 presents a formal grammar for a tiny fragment of English, using one standard notation called Context Free Grammar (CFG). The lexicon on the left lists the grammatical type of all possible words for this tiny fragment. For example, the first rule gives the four common nouns of the fragment, separated by the | symbol, which should be read as "or." The grammar rules on the right specify how to build larger grammatical constructions from smaller ones. For example, the first rule can be read as: A sentence (S) can be a noun phrase (NP) followed by a verb phrase (VP) or it can be a smaller S, followed by a Conjunction

A Tiny NL CFG

Lexicon	Grammar Rules
Noun → soul | pipe | fiddlers | bowl	S → NP VP
ProperNoun → King Cole	| S Conjunction S
Verb → was | called | play | plays	
Adjective → old | merry | three	NP → Adjective* ProperNoun
Article → a | the	| Possessive Adjective* Noun
Possessive → his	| Article Adjective* Noun
Conjunction → and	| Pronoun
Preposition → for	
Pronoun → he	VP → Verb NP | Verb PP
	PP → Preposition NP

The complete tiny grammar. It can generate lines from the *Old King Cole* nursery rhyme.

Figure 21.1
A tiny grammar for a fragment of English.

followed by a second smaller S. If these rules remind you of the Turing machine program discussed earlier, they should; they are alternative notations for essentially the same computations.

Figure 21.2 shows the analysis or *parse* of the sentence, "Old King Cole was a merry old soul," according to the formal grammar of figure 21.1.

There is nothing at all remarkable about this analysis. Starting from the input text at the bottom, it shows how words should be grouped, following the rules of the grammar. Linguists developing such grammars choose groupings (such as NP) that will be useful for later semantic processing, but semantics plays no direct role in the analysis. An almost identical analysis would result for the input string, "Old King Cole was a merry old fiddlers." This is equally good according to the grammar of figure 21.1, but obviously not to us. The basic task of grammar writing is to specify a set of formal rules that corresponds to what native speakers accept as their language. The task is analogous to that of a scientist trying to write formal laws covering all the observations in some domain.

Before delving too deeply into the technicalities of formal grammar, we should notice that, in an appropriate context, many officially ungrammatical utterances are perfectly acceptable. A famous (among linguists) example is

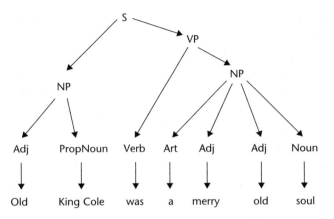

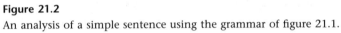

Figure 21.2
An analysis of a simple sentence using the grammar of figure 21.1.

Virginia thinks vanilla.

This seems strange in isolation, but is fine following a question like "What flavor of ice cream does Georgia want?" In languages with stronger grammatical markings, which depend less on word order, and also in East Asian languages, it is sometimes acceptable to omit any elements that can be determined by context. Japanese children are taught how to determine meaning from context as part of learning their language. Context plays a different, but equally crucial, role in Hebrew. Adult Hebrew is written without vowels, and readers effortlessly pick the right words from context. Interestingly, most Hebrew poetry is written with explicit vowels, presumably because there is not enough context to allow a reader to fill them in.

The problem of writing formal grammars that approximate real languages is still unsolved, but quite a lot is being learned about the task. Let's look at one particular issue that is now well understood. Our problem sentence, "Old King Cole was a merry old fiddlers," is acceptable until the last word. In fact, it is grammatical until the final letter of the final word; "fiddler" would be a perfectly appropriate English word in this context.

The difficulty is one of *number agreement*. Semantically, we know that "king" is singular and "fiddlers" is plural, and so they don't agree on grammatical number. But from the perspective of formal grammar, the situation is more complex. For example, it is perfectly all right in English to say, "Old King Cole was one of the merry old fiddlers." The agreement rules depend on the structure of the sentence. In addition to singular and plural, other languages, including Slovenian and Arabic, have separate grammatical markings for a pair of something. Russian has quite complex rules of agreement, depending on the number of objects being discussed.

Let's look briefly at how we might modify the tiny grammar of figure 21.1 to require agreement, first just for grammatical number. One rule that obviously needs to be modified is the one defining NP (noun phrases). As in our example, if the article is singular, "a," then the associated noun must also be singular—this is why "a . . . fiddlers" sounds so strange. We could try to fix our grammar by further refining the categories, perhaps by adding SgArticle and PlArticle, along with SgNoun and PlNoun. Then the rule for NP could also be refined into two rules, one for SgNP and one for PlNP. But that wouldn't be enough, because another rule of English is that grouping an NP and a VP requires that these constituents also agree in number; we can't say "fiddlers plays." So we would also need to split the categories verb and VP by grammatical number.

If number agreement were the only problem, splitting up grammatical categories might be an adequate solution, but it isn't. English is relatively simple in its agreement rules, but it still has requirements for number, person, grammatical case (subject, object, etc.), and gender agreement. Recall from our discussion of linguistic determinism in chapter 15 that "apple" is grammatically masculine in German (der Apfel) and feminine (la manzana) in Spanish. These languages require articles and adjective forms to agree with the noun they modify:

der rote Apfel
la manzana roja

English makes much less use of grammatical gender than does German or Spanish, but it is still illegal to say "He called for her bowl" in the context of the nursery rhyme. We also cannot use third-person singular verb forms like "plays" with the first-person pronoun "I."

Grammatical case is much more important in many other languages than it is in English. But even for us it is ungrammatical to use a pronoun in nominative case "he" instead of the possessive case in an expression such as "he bowl." In German or Russian, as well as in Latin and other languages, case markings capture the essential *"who did what to whom"* that relies on word order in English. So the Russian translation of

The good girl loves the poor boy.
Chorosaya devochka liobit bednovo mal'chika.

would mean the same if the order of the words were changed. The case endings tell us that it was the girl loving and the boy being loved.

Additional rules of English grammatical form arise even in our tiny example. The grammar of figure 21.1 treats all verbs identically, but this is wrong. One major distinction is between (transitive) verbs that normally require an object, for example, "played," in "He played his pipe," and (intransitive) verbs such as "sleep" that do not normally take an NP to be the object of the action.

So, to get a good approximation to English grammar using rules such as those in figure 21.1, one would need to add many combinations of different properties to the names of the grammatical categories. Even for our tiny grammar, we would need to have rules like

3rdSgMaNomPronoun → he

and also accompanying collections of rules for NP, S, and so on. This clearly gets out of hand, motivating linguists to develop a general clean and simple way to describe agreement conditions in formal grammar.

First, notice that the person, gender, and number agreement conditions all require that the components have the *same value* for each of the three features. We can exploit this fact to write a shorthand version of the painful explosion of rules just described. For example, we could revert to the original rule "S → VP NP" as long as we can also specify that, in each case, the VP and the NP to be combined must agree in person, gender, and number. The notation we will use for stating this is the following:

VP.person ↔ NP.person
VP.gender ↔ NP.gender
VP.number ↔ NP.number

The double-headed arrow notation is called *unification* and actually needs to be a bit more general than we have described so far. In English, and in other languages as well, a particular word form often agrees with more than one combination of features. For example, we use exactly the same form of a noun such as fiddlers in either the nominative (Fiddlers called . . .) or objective (. . . called the fiddlers) case. Similarly, a verb in English is not marked for grammatical gender but does have values for person and number. The full definition of unification is designed to cope with these multifaceted characteristics of words. Here's how it works.

A unification condition denoted by ↔ is satisfied whenever the feature values of its two constituents are compatible, not just when they are identical. Let's examine the case of a simple sentence: "He sleeps." The lexicon will contain the information that the verb, "sleeps," is a third-person singular verb, but has no restriction on its gender. The pronoun, "he," will be listed as having masculine gender, singular number, and third person. The sentence, "He sleeps," is grammatically acceptable because there is no contradiction on any of the feature values. The string, "They sleeps," is not acceptable because "they" has plural number and therefore cannot unify with the singular verb "sleeps."

As we will see in chapter 23, this idea of specifying grammatical rules using unification of feature values is used in much more general ways and is the foundation for most contemporary approaches to formalizing grammar. It is not important for us whether these unification conditions are called grammar or meaning, they have aspects of both. For the basic features of person, number, and gender agreement, the feature unification rules are often assumed and not written explicitly in the grammar. This allows linguists to specify some simple parts of a grammar using rules that again look more like our original rules in figure 21.1.

The idea of formalizing grammar is convenient for linguists and for computers, but what is the status of formal grammar as a theory of language in the brain? Before getting into the details of these technical arguments, it is worth reminding ourselves of how much of meaning is conveyed by mechanisms other than words and formal grammar.

Even within the realm supposedly treated by formal grammar, a number of language uses cannot be handled. For one thing, context plays a crucial role in language understanding. The meaning of the so-called indexicals such as *here* and *now* obviously depend on the situation, as do the referents of expressions such as *they* or *that question*. An ambiguous sentence like

Harry walked into the café with the singer.

could be describing either Harry's companion or a feature of the café, and grammar cannot tell us which. And the metaphorical use of language is not described in standard grammars.

Intonation and gesture also play major roles not captured in standard grammars. For example, think about how many different meanings you can get for the following simple sentence by using different intonation patterns:

Harry walked into the cafe.

You can easily get ten distinct meanings by stressing each of the five words in both question and statement form—try it. If you group *"walked into"* as a unit, yet more meanings result. It is also interesting to think about *negation*. How would you interpret

Harry did not walk into the cafe.

As before, there are several quite different possible meanings, depending on which words are stressed. This example also reminds us that the mathematical abstraction of semantic notions such as negation don't do justice to the natural phenomena.

In addition, you can imagine saying the sentence in various social situations—to a child, parent, judge—and notice more intonational differences. In face-to-face conversation a wide range of hand, head, and body gestures also convey additional elements of meaning and speaker attitude. Considerable research is now being done on understanding and encoding gestures, notably by David McNeill at the University of Chicago. Ultimately, grammar should encompass all these things, but we will revert to the standard limited treatment for the next chapter on the language wars.

In the last chapter, we saw how linguists can describe some parts of the syntactic structure of language in terms of rules of grammar. Some such formal rules are necessary for linguists to do their work, and formal grammars work quite well for them as well as for computers. But do our brains use formal rules in understanding language? Does our grammatical ability constitute an autonomous "language faculty," or is it inextricably linked to meaning and thought? Is the human language capacity largely genetically specified or is it learned, based on the same neural structure and adaptation techniques as all of our other mental abilities?

These three related questions continue to generate heated arguments in both the technical and the public press—heated enough that "language wars" is not an overstatement. The chapter title was inspired by the book *The Linguistics Wars* (Harris 1983). That book discusses an earlier controversy, with Noam Chomsky and George Lakoff as central protagonists. Like any true book about war, it gets nasty in places and is recommended only if you are considering a career in linguistics. The substance of the argument has progressively narrowed to the point where most linguists and cognitive scientists have lost interest, but we can learn a great deal from looking at the core issues involved.

The basic facts about language acquisition and use are not in question. Any normal child living in a language community will become fluent in the local language or languages without formal instruction, independent of her ancestry. Some other animal species have or can acquire considerable communication abilities, but nothing approaching the expressiveness of human language. In the few known tragic cases where children were deprived of language interaction throughout childhood, they never achieved fluency. So, there is something special about human language and thought, and it depends on both nature and nurture, as you already know.

Given the overwhelming evidence, everyone also now agrees that many, but certainly not all, parts of the brain are active during language processing. It is clear that various kinds of language (and vision, planning, etc.) processing involve different neural circuits, and damage to different brain areas results in diverse symptoms. And, as Antonio Damasio (Damasio 2003) states, "Any complex mental function results from concerted contributions by *many* brain regions at various levels of the central nervous system rather than from the work of a single brain region conceived in a phrenological manner."

The agreed-upon facts go much further. No one believes that the meaning of words, say *Internet*, are innate; they are obviously learned. No one even suggests that the specific rules of grammar for each language are genetically specified; they clearly are not. However, linguists have long noted that all human languages have some structural similarities; there could be some genetic basis for this. In fact, everyone agrees that there is *some* genetic basis for the commonality of human languages—how could it be otherwise?

But perhaps what the human genes specify is a unique learning ability that is in no way specific to language. Everyone also accepts that there must be some uniquely human learning ability since there is a vast range of activities (calculus, chess, concertos, etc.) that only humans learn to do. It could be that no special genetic basis exists for language at all, any more than for chess. Languages would turn out to be structurally similar because the human condition is shared and our common learning mechanisms give rise to similar grammars.

The current battles partially continue traditional philosophical arguments over the relative importance of nature and nurture in human development. But as we discussed in chapter 6, the intricate interaction of genetic and environmental factors is now so well understood that the notion of an "innate," unmodifiable capacity has disappeared from the developmental biology literature.

The related old rationalist/empiricist controversy concerned the extent to which the senses or pure thought was the more reliable source of truth. Although minor elements of this remain in the present debate, the general scientific method, involving cycles of reasoning and observation, is universally accepted as the preferred methodology for answering the questions at issue, despite continued controversies over what should be considered scientific.

The core questions in dispute can thus be expressed succinctly:

(a) Are formal grammar rules expressed in the brain?
(b) Is grammar independent of other brain structures?
(c) Is there some special genetic encoding specifically for grammar?

The language wars are fought between people who strongly argue that the answer to all three questions is Yes and those who are equally vehement in asserting that they are all No. We can think of the Yes camp as portraying grammar as a *special* ability and the No camp as suggesting that it is part of our *general* intelligence. More nuanced positions, of course, are available, and I will sketch one of them in the next chapter.

The Autonomy of Syntax

A central issue is the claim that syntax, formal rules like we explored in the previous chapter, are logically and biologically independent of all other aspects of language and thought. There must be some interaction, but it is claimed to be extremely restricted. Before getting into the technical issues, we should acknowledge that the language wars have a significant component of personal and institutional power struggles. Research funding, the careers of individuals, and the standing of departments, journals, and so on are at stake. There is a widespread belief that the "autonomy of syntax" stance is really a cover for the autonomy of linguistics from the findings of other disciplines. Linguists, understandably enough, want to believe that language is uniquely important and they own the only viable way to study it. Everyone pushes his or her beliefs—this book can be seen as an attempt to establish the centrality of neural computation in cognitive science.

These "academic" power struggles are ubiquitous and often harmless, but not always. Doctrinal differences among academic economists frequently influence major policy decisions. In the case of grammar, how we think about language has direct effects on teaching, law, therapy, and many other aspects of public and private life. Some of these are discussed in the final chapter.

Certainly part of the energy behind the language wars comes from people defending the style of work to which they have dedicated their lives. But there is no inherent reason this requires disparaging other approaches. Most of what we know about language has come from detailed analysis of linguistic regularities by professional linguists, and there is no substitute for this kind of empirical work. It is also true that human learning is a remarkable and powerful capability and we need to know much more about how it works and what it is capable of. But, unfortunately, the human genome does seem to code for a tendency to engage in bitter wars that are senseless to an outsider.

The Substantive Issues

Leaving motivational issues aside, let's look at the substance of the arguments. The "grammar is special" position is easy to state—that formal structures like those described in the previous chapter are represented as such in specific parts of the brain and function as a separate module of the language faculty. In this view, learning language has many facets, but much of the structure of the grammar module has been specified genetically. To learn the essential core of the local grammar, a child only needs to learn the values for a couple dozen binary parameters. For example, do modifiers come before or after the word they modify.

The position that language, including grammar, is a genetically undifferentiated part of our general intelligence requires a longer explanation. Before getting into this, we need to understand one of the central arguments used to defend the stance that some explicit knowledge of grammar must be specified in the genome—*the poverty of the stimulus*. The contention is that children learn grammar (which is assumed to be formal and autonomous) based on such an impoverished set of examples that they must have some built-in biases that amount to grammatical knowledge. One positive outcome of the current language wars is that very detailed studies now exist of what kind of utterances children do hear early in life. As you would expect, the warring factions differ on how to interpret all the data, but a more fundamental issue is the theoretical feasibility of learning grammar from examples at all.

Among the many weapons used in the language wars, mathematical theories of learnability have played a surprisingly large role. The basic arguments are phrased in terms of general computation, often using Turing machines as described in chapter 2. One result, called Gold's theorem (Gold 1967), shows that, under appropriate assumptions, no computational device can learn nontrivial formal grammars when given only examples of correct sentences. Since there is general agreement that babies get very little direct information on the sentences that *are not* in their language, this is claimed to prove that children must have some built-in knowledge of grammar. All of this discussion assumes that grammar is represented as an explicit set of abstract rules; we will question this assumption later, but not yet.

The basic ideas behind Gold's theorem are simple. We assume that some computer is presented with a series of sentences and must guess a grammar that yields exactly those sentences. If the computer is given all examples of well-formed (positive) sentences in the language and also all (negative) example strings that are not in the hidden language to be learned, it can easily guess a correct grammar using the following algorithm. As it sees more sentences, it makes successive guesses on the source grammar.

We assume that the computer can generate a list of all candidate grammars and can also check if a given example string can be parsed by a candidate grammar. Here's how it can eventually guess a correct grammar. Suppose the first example the computer sees is labeled positive; the computer tries to parse this example with the first candidate grammar. If that doesn't work, the computer continues down the list of candidate grammars until it finds one that does accept the first example. The same procedure is followed for all subsequent examples—guess the first grammar on the candidate list that can parse all the inputs seen so far. Although the list of possible grammars is potentially infinite, the machine only needs to generate candidates until it finds one that fits the data.

Now suppose a negative string not in the hidden language is presented. The computer checks if this is accepted by the current candidate grammar; if so, this candidate grammar is rejected and the next grammar is tried. A lot of candidate grammars will be rejected, but by our assumptions, somewhere in the list is a grammar that will parse all of the sentences and none of the nonsentences seen so far. As this process continues, a first grammar, G*, that happens to yield exactly the hidden language will be found. Once this first correct grammar becomes the candidate, the computer will never need to change its guess. Grammar G* will parse all of the positive examples and none of the negative ones, remaining the computer's correct guess.

However, children are not given (enough) explicit negative examples for this to work in real life. If the computer we just described were given only positive examples, it would almost certainly stop changing its guesses too soon. As soon as it reached some grammar, G+, that could parse *more* than the hidden language, it would continue to guess G+ forever because there would be no example where G+ fails. This is basically Gold's theorem.

Mathematical theorems, like experimental results, are subject to interpretation in how they might apply to a contested situation. Several assumptions are made in Gold's theorem that can be altered to yield a quite different result, although this line of argument is not common. For example, the computer need not guess the first adequate grammar on its list; some notions of "best" grammar do allow learning from positive data only (Feldman 1971).

Gold's result also assumes that the computer needs to guess a correct grammar for any arbitrary order of presentation. If we assume, instead, that the sentences are presented in order of increasing length, this is equivalent to presenting all positive and negative examples, which was shown above to be an easy learning task. If the examples come in order, after you have the first example of length five, you know that all unseen sentences of length four are not grammatical. In general, there are enough formal variations to ensure that computation theory is not the place to look for a definitive answer to whether or not grammar could be learned from the input children receive without some specific genetic constraints.

Are Explicit Grammar Rules Encoded in the Brain?

But there is a much more fundamental challenge to the perspective of Gold's theorem and treating language learning as a problem of symbolic computation, like the Turing machines introduced in chapter 2. Given all that we know about the massively parallel, quantitative, adaptive nature of neural computation, why should we believe that anything like symbol processing is actually happening in the brain? The most far-reaching opposition to the position that grammar is symbolic, autonomous, and genetically specified comes from a group of researchers in computational neural modeling, often called *the connectionists*. This labeling is somewhat confusing, because there are various connectionist research programs, some of which have quite different approaches to modeling, as described in chapter 9.

All connectionist research starts from the same assumptions that the known properties of individual neurons (chapter 4) and of brain circuitry (chapter 5) demand a computational theory and practice that is quite distinct from the traditional symbolic rules that have been used, for example, in writing grammars. Where connectionists differ among themselves is on the relative emphasis placed on learning versus prior structure in examining a capability such as language, as was discussed in chapter 9. At one extreme, the PDP research program pushes the limits on what can be accomplished by learning alone, with the simplest possible initial structure. Unsurprisingly, it is this pure-learning style of connectionist research that directly challenges the hypothesis that grammar is symbolic, autonomous, and genetically specified.

From the perspective of these PDP connectionists, grammar is one of many remarkable human skills that are achieved by learning from experience. There is no need to postulate any special genetic precursor explicitly for grammar, and it is against the research program to assume any prior structure before learning. Perhaps more important, grammar rules aren't represented explicitly in the brain at all—there are just neural networks whose weights have been modified to produce results similar to those experienced before. The long-term research goal is to demonstrate that initially uniform networks can be trained to capture all the regularities of grammar, as well as (with different training) all other mental functions.

The basic PDP approach relies on the *error backpropagation* technique, described in chapter 9 as one of the standard connectionist modeling methods. Networks such as the one depicted in figure 9.3 are trained to capture various aspects of grammar and other language and cognitive functions. Unsurprisingly, none of these models has yet attained a significant fraction of language learning or understanding. But there have been enough impressive results to challenge the contention that language learning from examples alone is simply impossible.

The English Past Tense

One particularly active battlefront in the language wars has revolved around two competing models for explaining the structure of the past tense of English verbs. The state of the debate as of 2002 is nicely summarized in an exchange of articles in *Trends in Cognitive Science* between Steven Pinker and Michael Ullman (P&U) defending the symbolic rule method (Pinker et al. 2002) and James (Jay) McClelland and Karalyn Patterson (M&P) taking the PDP approach (McClelland & Patterson 2002). I will first quote from the two sides and then try to summarize.

The formalists P&U lay out the problem nicely and fairly:

The past tense is of theoretical interest because it embraces two strikingly different phenomena. Regular inflection, as in *walk-walked* and *play-played*, applies predictably to thousands of verbs and is productively generalized to neologisms such as *spam-spammed* and *mosh-moshed*, even by preschool children. Irregular inflection, as in *come-came* and *feel-felt*, applies in unpredictable ways to some 180 verbs, and is seldom generalized; rather, the regular suffix is often overgeneralized by children to these irregular forms, as in *holded* and *breaked*. A simple explanation is that irregular forms must be stored in memory, whereas regular forms can be generated by a rule that suffixes *-ed* to the stem. Rumelhart and McClelland challenged that explanation with a pattern-associator model (RMM) that learned to associate phonological features of the stem with phonological features of the past-tense form. It thereby acquired several hundred regular and irregular forms and overgeneralized *-ed* to some of the irregulars.

The past tense has served as one of the main empirical phenomena used to contrast the strengths and weaknesses of connectionist and rule-based models of language and cognition. More generally, because inflections like the past tense are simple, frequent, and prevalent across languages, and because the regular and irregular variants can be equated for complexity and meaning, they have served as a test case for issues such as the neurocognitive reality of rules and other symbol-manipulating operations and the interaction between storage and computation in cognitive processing.

We can see this as a special case of the general controversy around our points a–c about the nature of language. The arguments back and forth get rather intense, in their academic way, with each side challenging the assertions made by the other or citing conflicting results. For our purposes, we present some summary statements that capture the essence of the two positions.

P&U focus on the fact that each of the various PDP models to date is designed to model a particular phenomenon:

At the same time, the post-RMM connectionist models have revealed the problems in trying to explain *all* linguistic phenomena with a single pattern-associator architecture. Each model has been tailored to account for one phenomenon explained by the WR theory; unlike RMM, few models account for more than one phenomenon or predict new ones. And modelers repeatedly build in or presuppose surrogates for the linguistic phenomena they claim to eschew, such as lexical items, morphological structures and concatenation operations. We predict that the need for structured representations and combinatorial operations would assert itself even more strongly if modelers included phenomena that are currently ignored in current simulations, such as syntax and its interaction with inflection, the massively productive combinatorial inflection of polysynthetic languages, and the psychological events concealed by providing the models with correct past-tense forms during training (i.e. children's ability to recognize an input as a past-tense form, retrieve its stem from memory, compute their own form, and compare the two).

The PDP modelers, M&P, respond by saying that, of course, more work needs to be done and there are also no implemented symbolic models that match the full range of experimental findings. Their main point is not about rules per se, they state, but about absolute symbolic rules:

We do not claim that it would be impossible to construct a rule-based model of inflection formation that has all of the properties supported by the evidence. However, such an account would not be an instantiation of Pinker's symbolic rule account. In fact, rule-based models with some of the right characteristics are currently being pursued. If such models use graded rule activations and probabilistic outcomes, allow rules to strengthen gradually with experience, incorporate semantic and phonological constraints, and use rules within a mechanism that also incorporates word-specific information, they could become empirically indistinguishable from a connectionist account. Such models might be viewed as characterizing an underlying connectionist processing system at a higher level of analysis, with rules providing descriptive summaries of the regularities captured in the network's connections.

Neither side in this battle or the broader war worries explicitly about the details of how language and thought are processed in the brain. The linguists do analysis of language as such, and the PDP connectionists focus on learning rules. By keeping the issues narrowly focused, both sides are able to pursue their argument without dealing with questions that would be compelling from any broader perspective.

For example, consider the knee-jerk reflex, whose circuit was described in figure 5.1. It implements a simple rule: if one leg is slipping, put more pressure on the other leg. But this clearly isn't stored as some symbolic rule; it is a hard-wired circuit that responds quantitatively and interacts with other circuits. Neither of the contending formalisms have any way to treat such circuits, and much more.

If this example seems too primitive, we can consider walking or, even better, *dancing*. Dancing is clearly learned and can be described by rules. Dancing appears to exist in all cultures and can be learned without formal instruction. On the other hand, there are obviously genetically specified limitations on the range of human movements and thus of dances. There may well be a human proclivity to dance—a dancing instinct. Suppose we recast issues a–c for dancing:

(a′) Are formal dance rules expressed in the brain?

(b′) Is dancing independent of other brain structures?

(c′) Is there some special genetic encoding specifically for dancing?

These questions don't seem to make a whole lot of sense, do they? Each one might be true to some extent, but none tells us much about how dancing is actually carried out and learned. More generally, it has often been noted that other cultural artifacts, most notably music, share many of the structural properties of grammar.

For different reasons, both sides in the language wars reject detailed operational theories. From the PDP general learning position, the only interesting issue is learning from a blank slate or some other totally neutral configuration. The fact that the brain has a great deal of elaborate structure before learning begins is ignored, because any structure built into the model interferes with the learning claims.

The extreme believers in innate, autonomous, rule-based grammar can ignore any conflicting biological evidence because of their conviction that neuroscience is not nearly developed enough to be taken seriously. Noam Chomsky (Chomsky 1993, p. 85) made the following statement in 1993, and repeatedly restated the same idea in his 2003 Berkeley lectures:

In fact, the belief that neurophysiology is even relevant to the functioning of the mind is just a hypothesis. Who knows if we're looking at the right aspects of the brain at all. Maybe there are other aspects of the brain that nobody has dreamt of looking at yet. That's happened often in the history of science. When people say that the mental is the neurophysiological at a higher level, they're being radically unscientific. We know a lot about the mental from a scientific point of view. We have explanatory theories that account for a lot of things. The belief that neurophysiology is implicated in these things could be true, but we have very little evidence for it. So, it's just a kind of hope; look around and you see neurons; maybe they're implicated.

The scientific path to truth described in this passage is formal linguistic analysis based on positive answers to questions a–c. If neuroscience is incompatible with this formal analysis, neuroscience must be wrong. The same belief system provides a rationale for ignoring inconvenient results from psychological experiments or corpus studies. These are said to reflect only linguistic *performance*, which is highly variable and uninteresting. The deep questions concern linguistic *competence* and can be addressed only by the orthodox methodology of formal grammar. This is the extreme form of the argument; other nativists, including Pinker and Ullman, experiment themselves and employ empirical results in their arguments.

One reason the war is so heated among participants and meaningless to most other cognitive scientists is that the two sides come from traditions that are radically different, as described earlier. And they both ignore uncomfortable findings. As with any effective belief system, positions on both sides are unassailable from within. Each side has an almost impregnable minimal stance to which true believers can remain committed indefinitely. For the language organ side, any aspect of grammar, however limited, that satisfies conditions a–c will suffice to establish the validity of their position. For the general learning side, there is always the hope that additional learning techniques will prove their side is right after all and grammar can be acquired without any precursor structure. The fact remains that both groups do good work within their methodological limitations, and everyone would be better served by a permanent peace. In fact, the actual beliefs by participants on both sides of the debate are much more balanced than you might judge from their fighting stances.

Beyond the Battlefield

Of course, no one knows exactly how the brain processes language, but enough has been discovered to support general answers to questions a–c that are internally consistent and in harmony with everything that is known. We know that current scientific knowledge is incompatible with either side of the current language wars. The basic theories arising from such an analysis are not as definitive as one would like, but they are unlikely to be refuted without major change in our understanding of neuroscience.

As I have discussed, current knowledge in the brain and behavioral sciences makes it clear that language, like all other human mental capacities, involves an intimate interaction between nature and nurture. We are not born a blank slate, nor is learning just selecting values for a few parameters. It also makes no biological sense to talk about an autonomous module for grammar or any other capability. The brain clearly does rely on specialized neural circuits, but these interact massively with one another and almost always have overlapping functions, at least partially compensating for damage to one circuit by other circuits.

We don't know which aspects of neural language processing involve specific evolutionary adaptations, but it would be amazing if there were none at all. We do have detailed knowledge about several physical adaptations in the throat, tongue, and other body parts that facilitate language, and we also know that such adaptations are always accompanied by related neural changes. If language is, as the neural theory suggests, continuous with other mental activities, it makes no sense to ask if certain evolutionary adaptations are specialized only for language. There is no such thing as language in isolation from thought. In chapter 26, I suggest a specific evolutionary adaptation that could have triggered our unique human abilities in language and much else.

Even more basically, the energy of much of the current debate is retained because both sides agree to focus on isolated problems in grammar, uncoupled to any effects of meaning or use of language. Though progress continues to be made within this restricted view, an embodied neural theory of language starts from the opposite perspective—grammar is inherently coupled to the form, meaning, and use of language. Many classical problems are greatly simplified in the framework of *constructions* that explicitly link all aspects of language. The remainder of the book explores this stance and some of its consequences.

23 Combining Meanings—Embodied Construction Grammar

For a book about embodied language, the last two chapters have been off the main track in discussing grammar divorced from meaning. This follows the traditional treatment of grammar, particularly syntax, as a separate area of study, if not an autonomous module in the brain. The view put forth here is the opposite. My contention is that the central role of grammar is to help specify how meanings are combined. As part of the process of connecting form and meaning, some strings can be labeled ungrammatical because they violate the grammar rules of the language, but that judgment is only loosely related to whether the utterance is meaningful in context.

Any theory of language will need some way to express its claims so that they can be evaluated. Meaning, in an embodied theory of language, must be grounded in behavior and neural circuitry. Ultimately, the meaning of any utterance is its effect on the (physical and emotional) well-being of the person saying or hearing it. Of course, human societies have developed a vast array of intermediate structures (i.e., culture) that affect meaning, but everything that matters is represented in each individual person's brain mechanisms.

It would not be feasible to write out the neural circuitry underlying the meaning of words even if we knew it. The brain is massively connected, and meanings are always linked to other concepts. As we saw in chapter 11, there is a fairly standard means of expressing a symbolic rendition of embodied meaning—*schemas*. My attempt to explain how meanings are combined will thus be stated in terms of rules for combining or linking schemas. As always in this book, any such symbolic notations should be viewed as shorthand for neural operations that link the activity of the circuits symbolized by the schemas.

Back in chapter 11, we saw how some spatial relation words, such as *into* and *through*, evoke multiple image schemas with explicit links between them. The meaning of *into* was shown to involve both a container schema and a source-path-goal (SPG) schema, with the goal feature of the SPG linked to the interior of the container, as depicted in figure 11.1. We also mentioned in passing that the phrase *"out of"* had a similar meaning representation, although it has a different grammatical form—a phrase instead of a single word.

The representation of meaning as a collection of linked schemas is just an intermediate step, but a crucial one. We call such a network of interconnected schemas a semantic specification (or SemSpec when we are lazy). The SemSpec doesn't say how we should actually respond to any particular utterance, but it does provide the information needed to do so. The way a person (or computer system) responds to language depends on many things beyond the utterance itself—the goals of the hearer, the context, accompanying gestures, and so on. The SemSpec is a hypothesized intermediate structure that captures, in a way that can be used for any appropriate response, all the crucial structures and relations specified by an utterance.

Figure 23.1 depicts how the components of the system work together to produce the inferences that are implied by a news story. Starting from the

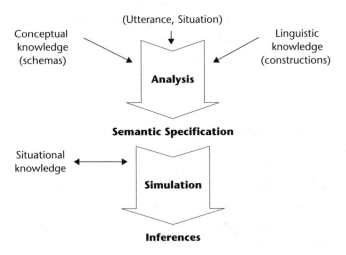

Figure 23.1
Overview of the language understanding process.

top left, one crucial requirement is conceptual knowledge, including both the universal schemas and cultural frames described in chapter 11. In addition to the input text, the system is assumed to know something about the general situation. At the upper right are the constructions, which are our primary concern in this chapter.

The *analysis* arrow portrays the process that was just loosely described, fitting together the appropriate constructions and schemas to yield a semantic specification of the meaning of the utterance. The *simulation* arrow represents the process described generally in chapter 18 and applied to news stories, in particular, in chapter 20. Much of the inference there resulted from the program simulating the metaphorical progress of an agent attempting to reach a concrete goal, which was then mapped metaphorically to economic progress. In that discussion, we had no way to describe how the input text was analyzed to yield the information needed for simulation. This chapter shows how this analysis can be done.

The focus here is on how meanings of words are combined in larger linguistic units such as phrases, clauses, and sentences. The basic idea is unchanged—the meaning of an utterance can best be expressed as a linked set of (embodied) schemas. We have seen repeatedly that languages differ widely in the way meanings are expressed. What is a specific word in one language might be a phrase in another. For example, in English we say *my house*, using the special first person possessive pronoun. In Hebrew, one can say *bayit shel lee* (house of me), where the pronoun is the same form (*lee*) as me and the possession relation is marked by a phrase. But one can also express the same thing in Hebrew as *bayitee*, where possession as well as grammatical person and number are marked by an ending, *ee*, on the noun.

This variability across languages is the standard, not the exception. A semantic theory needs rules for combining meanings that do not depend on the grammatical form that happens to be used in a given case: words, endings, phrases, and so on. Before getting into the technical details, let's explore some basic phenomena involving the combinations of meanings. We begin with what seems to be the simplest possible case, an adjective modifying a noun as in our example *red fire engine*. Even this first example has a small puzzle—what is the meaning of *red* that is somehow combined with *fire engine* to name a particular shade?

For most of us, a very specific shade of red is typical of fire engines. Unsurprisingly, it is quite close to the focal red that yields the strongest neural response; the color was chosen to be noticeable. This particular shade of red is not at all the same as those referred to in, for example, red hair, red face, or red sky. From our embodied neural perspective, the context-dependent meaning of "red" is natural; the activation of two words together causes the brain's neural best-fit mechanisms to settle on the most coherent overall pattern involving alternative concepts nameable by those words in the current context.

So, even in the simplest cases, we have *conceptual integration* or *blending*. The meaning of a combination of words can be a complex relation involving the surrounding context as well. Sometimes a two-word combination, like *Red Guard*, becomes a vocabulary item that evokes a complex frame only loosely related to the original word meanings. There are some much trickier cases, such as adjectives that negate essential features of the noun they modify, such as *artificial, fake, imitation, and toy*. Some thought is required to sort out the different meanings among these adjectives, and the distinctions seem to involve the intentions of the person making or using the object. Additional modifiers work this way for some objects, but not for others. So a *stone lion* is not a lion, but a *stone bridge* is still a bridge.

Our main concern in this chapter is with how meanings are combined. The simplest and still most widely accepted theory is that each word has multiple fixed meanings, called *word senses*. In this theory, all meaning resides in words; the rules of grammar are devoid of meaning and only specify which combinations of words are allowed. Referring back to the language wars, this position is part of the stance of autonomous syntax. According to this view, the meaning of any combination of words can be determined by first detecting which sense of each word is involved, and then using the appropriate rule for each word sense. So, we understand *stone lion* as referring to something made of stone that has the shape of a lion.

There is a major problem in trying to define word sense meanings for individual words that will lead to any such simple rules for the meaning of word pairs. Should each animal name, like *lion*, have another word sense covering lion-shaped objects? What about other animal attributes that are commonly used nonliterally—size (whale of a problem), habitat, aggressiveness, power, and mating habits? Should there also be separate word senses for toy lions, fake guns, and so on. There are also contextual usages; the stone lion could refer to the lion sitting on the stone, the one that ate a stone, or something else. If we include these contextual uses, there is literally no limit to the number of word senses that might be needed.

The embodied neural theory of language provides an alternative story on multiple word meanings that is much simpler and seems intuitively plausible. Each word can activate alternative meaning subnetworks, as we saw in the example of the two meanings of *rose* (flower and stood) in chapter 7. These subnetworks are themselves linked to other circuits representing the semantics of words and frames that are active in the current context. The standard neural best-fit matching mechanism activates additional related concepts as part of choosing the most appropriate meaning. The meaning of a word in context is captured by the joint activity of *all* of the relevant circuitry: contextual, immediate, and associated.

Computational Modeling of Neural Grammar

Even if we accept the basic validity of meaning as neural activation and combined meaning as (neural) conceptual integration, a major problem remains. How can we describe the regularities of any particular language— its grammar. There is no advantage to exclaiming that it's all neural activation; this won't help us teach the language, compare it with others, or build computer programs that allow people to communicate with systems using the language. Notice that the pure learning theories of language have the same problem—a massive neural network that somehow learned the grammar of a language would not in itself be usable for most purposes.

All neuroscientists and other scientists working on the brain confront the same problem: How can we produce understandable descriptions of what we know or propose? In our case the question becomes, how can we write down rules of grammar that are understandable by people and computer programs and that also characterize the way our brains actually process language? Much of the technical terminology and notation I have developed throughout this book has been directed toward solving this problem. Let's review some of the key ideas, and then see how they can be combined to yield what might be called *neural grammar*.

The first seven chapters tried to show how one could effectively model neural computation in understandable ways. A description of any mental ability, here grammar, must be reducible to the connectionist level and thus to the brain, as depicted in table 11.1 and discussed in that chapter. But the connectionist level is still too messy, so we also need a computational level, providing a fairly traditional way of describing structures in terms of feature–value pairs, as depicted in table 11.2.

A crucial observation came in chapter 13, where I pointed out that people understand their motor programs only at the feature (or parameter) level. We can control the force, direction, grip, and so on of hand actions, but have no direct access to the details of neural magic that execute the actions. If, as I hypothesize, languages encode only these observable features, the task of specifying grammar becomes much easier. The job of grammar is to specify which semantic schemas are being evoked, how they are parameterized, and how they are linked together in the semantic specification (SemSpec). The complete embodied meaning comes from enacting or imagining the content (chapters 18 and 20) and always depends on the context in addition to the utterance.

Given all this, we can see that some parts of the grammar specification methodology have already been outlined. In figure 11.1, we used the example of *"into"* to show how the meaning of a single word might involve multiple schemas with links (depicted as double arrows) connecting the appropriate features (or *roles*). This will play a central part in the methodology. It is no coincidence that the same double-arrow notation was used in chapter 21 in discussing grammar rules for specifying linguistic agreement in person, number, and so on. The technical term, *unification*, that I used there is standard and this idea, along with its double-arrow notation, is the key operation in our grammar rules, as in many other modern grammars.

Our proposed way of writing neurally plausible grammars is called *embodied construction grammar*, or ECG (Bergen & Chang 2005). We will see examples soon, but some preliminaries are needed. The basic unit of an ECG grammar is the *construction*, which is always a pairing of linguistic form and meaning. The idea of grammar as constructions that inherently link form and meaning has been important in linguistics at least since it was made explicit by Charles Fillmore around 1965 (Fillmore 1989).

In our formulation, all levels of linguistic form—from prefixes, to words, phrases, sentences, stories, and so on—can be represented as mapping from some regularities of form to some semantic relations in the SemSpec. The term *embodied* in ECG arises from the fact that the semantic part of a construction is composed of our various kinds of embodied schemas—image, force dynamic, or action schemas. To illustrate how ECG works, we will give a simplified, but basically complete, analysis of the sentence, "Harry strolled to Berkeley."

A Small Complete Example

The simplest and most basic kind of construction is the individual word, also called a lexical construction. For example, the construction *"to"* could be described as follows:

lexical construction To
   subcase of Spatial Preposition
   evokes SPG as s
   form "to"
   meaning Trajector-Landmark
     lm ↔ s.goal
     traj ↔ s.traj

The crucial starting point is that a semantic specification will consist entirely of linked schemas; the *constructions* are needed only to get from linguistic form to this meaning representation. There are often several quite different ways of expressing the same content, and such differences will be invisible in the SemSpec. For the *"to"* construction, there is some notation to explain, but the meaning is based on the SPG (source-path-goal) schema from chapter 11. There are alternative uses of the word "to" such as in the infinitive "to walk," but these have different associated meanings.

The words in boldface are part of the definition system and will always be used. When one construction is a **subcase** (or child) of another, it can be used wherever its parent type is called for (we will see an example soon). The **"evokes"** mechanism is an innovation introduced by ECG and is crucial. It is our way of writing down the fact that a word or concept will often activate other related concepts. As we have seen, the word *"to"* gets its meaning by linking and activating two primitive image schemas, a trajector-landmark and an SPG. An evoked schema also gets a local alias, here "s." The **form** line is very simple in this case; it just gives the spelling of the word being defined. We will see more complex form rules soon.

As I mentioned, the **meaning** section specifies the semantic schemas and relations that are introduced by the construction being defined. Here, the basic meaning is a trajector-landmark schema. The one extra bit of formalism is the dot notation, as in s.goal. The convention here is the standard one from programming: s.goal refers to the *goal* role of the particular schema s. The double arrow ($\leftrightarrow$) notation is doing the same job as the pictorial double-headed arrows in figure 11.1—showing which role pairs should be unified. For comparison, the lexical construction for the word "from" would have the alternative line:

lm $\leftrightarrow$ s.source,

indicating that the focus is on where motion started.

In addition to constructions for individual words, ECG allows us to specify the way in which meanings are combined in larger grammatical constructions. We have already seen the basic idea—grammar specifies semantic relations, represented by the double arrow notation. The first example of a grammatical construction is the following one for spatial prepositional phrases (PP):

construction Spatial PP
  subcase of Destination
  constituents
    r: Spatial Preposition
    base: NP
  form r < base
  meaning
    r.lm $\leftrightarrow$ base

This looks a bit more like a traditional rule of grammar, such as those about Old King Cole in figure 21.1. In traditional CFG form, the rule would be something like

Spatial PP $\rightarrow$ Spatial Preposition   NP

It is also traditional to call the spatial preposition and the NP **constituents** of the resulting spatial PP, as we do in ECG. There are two significant

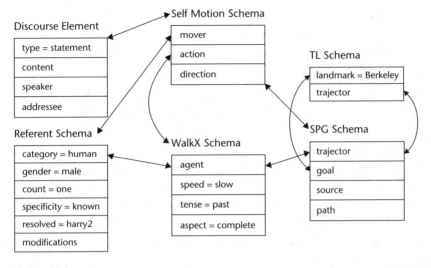

Figure 23.2
Simulation specification for "Harry strolled into Berkeley."

differences in the ECG treatment. In the **form** line, there is the looser requirement that the spatial preposition (named r) come at any position before the NP (named base). This doesn't matter much in this case, but can be important. The crucial difference is that semantics or meaning plays an equal role in ECG constructions. When the spatial PP construction is applied, the meaning condition must be matched in addition to the form requirement. In our example, the phrase "to Berkeley" would match as a spatial PP, leading to the bit of SemSpec (on the right side of figure 23.2), which expresses motion of some sort toward Berkeley.

Figure 23.2 captures all of the semantic schemas and relations needed to express the meaning of the sample sentence. We will continue to refer back to it as more of the analysis is explained. The representation for the proper noun *Berkeley* is abbreviated; the full treatment would be more like the following definition for *Harry*:

lexical construction Harry
  subcase of NP
  form "Harry"
  meaning Referent Schema
    type $\leftrightarrow$ person
    gender $\leftrightarrow$ male

count   ↔ one
specificity ↔ known
resolved   ↔ harry2

This introduces another kind of basic schema, the Referent Schema (on the lower left in figure 23.2), which encodes what has been expressed about the meaning of a noun phrase. In this example, we assume that the hearer knows the particular person being referred to. But the same general form works for many other cases. If the example were either of "The man/he strolled into Berkeley," the only difference would be a blank *resolved* role. A question about who strolled into Berkeley could be represented with a value of "questioned" in the *specificity* role, and so on.

The only other word in our example sentence is *strolled*; this denotes an action and its construction is a bit more complex.

lexical construction Strolled
  subcase of Motion Verb, Regular Past
  form "stroll+ed"
  meaning WalkX
    speed ↔ slow
    tense ↔ past
    aspect ↔ completed

As with the other words, the word "*strolled*" has, as its meaning, a basic schema—in this case the WalkX executing schema, which was described in chapter 13. This schema has various parameter roles including speed of motion, the grammatical tense saying when the action occurred, and grammatical aspect stating whether the action should be simulated as ongoing, completed, and so on. (chapter 18). We see that strolled is a subcase of motion verb, and this fact is needed for analysis. The **form** line shows the word strolled as being made up of a root, *stroll*, and a suffix, *-ed*. This is an instance of the English regular past tense construction, which we will discuss further in the next chapter.

To understand how all these constructions work together to produce figure 23.2, we must introduce one additional simplified construction. Recall that we defined *strolled* as a **subcase of** motion verb and spatial PP as a **subcase of** direction. In English, a complete thought or predication is normally expressed as a *clause*. There are many kinds of clauses, but here we just need one construction for tying together the constituents that describe directed motion of one's self.

construction Self-Directed Motion
  subcase of Motion Clause
  constituents
    movA: NP
    actV: Motion Verb
    locPP: Spatial PP
  form mover < action < direction
  meaning Self-Motion Schema
    mover   ↔ movA
    action   ↔ actV
    direction ↔ locPP

Here, a self-directed motion clause has three **constituents**, each of which is an instance of a (possibly lexical) construction. The *movA* must be an NP, the *actV* must be a motion verb, and the *locPP* must be a Spatial PP. The **form** line gives the ordering relations. The **meaning** section specifies a self-motion schema; as always we assume that people understand motion in contexts other than language, and this schema reflects that knowledge. For our purposes, we can envision the self-motion schema as having the three roles mentioned earlier: mover, action, and direction.

With all these mechanisms defined, figure 23.2 shows the resulting semantic specification (SemSpec) arising from our example sentence, "Harry strolled to Berkeley." The schema on the upper left describes what is known about the discourse properties of the example sentence—here only that it is a statement. The content itself is all based on the self-motion schema in the top center; it links together the actor (Harry), the action (strolled), and the direction (to Berkeley). The other links capture what has been expressed, namely, that the mover, the agent of WalkX and the trajector of the SPG are all the same entity, the referent schema that describes Harry.

Given a SemSpec like figure 23.2, various enactment processes, such as those described in chapter 20, could react appropriately to the utterance. Suppose this sample sentence occurred in the context of a news story; an understanding system could draw inferences about Harry's location, his health, state of agitation, and so on from this SemSpec.

This was a long explanation for a short example, but no one said language was simple. In any methodology, no complete description for a natural language is currently possible. For one thing, there is no agreement on exactly what should count as part of each language.

In the following two chapters, we will look at some ways that ECG and, more generally, an embodied neural theory of language can help us understand human behavior. Chapter 24 will explore how ECG can form the basis for programs and theories dealing with language and human language processing. Chapter 25 will show how the same theory provides a basis for theories of language acquisition and how this can be demonstrated in a program that learns ECG constructions from data.

But it is also worth briefly revisiting the previous chapter on the language wars with the ECG perspective. Recall that the three central issues were:

(a) Are there formal grammar rules in the brain?

(b) Is grammar independent of other brain structures?

(c) Is there some special genetic encoding specifically for grammar?

These issues were framed in terms of traditional definitions of grammar as independent of meaning. From our ECG perspective, grammar inherently links form and meaning, so questions b and c make little sense. If grammar *includes* meaning, then of course it is not independent of meaning. Similarly for question c, if grammar *includes* meaning, that is intimately linked to other knowledge, it can't have completely separate genetics. With respect to question a, ECG is closer to the positive answer. There is good evidence that grammar, in the ECG extended sense, is not just another product of universal learning. But there is equally strong evidence that what is genetically encoded is not a set of symbolic rules.

On the surface, the ECG notation might look like other formalisms for describing language. But the crucial point is that the conventional-looking constructions, like formalized schemas described earlier, are just our way of writing down hypothesized neural connections and bindings. The systematic reduction to connectionist, and ultimately neural, realization, as outlined in chapter 11, is the key to grasping ECG and, for me, is central to understanding language and thought.

IX | Embodied Language

It took all of the previous chapter just to introduce embodied construction grammar (ECG) and present some simple examples of its use. Suppose that ECG really does capture embodied meaning at the computational level. Is this of any value in practice? In this chapter, I will discuss the usefulness of ECG and the neural approach to language in three related domains: linguistic analysis, computer understanding systems, and models of human language processing.

There is a large and very productive subfield of language studies called cognitive linguistics. For several decades now, cognitive linguists have been studying phenomena that are not covered in the traditional formal linguistics of chapters 21 and 22. Many of the key ideas forming the basis for this book come from cognitive linguistics: schemas, conceptual blending, unified constructions, and metaphors, to name some of the most important. However, until recently, there has been no precise way to specify exactly what was being stated in a cognitive linguistics analysis. The standard means of expressing insights has been through pictorial diagrams and accompanying discussions.

A major goal of ECG development has been to provide a formal notation for cognitive linguistics. This has turned out to be surprisingly easy. It appears that only four basic formal structures are needed to express the results of cognitive linguistics in a precise and tractable notation. We have made extensive use of two of these—*schemas* and *constructions*. The constructions of the previous chapter and the semantic schemas used there are examples of how ECG formalizes cognitive linguistics.

Metaphors, which we have used in several places, provide an example of the third primitive structure, called *maps*. The final ECG primitive used for cognitive linguistics is the *mental space*, as discussed in chapter 17.

These are needed for analyzing statements about other people's thoughts, other times and places, and a variety of other ideas, a few of which I discuss later in this chapter.

ECG and Construction Grammar in Linguistic Analysis

In addition to its close ties with cognitive linguistics, ECG is part of a larger effort on construction grammars (Goldberg 1995) whose goal is to simplify and improve linguistic analysis. Recall from earlier chapters that conventional grammars and theories place all semantics in (various senses of) individual words, and then try to derive the meaning of any utterance from combinations of word senses. Construction grammars explicitly allow meaning to be added by larger grammar rules, and this improves analyses for various simple and complex problems in language.

Let's start with the simple problem of adjective–noun combinations such as red ball or stone lion. We saw in the previous chapter that even simple pairs like red ball involve considerable mental simulation and conceptual integration. When you read the phrase "red ball," you probably imagined a round, shiny, resilient ball of human scale. Since the conceptual combination evoked by a phrase will vary from context to context and person to person, it seems impossible to write down all the rules that determine form and meaning for a language.

The ECG solution to this class of problems explicitly acknowledges that language is always interpreted in an active neural context and postulates a linking semantic specification (SemSpec). The SemSpec is intended to capture exactly those semantic relations that can be derived from the input sentence in context. The simulation semantics process, discussed in chapters 18 and 20, uses the SemSpec and other activated knowledge to achieve conceptual integration and the resulting inferences, as we discussed in the previous chapter.

Going from linguistic form to meaning can get even trickier when we look at *measure phrase* examples such as "bottle of beer." The traditional view is that every phrase has a "head," which is the focus for all modifiers and actions. Even a complicated phrase such as

the big old red frame house on the corner near the church

is unequivocally about the house. But it isn't clear whether we should view "bottle of beer" as being basically about a bottle that contains beer or about beer that happens to be in a bottle. Consider a simple sentence such as

She opened and drank an expensive large bottle of beer.

We can see that it is the *bottle* that was large and that was opened, and it was the beer that was consumed and was expensive. But this depends on semantic relations among the nouns, adjectives, and verbs involved. There is no obvious way to handle this kind of construction in conventional grammar. In ECG, it is natural to introduce a *measure phrase construction* and an accompanying containment schema, each of which has two head roles, a measure of some sort and the substance being measured (Dodge & Wright 2002).

The ECG semantics-based unification process will work correctly because the various verbs and modifiers involved are more semantically compatible with one or another head role. In our example above, *opened* and *large* do not apply to the substance, *beer*. This semantic-based matching can also work when the sentence is given in the abbreviated form:

She opened and drank an expensive large beer.

assuming that the grammar covers the possibility that *beer* sometimes means a container of beer. In the ECG notation of the previous chapter, the measure phrase construction could be written as

construction Measure NP
  subcase of NP
  constituents
    m: Measure NP
    "of"
    s : Substance NP
  form m < "of" < s
  meaning Containment Schema
    vessel   ↔ m
    contents ↔ s

Notice that because constituent *m* is itself a measure NP, this construction can describe complex cases such as

truckload of large cases of small bottles of Czech beer.

The meaning of the containment schema depends on the fact that the measure m is (or can be construed as) a container. It should seem natural, after a moment's thought, that a *herd* can be construed as a container of zebras in our sense. There is a special English construction, "*–ful*," that is used when m is not ordinarily thought of as a measure, as in *mouthful* of beer.

A somewhat similar class of problems arises with verbs of action when they are used in nonstandard constructions. Some verbs, like *eat*, are commonly used both with and without a direct object:

I love to eat (Pizza).

In contrast, the similar verb, *devour*, can be used only with an object, so

I love to devour Pizza, but not **I love to devour.*

Now, we know that *sneeze* is a so-called intransitive verb, which means that it normally takes no object. But what about a sentence like

She sneezed the tissue off the table.

This seems perfectly grammatical and understandable, but how can it be analyzed?

The conventional answer is that (as in the case of nouns) there is a separate word sense for sneeze as a transitive verb. But unless you are a linguist, you probably have never heard sneeze used this way. The construction grammar answer is different in kind and is revealing. It suggests a *caused motion construction*, similar to our directed motion construction of the previous chapter:

construction Caused Motion
   subcase of Motion Clause
   constituents
      causer: Agent
      action: Motion
      trajector: Movable object
      direction: SpatialSpec
   form causer < action < trajector < direction
   meaning Caused Motion Schema
      causer   ↔ action. actor
      direction ↔ action. location

The important point is that it is the construction that introduces the possibility of a direct object (the extra role *trajector*) for a normally intransitive verb. Since this is a general rule and does not need to be learned separately for each word, you had no trouble understanding "She sneezed the tissue off the table," even if you had never heard sneeze used this way. Sneeze is usually an intransitive verb, but can be used transitively (with a direct object) in certain constructions.

Beyond Strings of Printed Words

Language includes a variety of expressive mechanisms in addition to the strings of words treated by formal grammars. Meaning is also conveyed by changes in word form, by intonation patterns, and by gestures. ECG has been designed to allow constructions that permit any combination of form elements, and this is needed in many cases. We will look at several examples.

The ECG approach has proven to be of value in *morphology*, the study of how meaning is conveyed by changes in the form of a word. The discussion of the English past tense in chapter 22 was about morphology. If you know another language, morphology is likely to be much more important in that language, unless it is Chinese, which has almost no morphology.

Chinese, along with many other languages, uses *tones* as additional way of specifying meanings. Mandarin Chinese has four distinct tones and the meaning of words can differ widely depending on the tone used. In addition, the exact same sound can have multiple meanings, as with the English *bank*. For example, Mandarin words include

ma1 = mother
ma2 = toad, hemp
ma3 = horse, yard
ma4 = scold

This is parallel to the difference in meaning of different vowel occurrences in English, for example, ma, me, my, mow, moo. Of course, Mandarin uses vowel distinctions as well as tones to convey meaning.

Traditional morphology has followed formal syntax in assuming that each operation has an independent meaning, and these are combined to yield the overall meaning of the changed form. Morphology was briefly mentioned in the last chapter when we described *strolled* as "stroll + ed." It would obviously be better to have a single construction for all regular past tense verb forms, and we do.

construction Regular Past Tense
  subcase of Verb
  constituents
    Root: Verb Stem
    "ed"
  form Root + "ed"
  meaning Root.meaning
    tense ↔ past
    aspect ↔ encapsulated

This construction specifies that the regular past tense is formed by adding "ed" to the verb root. More interestingly, it also says that the *meaning* of any such construct is found by taking the meaning of the root verb and changing the value of its tense and aspect roles. So, we don't need to do this explicitly for every regular verb, and could simplify the example from the previous chapter. Defining additional constructions for the other forms of past tense is straightforward. Some irregular forms such as *"go, went"* do need specific lexical constructions, of course.

English has fairly simple morphology, and many approaches will suffice, but ECG has also proven to be effective for such complex systems as that of Georgian. Using an approach based on ECG, Olya Gurevich (2003) has shown how complex morphological systems can be much better understood as involving structured constructions, analogous to the caused motion construction that we have discussed. As with grammar, morphology sometimes requires consideration of complex constructions involving both form and meaning.

Written declarative language is complex enough, but it is only part of the story. Let's think about questions; the discourse type shown in the upper left of figure 23.1 was a *statement*; one alternative type is a *question*. There are several explicit question constructions in English, but you can also change a written statement into a question by adding a "?" as in "Harry strolled to Berkeley?" There are no punctuation marks in spoken language, and a question like this one is signaled by a rising tone at the end. There are standard ways of recognizing and labeling such intonation patterns, and these can be used in ECG constructions. A rising tone is a form feature just like a word or ending and can be constructionally paired with a meaning effect.

Another interesting intonation issue comes up in connection with the preceding example question. Try reading the question aloud with equal stress on each word—it will probably seem odd. The reason is that the question makes sense only if one or more words are stressed. If you stress each word in turn, you get different meanings—the stressed word is the one being questioned.

Also, try reading the statement form with stress on each different word. In this case, the stressed word suggests a *contrast* set. For example "Harry strolled TO Berkeley" emphasizes that he didn't stroll *from*, *through*, or *around* it. ECG has mechanisms to represent these contrast sets in the semantic specification, but no one has yet worked out how to make all the proper inferences from them.

Discourse features can also be used to analyze more complex sentences such as "Josh said that Harry strolled to Berkeley." This statement has an embedded sentence as the subject of "said." ECG follows cognitive linguistics practice and expresses such meanings with two *mental spaces*, one for Harry's action and another for Josh's statement. The discourse mental space mechanism is also used for language about other times and places, other people's thoughts, paintings, movies, and so on (Mok et al. 2004).

When people have visual contact while talking, gesture also plays a large role in conveying meaning. In fact, children communicate by gesture well before they can talk. Some gestures, like pointing, are universal, but many are cultural. Understanding a pointing gesture is inherently situational— you need to be there to know what is being indicated. One can add notation for such gestures to ECG, but their meaning goes beyond language, involving visual perception. The same is true for some linguistic constructions such as the demonstratives *"this"* and *"that"*—their meaning is often situational.

But a number of gestures can also be captured as linguistic form-meaning pairs and added directly to ECG. For example, raised eyebrows to express skepticism or a flat rotating hand to suggest uncertainty. These gestural forms can be combined with structural and intonational forms in constructions that describe the full richness of language use. Shweta Narayan has shown how to extend this idea of multistream ECG constructions to signed languages and such multimedia forms as cartoons.

Summing up, the embodied neural approach to language and ECG formalism have established new methods for working on hard problems at all levels of linguistics, and especially on problems that cross traditional research boundaries.

ECG in Computer Understanding Systems

I have also claimed that ECG and the neural approach to grammar can directly help in computer systems for understanding natural language. For this to work out, computer programs that use an ECG grammar to produce a semantic specification (SemSpec) are needed. Because each ECG construction explicitly links form and meaning, we already know that this is possible in principle. Any program that could successfully analyze English input using ECG will automatically produce an equivalent SemSpec.

The problem is that ECG is significantly more complex than traditional grammars, partly because it includes deep meanings, but also because it allows more flexible rules of form. It was not obvious that a program for efficient ECG analysis could be written, but John Bryant has recently done this (Bryant 2004). Again, the details of this accomplishment are beyond the scope of this book, but it is useful to understand some of the key ideas.

All parsing programs confront the same basic problem. They have a large collection of grammar rules that might be useful in analyzing any given input sentence. An average sentence will require the combination of several rules in its analysis, as we saw in chapter 23. Even on the fastest computer, it is totally impractical to just try all possible combinations of grammar rules. So the problem is to find a method for choosing the right collection of constructions for analyzing any sentence the system might be given.

The grammatical analysis problem is made harder by the fact that many words, phrases, and sentences can have more than a single meaning, as we saw in the preceding examples. The brain, being massively parallel, is able to maintain activity patterns for several possible analyses, but it requires some cleverness to do this on a serial computer. Bryant uses the standard trick, called a *parse chart*, for keeping track of potential parses. His program starts in the obvious way by placing (one or more) meanings in the parse chart for each word in the input.

Let's consider how Bryant's program might produce the SemSpec of figure 23.1 from the tiny sentence, "Harry strolled to Berkeley." Suppose that each of the four words had only one meaning in the lexicon, except for *to*, which could be our spatial relation term, but could also be the infinitive marker. The chart must allow for either possibility, and the program would start looking for constructions that matched some of the information in the chart. The only direct match (from chapter 23) would be the spatial PP construction, which matches the preposition sense of *to* followed by the NP, *Berkeley*. An important innovation in Bryant's system is using a measure of semantic coherence to evaluate potential matches in the chart.

After this match has been found, the chart is expanded to note the possibility of a spatial PP covering the last two words. Now, the big self-directed motion construction (from chapter 23) will match the chart, because

Harry is a person and thus a good agent
strolled is a Motion Verb
"to Berkeley" is grouped in the chart as a spatial PP

As we described in the previous chapter, the process of matching constructions like this automatically involves unifying their meanings, so that the desired SemSpec of figure 23.1 will result.

Of course, this example is very close to the simplest possible case. A typical sentence might have many possible analyses, and the chart can grow quite large even if there is only one possible parse at the end. One significant feature of Bryant's system is that it can analyze and produce a SemSpec for input strings that cannot be fully analyzed using the given grammar. This is important for understanding less-than-perfect sentences, and also a crucial component of Nancy Chang's model of how children learn grammar, the topic of the next chapter. Since a young child is just starting to learn grammar, the child's current grammar often does not completely explain a sentence that she or he hears.

We have now seen how a program can use ECG grammars to derive the semantic relations that underlie English sentences. This allows us to fulfill a promise made in the discussion of story understanding in chapter 20. Recall that Narayanan's program was able to draw complex and subtle inferences from news story text, using several NTL ideas such as active simulation, metaphor mappings, and probabilistic inference. But that system required a person to analyze the natural language sentences and present the program with the underlying semantic relations. This is exactly the job that Bryant's ECG analyzer can do automatically.

It is natural to combine these two programs, and Bryant, Narayanan, and Sinha have recently carried this out. The resulting demonstration system can take unprocessed English sentences (as in chapter 20), analyze them, simulate the resulting semantic specification, and draw appropriate inferences. This language understanding system goes well beyond the abilities of any other program in some ways, but it is still just a prototype. To scale this program up to a practical system for understanding English would require solving several hard problems in linguistics, knowledge representation, inference, and computer science. But we do now have a framework in which this effort can be undertaken as routine science and engineering with reasonable prospects for success.

ECG and Human Language Processing

It's nice that the neural theory of language seems useful for artificial intelligence systems, but what can it tell us about natural intelligence? Various partial answers to this question have been presented throughout this book, particularly in chapter 7, which discussed some of the psychological experiments that led to the connectionist revolution in cognitive science. But some findings could not be discussed until we knew about construction grammar and ECG. In the next chapter, I present Nancy Chang's neural theory of grammar *learning*, which is a major result of the entire project.

Here, I briefly describe some results on adult language processing that, as far as I know, can be explained only by a theory that has integrated form-meaning constructions in a quantitative best-match computational system. Let's first consider an example from *phonology*, how sounds are put together in language. A well-studied problem is French *liaison*, in which the final sound of one word is sometimes joined with the first sound of the next word. It is common in French for the last sound to be unspoken, for example, the first word of "Les Miserables" is pronounced "ley" and not "lez." But the same word is treated differently in an example such as: "les enfants" (the children), where the final "z" sound of "les" is usually pronounced and joined to "enfant" as a single word, yielding roughly "lezenfan."

Whether or not a native French speaker will pronounce the final liaison sound in this fashion is known to depend on many factors, including the particular words and sounds involved, the speech context, and the age, gender, and social class of the speaker. Ben Bergen (Bergen 1999) was able to use belief networks, of the kind described in chapter 19, to build a computational model that could predict the probability of liaison from values for such parameters as those described here. This provides a much better fit to the data than any previous theory, apparently because the belief networks model the complex, context-dependent neural computations underlying speech.

There are many ways to study human language processing and a significant field, *psycholinguistics*, is dedicated to this pursuit. Most of the results in chapter 7 would be called psycholinguistic findings. But this is also a field in which there are quite a few demonstrations, and you can experience interesting phenomena. Consider the three sentences:

Harry walked into the café with the invoice/fireplace/singer.

In the first case, we naturally assume that the invoice is in Harry's possession. In the second case, the phrase *"with the fireplace"* is clearly a description of the café. But the third case is ambiguous; without more context, there is no way to know whether the singer is Harry's companion or a feature performer at the café. These are called *attachment* ambiguities because it is often not clear whether some "with" phrase should be constructionally attached to the verb (walked) or to the object (café).

There are even more striking cases. Please read the following sentence aloud slowly, word by word:

The   horse   raced   past   the   barn   fell.

Sentences like these are called *garden-path sentences* because, in slow reading, we often notice that we have followed an analysis path that turned out to be wrong.

This famous example exploits an attachment ambiguity, and the fact that English allows reduced relative constructions, omitting the relative pronoun, *which*. You would have no problem with the unreduced sentence:

The horse, which raced past the barn, fell.

As you would guess, psycholinguists love this kind of example and have done many studies of the garden-path phenomenon. As in the preceding café example, garden-path sentences have differing degrees of difficulty. Psycholinguists measure difficulty of understanding using the techniques we have discussed before—error rates, reaction times, attention, and others. The difficulty of a garden-path sentence has been shown to depend on several separate factors in addition to grammatical form. These include the frequency of the individual words involved, the likelihood that they occur in certain constructions, and the probability that they appear as pairs.

Using several of the ideas from ECG and the neural theory of language, Srinivas Narayanan and Dan Jurafsky (Narayanan et al. 1998) developed a computer model that gives quite detailed predictions of how these various factors interact in determining the difficulty of a garden-path situation. The first step was to explicitly recognize that both form and meaning play a major role in selecting the best construction match for some text, following the tenets of construction grammar. The second step was to use numerical values to compute the relative goodness of alternative analyses, in this case the reduced relative construction versus the standard one in which the verb (e.g., *raced*) is the main verb of the sentence. Finally, to build a testable model, they used Bayesian belief networks, described in chapter 19.

Recall that belief networks are a computational approximation to the quantitative neural activity postulated to support language understanding. To approximate the relative strengths of various words and constructions, Narayanan and Jurafsky used the relative frequency of their appearances in corpora of English usage. Thus, they built a model that could give a numerical score on which construction was more likely in a given situation.

But why are people surprised in garden-path situations? The brain is a massively parallel information processor and is able to retain multiple active possibilities for interpreting a sentence, scene, and so on. Well, there must be a cutoff after which some possible interpretations are deemed so unlikely as to be not worth keeping active. The final piece of their model was an assumption that a hypothesis was abandoned if its belief net score was less than 20% of that of its rival. We experience surprise when the analysis needed for a full sentence is one that was deactivated earlier as unlikely. This is a complex computational model, but nothing simpler can capture all the necessary interactions.

Consider another concrete example:

The witness examined by the lawyer turned out to be unreliable.

Upon reading the word *"examined,"* several considerations make it most likely that examined is the main verb. For one thing, this construction is much more common than the reduced relative. *Witness* is a very common subject for the verb examine and is a good example of an agent. So this sentence might well lead some people to garden-path at the word *by*, and the model predicts this. In contrast, the quite similar sentence,

The evidence examined by the lawyer turned out to be unreliable.

causes no such problem. This is because *evidence* is not a good agent or subject of examine, and the model predicts this as well. Computational models such as this are becoming increasingly important in studying human language processing.

   This is a sample of some of the ways in which an explicitly neural theory of language can help us understand the relation between brain and mind in language use. But what about language acquisition? Does the neural theory provide any explanation of how children everywhere can learn their native language or languages without formal instruction? The current answer, outlined in the next chapter, relies on almost every topic discussed in the book and should be viewed as the acid test for the ideas. If the theory is good, and its exposition not too bad, you should come away from chapter 25 with an *aha* experience.

25 | Learning Constructions

With the previous two chapters on the definition and use of embodied construction grammar (ECG), we have completed the neural theory of language promised at the beginning of this book. I also suggested that such a development would form the basis for a theory of child language learning. As we have seen, the question of how children learn language is at the center of much of the discussion about the nature of human language.

After the background laid out in the first seven chapters, most of the material of chapters 8 through 17 was about how children learn individual words and how this can be simulated using the embodied neural theory. But the more difficult and controversial issues concern the child's learning of *grammar*. The battleground in the language wars of chapter 22 is largely focused on the nature of grammar and how it is learned by children. I suggested in that discussion that an embodied neural approach to language can provide novel and promising answers to some of the deepest questions about grammar learning. This chapter is an attempt to provide these answers.

A wealth of data on child language and grammar acquisition now exist in a wide range of languages. Although the grammars of various languages differ greatly, the general pattern of grammar learning is similar everywhere. As we discussed earlier, children pick up some general information about the sound patterns of their native language even before birth. They learn to respond to emotional and interpersonal cues quite early, with some reactions being present at birth. By the first year, all normal children have learned to respond to some words, whether spoken or signed. Chapters 10 through 14 talked extensively about how children learn the meaning of individual words as labeling their direct experience.

Sample input prior to 1;11.9:
don't throw the bear.
don't throw them on the ground.
Nomi don't throw the books down.
what do you throw it into?

Sample tokens prior to 1;11.9:
throw
throw off
I throw it.
I throw it ice. (= I throw the ice)

Transcript data, Naomi 1;11.9

Par: they're throwing this in here.
Par: throwing the thing.
Child: throwing in.
Child: throwing.
Par: throwing the frisbee. . . .
Par: do you throw the frisbee?
     do you throw it?
Child: throw it.
Child: I throw it. . . .
Child: throw frisbee.
Par: she's throwing the frisbee.
Child: throwing ball.

Sachs corpus (childes.psy.cmu.edu)

Figure 25.1
Sample data on early instances of "throw."

By the child's second birthday, she will be responding to language communication in sophisticated ways and will be producing some language. The amount and level of production at age 2 varies widely; the girl Naomi of figure 25.1 is fairly typical. The figure presents examples of language spoken to Naomi by her parents and some of her responses around the age of 1 year, 11 months, and 9 days (1;11.9). Like all children, Naomi first spoke individual words. The next stage is normally two-word combinations, like *throw off, throw it*, or the equivalent in languages with more complex word structure. These combinations are not restricted to particular constructions of the adult grammar.

A fairly recent discovery by Michael Tomasello (Tomasello 1992) suggests that the child first develops more complex constructions centered on individual heads (verbs in English). So Naomi will say "*I throw it ice*," but not the equivalent with other actions like *eat* or *wear*. It is only later that the child's grammar will incorporate general rules for combining any transitive verb with any suitable agent and object. In languages that use morphology more than word order, children start with simple forms and learn complex rules at roughly the same rate as English-speaking kids learn their grammar.

Starting with these basic findings and the theory of language described in this book, Nancy Chang built a model of how children learn their first rules of grammar and then generalize these to more adultlike rules (Chang 2006). This is the most complex model I will discuss, and one of the more ambitious cognitive models ever built. But it does provide an answer to the central question of grammar—How are children able to learn their native language with so little direct feedback?

As with the other computational models discussed here, Chang's system tests her theory of language learning by simulating the child's behavior. If the program performs like the child, there is reason to believe that the underlying theory is at least plausible. If the theory has other independent support from biology, psychology, and so on, it might be worth taking seriously. Let's explore the theory and see how well its implementation works. The test will be on a subset of the real data from child language acquisition studies.

Figure 25.2 presents an overview of the language learning theory. The top half of this figure is identical to the top of figure 23.1, which characterizes language understanding. Chang's theory postulates continual "bootstrapping," with the child using the constructions that she already knows in trying to understand what is being said, always in context. Of course, the child will often not fully understand the utterance, but Chang observes that the child will often know quite a lot about the situation and therefore what the utterance might be about.

Referring to the bottom of figure 25.2, we see a two-way link between situational knowledge and the child's partial interpretation of the

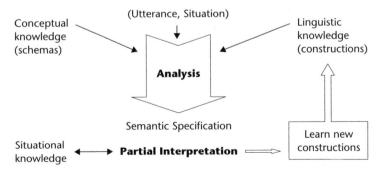

Figure 25.2
Overview of Chang's grammar learning theory.

utterance. This was already the basis for the models of individual word learning in chapters 12 and 14. In Regier's model, the child was assumed to be looking at a scene and to have the situational knowledge of the objects and their spatial relations. In that model, the child learned to associate a spatial relation term with a visual situation. This is a special case of figure 25.2; the construction learned in Regier's system is a *lexical* construction, or word sense. In a language such as Finnish, in which some spatial relations are marked as word endings, a *morphological* construction would be learned for these situations.

Essentially the same story can be told relating figure 25.2 to Bailey's system for learning the meaning of verbs of hand action in different languages. Bailey modeled a child carrying out a hand action and having it labeled by a parent. In that case, the situational knowledge is the child's (again subconscious) familiarity with the X-schema and parameters involved in the particular action. The construction that is learned is again lexical, but it will tend to be more complex because verbs have more elaborate parameters and argument structure.

Learning Complex Constructions

Now, our current concern is how a neural theory can explain the acquisition of more complex constructions such as those for the phrases and clauses, that we know to be part of adult grammar. I will illustrate the basic ideas using an extended example, based on the corpus of figure 25.1. Let's suppose that we are modeling the situation in which Naomi hears the sentence, "You throw the ball." We suppose that Naomi has learned lexical constructions for the individual words *throw* and *ball*, but does not yet have a construction for the phrase *throw ball*. Following chapter 23, her known constructions might be represented in ECG as follows:

construction Throw
  subcase of Verb
  roles
    thrower: Self
    thrown: Small Object
  evokes Hurl-X as h
  form "throw"

meaning
    agent   ↔ h.thrower
    trajectory ↔ h.thrown

construction Ball
    subcase of Small Object
    form "ball"
    meaning <my lovely red ball>

Of course, the ECG description is just our way of writing down what the neural circuitry in Naomi's brain might embody, but let's examine it. The *ball* construction is simple; Naomi believes that "ball" refers to her particular toy ball and knows it is a small object. The *throw* construction involves two roles and a more complex meaning. We assume that she has learned (ala chapter 14) that the sound "throw" is identified with a motor routine (X-schema) that she can carry out, which we have written as Hurl-X. In the meaning part, we assume that she knows throwing is a kind of action and how the general verb roles fit the specifics of throwing. So the agent mentioned verbally is identified with (↔) the thrower in the embodied Hurl-X schema.

So, the knowledge of the individual words tells Naomi quite a lot about the utterance. In addition, she knows full well what is going on in the situation—she just threw the ball and the utterance is quite likely about that, especially if some of the words fit perfectly. What she doesn't know yet is how English grammar marks which words fill the various roles, here for the verb throw. Let's assume for now that she believes that English uses word order rather than special endings to label the agent and object of an action like throw.

This is all portrayed graphically in figure 25.3. On the right side of the figure is Naomi's situational knowledge—her mother is talking to her and, also, she herself has just thrown her favorite ball. She has no doubt about what the thrower (herself) or thrown (the ball) of the action are in the situation. For Chang's model, the situational knowledge is assumed to have a form similar to that of the semantic specification produced by analysis. If an utterance is completely understood, there should be a close correspondence between the meaning of the sentence and the current situation, for this direct kind of language.

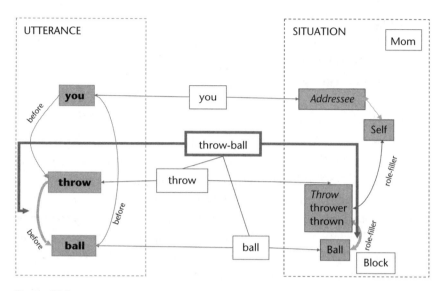

Figure 25.3
Matching form relations to meaning relations. The arrows labeled "before" denote the order in which the child heard the words.

On the left side of the figure, Naomi knows the order in which the words appeared, and we assume she views this as important for English grammar. The crucial step, according to the theory, is when the child (subconsciously) compares what she knows to be true with what she understands to have been said. In Chang's model, Bryant's best-fit construction analyzer tries to analyze the input sentence using the currently known constructions. If it can't find a complete analysis, it returns the partial analysis that is the best semantic fit.

So, in this case, Naomi's current grammar allows her to connect the words throw and ball with the corresponding concepts, as shown with thin arrows. The boxes in the middle of the figure depict the lexical constructions presented just above. The figure also assumes that Naomi knows a lexical construction that links *"you"* to herself. The right side of the figure represents her knowledge of the situation. We are interested in how she might postulate the *throw-ball construction* and its links, shown as thick dark arrows and border in figure 25.3.

The crucial insight is that a grammatical construction is based on a correspondence between some form relation and a matching meaning relation—*a relation of relations*. In this case, Naomi knows the ball is the thrown of the action (meaning relation) and also the word "throw" came before the word "ball" (form relation). She might well guess (subconsciously, of course) that the thing being thrown is specified in English by coming after the word "throw." According to the findings of Tomasello and others, it would be rather later that this rule might be applied more generally. Before getting into broader questions of learning, let's review what we have in this particular case. In terms of our ECG notation, Naomi's new grammar rule might be written:

construction Throw-ball
  constituents
    action: Throw
    trajector: Ball
  form action < trajector
  meaning
    trajectory $\leftrightarrow$ Throw.thrown

This is a grammatical construction with multiple constituents, and could have been Naomi's first such. It could be that all her previous constructions were just one word or a fixed phrase. The significance of this is that, in this construction, she would have learned that a particular form relation (action < trajector) specifies that the second word (which we call the trajector) determines which object fills the thrown role of a throw action. Only later does the child learn the generalization of this construction that works for any transitive verb.

The process of learning an early grammar rule was a bit complicated to describe, but it does not require any magic on the learner's part. The fundamental operation is to map a relation in one domain (here, speech or sign) to a relation in another domain, here embodied meaning. The child can learn grammar rules because they mark relations that the child already knows and cares about from experience. Grammar learning seems mysterious only if syntax is viewed as separate from meaning—how would kids learn these arbitrary rules?

The key to understanding grammar acquisition is not the famous *poverty of the stimulus* (chapter 22), but rather the *opulence of the substrate*. The child comes to language learning with a rich base of conceptual and embodied experience as well as a supportive social environment. Words and rules that describe this experience can be learned without formal training, although not without years of focused effort on the child's part. As the child expands his or her scope and deals with abstract concepts and others that are not directly experienced, language coevolves, always maintaining the grounding in direct experience. It makes a simple, lovely story and most likely captures much of the truth about language acquisition.

We have only introduced Nancy Chang's theory and computer model of grammar learning and have not yet discussed several important issues the model addresses. The example we considered was as simple as possible, but the same basic ideas carry over to learning more complex constructions, such as the directed motion construction of chapter 24. Sometime after Naomi learned the throw-ball construction, she might try to build a single construction that captured all the relations in the scenario of figure 25.3. This would produce a construction with three constituents: agent, action, and trajector, with the form rule agent < action < trajector, and the related meaning connections. There is no barrier in principle to the child learning arbitrarily complex constructions. We will shortly discuss the question of why children seem to all learn pretty much the same constructions for the local language.

The story so far on grammar learning has assumed that the child already knows the meaning of all the individual content words when learning a new construction. Children also use the grammar they already know in learning about novel words. Some of this was discussed in connection with figure 10.2, where information about the part of speech of an unknown word can be inferred from its grammatical setting. And, of course, as children learn more language, they are directly told about words and concepts.

A concern about the theory might be that the only form relation used in our examples was word order; what about languages that mark meaning relations differently? It is true that the theory needs to be extended to incorporate other kinds of form relation, but there appear to be only four ways that languages mark these. In addition to word order, meaning relations are often marked by changes in form (morphology); an example is the English possessive, as in *"Naomi's ball."* The English possessive can also be expressed using the third kind of form marking, a specific word, as in "*the ball of Naomi.*" The fourth general kind of marking a semantic relation is through intonation. In English, this is used mainly for discourse marking, as we have seen in earlier examples.

Construction grammar in general, and Chang's theory of acquisition in particular, explicitly includes the notion that constructions can have form relations of any of the four basic types. Many constructions, including English questions, have form markings of more than one basic type. For example, the question

Did you throw the ball?

is marked by a function word "*did,*" a morphological change (threw → throw), a word order change that puts *did* first, and a rising intonation at the end of the question when spoken. There are a number of question constructions for English, involving varying combinations of form markings. For language situations involving direct human interaction, constructions can also include gestures that carry meaning as form conditions, as we discussed in the previous chapter.

The computer model based on Chang's theory does not support full intonation marking because it is technically too difficult to do the required analysis of the speech signal. The other three types of form marking (words, word order, and morphology) are included to some degree. Implementation aside, the theory says that a child learning grammar needs to attend to all four kinds of form cues and to postulate constructions using them. Of course, languages tend to be systematic about the use of form markings, and children are known to learn to exploit these regularities.

The entire discussion so far has focused on language *understanding*, but the theory suggests that very similar operations underlie the child's *production* of language. We again assume that the child understands the situation and that his or her knowledge of it has the form of linked schemas, which we write as a semantic specification, as on the right side of figure 25.3. When children want to express something, they (like adults) attempt to find constructions that will map their intentions into language. Normally, they will do the best they can with the constructions they know, but sometimes children will want to express more than this permits. Chang's theory proposes that a child will then guess a new way of linking meaning and form—a possible new construction.

According to the theory, the constructions proposed for speaking look exactly the same as those used in understanding. In this case, the child proposes and tests new constructions in both production and comprehension. The reason that understanding is ahead of speaking is that the child can (partially) understand complex sentences by matching constructions to only parts of the utterance.

Of course, some of the child's early guesses at grammatical constructions will turn out to be wrong and those that do match adult grammar will need to be generalized. But these are the standard questions that arise in learning anything from experience. Chang's computer program makes use of some current technical advances in computational learning theory, as did the Regier and Bailey programs described in early chapters. No one knows the neural details of how people's brains do learn, but existing computational and cognitive theory tells us a lot about how brainlike systems *could* realistically learn language. I will briefly summarize some of the key issues and how they are addressed in the model and the theory.

As I have stated several times, a key fact is that children receive very little direct feedback on any language errors they might make. So how could they learn to abandon a proposed construction that isn't consistent with the adult language? The computational solution in the model uses a standard technique, decay of unused knowledge. As we saw in chapter 24, people always need to choose the set of constructions that best fits an input utterance. Suppose the program (and people's brains) kept track of which constructions were used in the best match for the input each and every time. In addition, imagine a learning rule that increases the potential value of successful constructions and decreases probability of trying constructions that had not proved useful. Then, any construction that did not match the adult grammar would eventually wither away because there would always be a better choice.

In general, an adaptive best-match system can learn without negative evidence because good choices will continue to get better. Notice that such a system can also adapt to the changes in grammar we encounter as adults. When a new language fad becomes popular, we learn constructions for it and they become active in our understanding and speaking for a time. They then usually fade away from lack of use, like the child's early guesses at grammar.

How Chang's Program Generalizes

We also need to consider how a child goes from a very specific construction, like the throw-ball construction, to quite general ones like the directed motion construction from chapter 24. Again, generalization from instances to parameterized rules is required for any nontrivial learning by people or machines, not just for grammar. In chapter 11, we saw that it was essential for a child to learn superordinate concepts like *tool* or *animal*, rather than try to deal only with knowledge about basic categories. The required information processing operation is called *lifting*, and involves taking a collection of relations of similar form and replacing the common element with a parameter, which can stand for any of the particular instances. So, after learning that cows, dogs, horses, and pigs, all move and eat and make noises, a good learning system will postulate a category (known to us as *"animal"*) and just remember what goes in the category and what relations apply to anything in that category.

The theory (and all other theories) assumes that a similar generalization process happens for grammatical categories. Even very early, children tend to generalize a construction such as throw-ball to encompass other small objects. They obviously do not have a name for the category "noun," but many adults don't either. Moving from verb-specific constructions to more general ones is more complicated and occurs later. The theory assumes that this happens for the same two reasons as other generalizations: it allows for a much more compact encoding of (grammatical) knowledge and yields rules that can then apply to novel examples. There are many computational realizations of parameter lifting, and something like this must be happening in people.

At this point, we have a story (and Nancy Chang has a model) for how children might learn early constructions, extend them in both speech and hearing, reject those that aren't appropriate, and generalize those that do fit adult language. But why do all children in a language community learn essentially the same grammar? One possibility is that the input data are so exhaustive and complete there is only one grammar that works. Most workers in the field reject the idea that children receive such compelling input data, and linguists also cannot agree among themselves what the grammar of English or any other language should be. So there must be some mechanism that leads children to converge on very similar grammars.

How the Program Chooses the Best Grammar for Sample Data

This brings us perilously close to the language wars of chapter 22. Even if we agree that grammar is inherently embodied and individual constructions are naturally learned, a question remains about which set of constructions becomes the grammar. According to Gold's theorem, the child will not be able to choose among all the potential construction grammars, given only positive examples. Do we still need to postulate that construction grammar is innate so the child's choice is limited in advance?

Chang's theory and her model incorporate yet another bit of computational technology that solves the problem of choosing the best grammar. Recall that people and programs both always need to choose the best set of constructions for analyzing each sentence. This is done using weights on the various constructions, indicating how useful each is likely to be. Using the ideas of probability theory, one can treat these weights as probabilities and formalize this best match process as follows:

@ Given a sentence S and a grammar G, the best analysis is the one that maximizes the probability of sentence S being generated by grammar G.

So far, this is just a mathematical way of expressing what the model does in choosing the best analysis. But there is an elegant computational trick that can be applied to any such system for choosing a best analysis for each example (sentence, picture, etc.). We can turn such a system inside out and use it as a way of choosing the best *grammar* for analyzing a collection of data. Let's see how this works.

Suppose we have a collection, C, of sentences that we know to be grammatical and two competing grammars, G1 and G2. We want to know which grammar does a better job of analyzing the whole set C of examples. Using our rule @ above, we can get a probability score for any individual sentence as analyzed by a particular grammar. Now we can compute the probability of the whole collection C, assuming that G1 is the best grammar, and then do the same assuming that G2 is the winner. If the total probability of C is higher using G1, then it should be chosen—it does a better job of explaining why the sentences in C are all grammatical. To really make this work right, we need to penalize more complex grammars, but that doesn't change the basic idea.

Now we have a principled way for the program, and presumably for the child, to select the best construction grammar for the data she or he remembers. There is also a way to update this choice of grammar as new data are encountered. Technically, this procedure is one that overcomes the limitations of Gold's theorem by choosing the *best* grammar, rather than the *first* one that fits the data. We discussed this kind of procedure in chapter 22 as part of the background to the language wars. This completes the catalog of technical concerns about the adequacy of Chang's theory as a plausible model for how children learn language.

Our story covered a wide range of considerations, but the basic ideas are simple. Language, including grammar, inherently links form to meaning. People, including children, are always trying to find the best fit between what they observe and what they know. In learning language, children fit linguistic input to the grammar they already know and to their knowledge of the situation. They can tentatively add new constructions and test them for usefulness. Straightforward ideas from learning theory explain how such processes can lead to learning adult language under realistic assumptions. In the final two chapters I suggest some implications of these results and touch on some fundamental questions that remain open.

We are now near the end of the story. Whether you worked through all the details at the various levels or just skimmed for conclusions, it should be clear that the neural basis of language is no mystery. Taken together, advances in our understanding of many subjects provide a compelling outline of the embodied nature of human language, although certainly not all of the details. This might be a good point at which to conclude the book. But two basic questions remain somewhat mysterious, one lesser and one greater.

The Origins of Language

The lesser mystery concerns the origins of human language: How did we come to develop a communication system so much richer than that of other animals? This hotly debated topic is related to the "language gene" controversy and is also popular in the media. Every few months, we get another story about how some new finding has solved the mystery of language origins. A recent example is the discovery that two unrelated languages from Africa and Australia use somewhat similar click sounds. This was claimed to show that clicks were the key to language origins. Of course, even if clicks were the first sounds, it tell us very little about the basic questions of how language got its start.

Language was spoken long before it was ever written down, so there is no record of what languages might have been like tens of thousands of years ago. We do know that all contemporary languages have essentially the same level of complexity and expressiveness—there are no fossil languages to give us clues on their origins. We also now have a rich and detailed literature on how languages can change rather rapidly. We can't work backward from current languages and preserved texts to some common precursor; language change is much too fast and varied.

Some relevant information can be gathered from paleontology, particularly from the shape of discovered skulls, jaws, and related skeletal remains. Producing the full range of human language sounds apparently requires some anatomical adaptations that are not present in early hominids and certainly not in contemporary apes. But, at best, this kind of finding can provide us only with some crude estimates of *when* human languages might have started evolving, not *how*.

As you would expect, such a compelling question with no serious constraints on possible answers has given rise to no end of speculations on how human language evolved. As early as 1866, the Linguistic Society of Paris issued a general statement that the society would accept no more articles on the origins of language. All the new results in various related fields, many discussed in this book, were bound to engender a new round of speculation about language origins. There is some commonality between the language wars of chapter 22 and the various theories of language origins, but the link is far from simple.

As usual, Noam Chomsky's position is the touchstone for most of the discussions within linguistics. His current stance is that there is a core linguistic competence that is unique to humans and disjoint from other neural systems; this is completely consistent with the modularist stance that we discussed in chapter 22. In a 2002 article in *Science*, written with Hauser and Fitch, Chomsky makes the reasonable argument that no animal rule systems approach the complexity of human grammar. The conclusion is that human language (core grammar) is the result of a single large mutation.

Other modularists, notably Steven Pinker, argue that continuous evolution produced the innate, autonomous, formal grammar module. The very detailed critique in Pinker and Jackendoff (2005) of Chomsky's current positions on the essence of grammar and the origin of language is completely consistent with the biological continuity stance of this book. But neither side in this latest argument says much about how language came to be the organizing force of human culture. Of course, if you believe that language is just one manifestation of a bigger brain with superior learning ability, there is nothing much to explain. Language got started somehow, and, because it is so adaptive, people learned to be better and better at it.

People also developed many other intellectual skills, some related to language and some not.

Among the many other theories of the origins of language, Derek Bickerton produced the most complete and widely regarded (Bickerton 1981). He started by looking at *Creoles*, languages that develop ad hoc when people without a common language are forced to communicate. He suggested that all Creoles start from the same simple grammatical structure, which might well be the prototype for the original human grammar. There are also claims that this same primitive grammar structure is universally found in small children and in great apes that are taught human language.

The proposed proto-grammar lacks grammatical function words and endings and relies only on word order to structure meaning. This is an attractive hypothesis and could even be right, but the evidence for it is lacking. English-speaking children do start like this, but children from cultures with morphologically complex languages such as Turkish and Eskimo use grammatical markings very early. There is also good evidence that bilingual children learn quite early to obey the different word orders used in their two languages, such as French and German. And the results from Michael Tomasello and his colleagues suggest that children's early grammar rules are not generalized at all, but are focused on individual constructions.

The evidence from the development of Creoles is also more complex than originally thought. It is true that the first generation to be native speakers of a Creole are much more fluent than their parents, and this is additional strong evidence for the special nature of first-language learning. But it does not seem to be the case that these children develop a totally new grammar. The elements of the Creole grammar can be seen in the base grammars of the languages from which it arises.

The most famous case of children building a language community concerns Nicaraguan sign language. Before the 1980s there were no schools for the deaf in Nicaragua and no common sign language. The first school cohort (around 1978–83) struggled to find ways to communicate in a partially systematized way. It was the children of the second cohort, being first-language learners, who developed and became fluent in a systematic language. This is good evidence that people tend to produce systematic grammars, but people also favor systematic explanations of other experience. The results on Creole languages do not provide insight into the possible special character of grammar or on how it may have evolved.

So, the mystery of the origins of human language is not likely to be solved any time soon. But it is not a profound mystery. Everyone agrees that expressive language conveys very significant evolutionary advantages on groups that can use it. Biological evolution moves too slowly to explain the rise of language (and modern civilization) in just some thousands of years, but cultural evolution is easily fast enough. In a general way, it must be true that the genesis of language was neither a biological event nor individual learning, but a social phenomenon. The biological precursors, whether specific to language or more general, were almost certainly evolving well before the rapid rise of language. The mathematics of this kind of rapid change from a slowly evolving base is well understood as part of dynamical systems theory.

Our neural theory of language suggests that *simulation* might well be a cornerstone in the evolution of human language and thought. As we have seen, converging evidence indicates that people understand language and other behaviors at least in part by simulation (or imagination). This ability to think about situations not bound to the here and now (*displacement*) is also obviously necessary for evaluating alternatives, for planning, and for understanding other minds. We have discussed this ability earlier, in terms of *mental spaces*.

I believe there is a plausible story about how a discreet evolutionary change could have given early hominids a simulation capability that helped start the process leading to our current linguistic abilities. Mammals in general exhibit at least two kinds of involuntary simulation behavior— dreams and play. While a cat is dreaming, a center in the brainstem (the locus coeruleus) blocks the motor nerves so that the cat's dream thoughts are not translated into action. If this brainstem center is destroyed, the sleeping cat may walk around the room, lick itself, catch imaginary mice, and otherwise appear to be acting out its dreams. There is a general belief that dreaming is important for memory consolidation in people, and this would also be valuable for other mammals. Similarly, it is obvious that play behaviors in cats and other animals have significant adaptive value.

Given that mammals do exhibit *involuntary* displacement in dreams, it seems that only one evolutionary adaptation is needed to achieve our ability to imagine situations of our choosing. Suppose that the mammalian involuntary simulation mechanisms were augmented by brain circuits that could explicitly control what was being imagined, as we routinely do. This kind of overlaying a less flexible brain system with one that is more amenable to control is the hallmark of brain evolution, and no one would be surprised to find another instance of this mechanism. Now, hominids who could do detached simulations could relive the past, plan for the future, and be well on their way to simulating other minds. Understanding other minds would then provide a substrate for richer communication and all the benefits that accrue from the use of mental spaces.

One crucial component of mental space reasoning is the ability to map ideas from one mental space to another. This is how we draw lessons from the past or change our plans after thinking about their consequences. People can predict what someone is likely to do based on what she says. So, our general simulation facility must include the ability to maintain and exploit *relational mappings*. We saw in chapter 25 that the learning of grammar could be very nicely modeled as learning relational mappings between regularities of linguistic form and the underlying meaning they convey, and some such mapping ability seems to be required under any theory of grammar. Even more speculatively, the combined ability to imagine separate scenarios and to map them together is perhaps one of the foundations of many human capabilities, including grammar. This is close to the proposal of cognitive scientists Gilles Fauconnier and Mark Turner in a recent book, *The Way We Think* (Fauconnier & Turner 2003).

Whatever combination of biological and cultural evolution gave rise to early human language, it is no mystery that it developed rapidly and, in all cultures, has a vast array of uses in human communication and thought. We would love to know more about how language evolved, but it is unlikely that any theory of language origins would change our basic ideas of who we are and how the world works. The second unsolved mystery concerning language is that fundamental.

The Nature of Subjective Experience

The remaining unresolved issue, the nature of *personal experience*, is the most profound question about the mind and arguably the deepest issue in all of science. Why do we experience everything in the way we do? This issue is so central to our thinking that there isn't even agreement on how to talk about it. Almost everyone believes their own personal experience has a quality that goes beyond what this book, and science in general, can describe. The pleasure of beauty, the pain of disappointment, and even the feeling of being alive do not seem to us like they are reducible to neural firings and chemical reactions. There is good reason to believe that higher animals have some similar experiences.

We saw in chapter 16 that children learn quite early to use metaphors based on physical sensation in talking about subjective experiences—hot for angry, for example. But how do we talk about that extra part of experience we believe to be beyond current science? People use terms such as *personal experience, subjective experience,* and *phenomenology* to label this idea. Philosophers have coined a technical term, *"qualia,"* to refer to exactly this currently unexplained residual, whatever it may be. When the focus is on self-awareness, the term *"consciousness"* is often used. I find this usage confusing and not helpful, because the same word is used to label the waking state in general. There are quite good scientific theories of sleep, attention, and so on that explain many things, but tell us nothing directly about qualia.

The nature of subjective experience has engaged some of the most illustrious thinkers throughout history. In our time, the rise of new methodologies, like those described in this book, has led to a wide range of books trying to "solve" the qualia problem by many of our leading scientists and intellectuals.

My personal favorite among the recent books is *Looking for Spinoza* by Antonio Damasio (2003). Damasio tries to relate the latest biological and clinical findings to subjective experience with impressive results. As with all current explanations, even if every detail in the book were exactly right, it wouldn't resolve the big question. We simply don't yet have a way to pose the question of subjective experience in a way that could yield a scientific answer.

A fundamental problem for any scientific approach to explaining subjective experience is the ineffability of qualia. Pretty much by the definition of the question, anything scientifically measurable can also be explained without evoking subjective experience. This is a huge philosophical issue that poses a central problem for a neural theory of language like the one described in this book:

If meaning is based on experience and we don't fully understand experience, how can we have a scientific theory of meaning?

The neural theory of language, along with much of contemporary cognitive science, is based on the *physiological correlates of experience*. We absolutely do not understand the nature of subjective experience, but there is overwhelming evidence that experience correlates with measurable brain events. Distinctive patterns of neural activity are correlated with seeing, speaking, emotions, dreaming, grasping, and increasingly detailed knowledge about the circuitry and activity underlying various experiences is now available. Until a conflict between the measurable and the subjective is found, theories of mental function will continue to use measurable activity and responses as indicative of experience. This is not completely satisfying, but it is productive in its own right, and is one of the most promising ways to address the deep problem of subjective experience.

The possibility still remains that scientists will be able to reformulate the question of subjective experience in a way that does lead to answers that are both scientifically and experientially satisfying. There seem to be three possibilities for the eventual outcome of the search for a scientific explanation of personal experience and currently no compelling evidence on which is more likely:

(a) Personal experience is not describable by science—it's just the way we are.

(b) There is a scientific explanation, but humans can't ever find it.

(c) The explanation will eventually be routine science.

As scientists, we have no choice but to pursue option c, but we should be aware that possibilities a and b are just as likely. If option b seems precluded to you, imagine that gorillas were trying to understand the brain; there is good reason to believe they simply don't have the mental capacity to grasp what we humans can. There is no inherent reason to believe that our brains can understand everything that some more advanced species could.

There are a number of other classical philosophical mysteries such as the nature of causality, free will, and so on. Patricia Churchland does a great job of examining them from a modern neuroscience perspective in her book, Brain-Wise (2002). None of them bear as directly on the concerns of this book as the qualia question.

It should not disturb us that some mystery remains in our theories of the mind; science is only one way of understanding the world. For anything that can be measured, even indirectly, science is the path to understanding. But for some (currently) immeasurable questions like what it would be like to be someone else, other approaches—introspection, interaction with others, the arts, and arguably philosophical arguments—can yield superior insights. It is profoundly unscientific to assume that our current science is able to provide the best understanding of all of human experience.

Cognitive science can not yet address all the mysteries of the mind, but an enormous amount has been achieved and the outlook for continuing progress is excellent. By exploiting many discoveries and insights obtained by various fields, I have been able to assemble a picture of language and thought that must be right in its essentials. In this final chapter, I briefly review the argument, discuss some applications of a neural theory of language, and assess the prospects for the unified cognitive science that seems necessary for further progress.

The first few chapters focused on three things: the richness of language, the astonishing complexity of the human brain, and the idea of computational models that help explain how language is realized in our brains. We saw at the outset that language is such a flexible vehicle for communication and thought because it maps new ideas to existing ideas and experience. It is essential to study language as an integral component of our bodies and their functioning, not just as an abstract formal system.

One fundamental fact is that our brains, though incredibly intricate, depend on many properties, including their underlying biochemistry, shared with all animals. Language and thought are crucially shaped by the kind of parallel, evidential, best-fit information processing that animal brains all do. Even the simplest animals evolved to have rapid adaptive responses to changing goals and environmental conditions. Neurons, the information-processing foundation of our minds, develop, compute, and modify their behavior much like those of primitive animals. This has enabled neuroscientists to learn an enormous amount of details of neural functioning, particularly for behaviors that we share with other mammals.

A major barrier to any neural theory of language is the conceptual gap between the components of language (grammar, metaphor, etc.) and the concepts and terminology of neuroscience, such as synapses and transmitters. Only recently has cognitive science developed computational theories and techniques that support the construction and testing of *adequate* models—ones that demonstrate the required behavior while remaining consistent with all anatomical and experimental findings.

Our language and conceptual systems are obviously acquired, and the adaptive processes of neural development largely determine how that comes about. Scientists now know a great deal about the intricate interplay between genetic and environmental factors at all stages of development. Learning language might well involve some specific genetic precursors, but it has the same basic interactive character as other learning by mammals.

With our basic understanding of language, the brain, and neural computation, we were able to look at detailed theories and models of how children learn their native language or languages. Everything depends on the intimate connection between form and meaning: children learn to associate sounds and gestures with their own experience. They bring a rich understanding of their physical and social environment to the language learning task, the opulence of the substrate.

Even so, it requires major effort to convert general insights about embodied language into an adequate model of how children's brains adapt to learn language. Our first detailed example, Terry Regier's model of acquiring spatial relation terms, involved an approximation of the human visual system, the idea of image schemas from cognitive linguistics, and a program incorporating innovations in the computational theory of neural learning. It did well at learning spatial words and concepts from widely varying languages, but had a number of limitations that were addressed in follow-up efforts.

To study the acquisition of verbs, we had to introduce a novel computational mechanism, X-schemas, which represented actions in a way that supports recognition, execution, or reasoning. Independently, the discovery of neural mirror circuitry in monkeys and humans suggests such a multimodal representation. With the X-schema representation, David Bailey was able to build a computational model of how children learn words describing motions of their own hands, again cross-linguistically. There appears to be no barrier to using similar ideas to develop detailed models of how children learn words and concepts that directly describe other aspects of their experiences, including social and emotional ones.

As the cognitive linguists have known for decades, people develop abstract and theoretical thought and language from the base of our embodied concepts and experiences—how else? There is a well-developed theory of metaphor that can be exploited to model how we understand abstract and figurative language, which is ubiquitous in all discourse, including news stories. The next section of the book explained Srinivas Narayanan's computational model that understands news stories about international economics, relying heavily on metaphor. The program required two additional technical developments, both of which are important for an appreciation of embodied language.

One requirement for understanding language is a proper treatment of the detailed shape of events and actions—what linguists call "aspect." Narayanan's program captures the difference between "is slipping" and "slipped," using the same X-schema mechanism that was postulated as the semantic basis of actions. Any adequate model must also reflect the fact that the world, and our reasoning about it, is uncertain. A modest extension of current computer science ideas on belief networks provides a reasonable model of the quantitative best-fit operations of neural systems.

The final section of this book focuses on grammar—the way individual words, phrases, and gestures combine to yield the marvelous expressiveness of human language. The hypothesis that grammar is innate continues to attract wide media attention. Certainly people have mental abilities, including language, that go beyond those of other animals, but there is no scientific support for the notion that language (or even some core grammar) is an abstract symbolic system unlike any other human capacity. The grammars of languages inherently relate linguistic form to meaning—what else could they do? It is possible to write down constraints on what is an allowable sentence in English, but these constraints are not absolute and could not function in isolation from the rest of language processing. It is equally clear that there is some genetic basis for the universal drive in children to learn their native language or languages. Language is not just the product of a universal learning machine.

The central idea of embodied language fits best with one particular class of grammar theories, called construction grammar, which posits that every element of language pairs form with meaning. If we assume that the meaning component is directly or metaphorically linked to direct experience, we get embodied construction grammar (ECG). I discussed some early results that suggest ECG can help solve problems in linguistics that seem otherwise intractable.

Most important, ECG is a form of grammar that is manifestly learnable by children in the course of their daily activities. Nancy Chang has built a complex computer program that models how this comes about. As with the early models of word learning, the key is the pairing of linguistic form with embodied meaning. After an English-speaking child has grasped the meaning of "push," she or he still needs to learn the difference between "I pushed Josh" and "Josh pushed me." Chang's model suggests that this comes about by the child noticing the correlation between a real-world relation in the current environment and a linguistic relation in parental speech. The fact that this program seems to learn much the way that children do is evidence that we are approaching an adequate neurally based theory of embodied language.

Any embodied theory of language rests on two fundamental principles and a related scientific stance:

Thought is structured neural activity.
Language is inseparable from thought and experience.
The study of language should be explicitly based on these principles.

The purpose of this book is to show how these insights can be combined to produce neural theories of language that are both scientifically adequate and highly productive. That is, we can build theories of language that are consistent with all experimental findings from relevant disciplines and that provide computationally plausible bridges between the various levels. Within these general constraints many open questions remain as to exactly how language works at the behavioral, computational, and biological levels. Importantly, these scientific questions can be posed with precision, separately or in combination, using an integrated neural theory of language.

Every human language is rich and changing. There are principles that appear to underlie all human languages and provide important cues on the nature of human thought. Even if everything in this book were exactly right, it wouldn't make linguistics simple any more than physics makes chemistry simple.

In fact, my (outsider's) vision for a future linguistics is modeled on organic chemistry. Like chemistry, the science of language involves the study of complex and elaborate structures and how they interact, develop, and change. With a sound scientific basis and some fundamental agreement on terminology, the field could become much more cumulative and productive. The study of language could occupy a central role in the unified cognitive science, which we all know is needed.

Even in its current nascent state, the embodied neural theory of language has applications in many domains. We have talked about major improvements in computer systems that communicate in language and will return to that. But several important applications of the *idea* of embodied language precede any detailed neural analyses or computer implementations.

Some Applications of a Neural Theory of Language

Many of the key ideas in this book were originally developed as part of cognitive linguistics. Long before there was an explicitly neural model for their ideas, cognitive linguists were making fundamental contributions to the cognitive sciences in general and linguistics in particular, some of which have been reviewed in earlier chapters. Because it explicitly links language to other mental activities, cognitive linguistics has given rise to lively interdisciplinary fields in areas such as literary criticism.

In addition, some cognitive linguists have made special efforts to show the important impact their results can have on fields as disparate as law, poetry, politics, and mathematics. The best known popularization of embodied language is the book *Metaphors We Live By*, by George Lakoff and Mark Johnson. Originally printed in 1977, it was republished in 2003 and is still in active use. It is an informal presentation of how metaphors, such as the ones discussed here, pervade ordinary language.

George Lakoff has written several additional books suggesting how embodied metaphorical language plays a central role in politics, poetry (with Mark Turner), and mathematics (with Rafael Nunez). Mathematics is often seen as a purely abstract discipline, but we now know that people use their same mental apparatus for all thinking. Much of higher mathematics is based on finding mappings, like metaphors, from a more complex domain to one that is understood. The importance of the cognitive basis of political metaphors and framing is now widely accepted by politicians as well as scientists and one can hope that it will also become public knowledge.

More recently, Mark Turner and Gilles Fauconnier (2002) have made a bold attempt to explain much of mental life in terms of the cognitive linguistic notion of conceptual integration (or blending) we discussed in chapter 24. Even more ambitious efforts have been made to use the ideas of embodiment and neural computation to address core questions of our existence.

We should expect a neural theory of thought and language to be used to confront the eternal questions of philosophy. The previous chapter discussed the most relevant one—the nature of subjective experience. In addition, two complementary books, between them, recently provide an embodied view of all the traditional philosophical issues. Patricia Churchland's *Brain-Wise* (2002) uses contemporary neuroscience as a base and shows how this provides partial answers to many of the standard deep questions such as free will and the existence of God. She does not get as far as language and thought, but Lakoff and Johnson's book *Philosophy in the Flesh* (1999) historically reexamines mainstream Western philosophy from the perspective of cognitive science. We have traditionally been taught to view philosophical reasoning as quite distinct from ordinary thought. But even the greatest philosophers used ordinary (embodied) language tools for developing and presenting their ideas. Using our current understanding of cognition and metaphor, Lakoff and Johnson provide new insights into past philosophical positions and discussions.

So, the embodied neural view of language can provide a systematic approach to answering many traditional questions about language and may also offer insights into how language shapes thought. It allows the findings of cognitive linguistics to be merged with the profound developments in cognitive neuroscience that are changing the way we understand and treat the brain. A powerful computational theory of language should lead to much better programs for human-computer interaction, and we saw examples of this in chapter 20. This leads us to consider what the ultimate limit might be on natural language communication with computers.

Will We Talk with Our Robots?

Given the impasse on the basic issue of subjective experience, we can still try to answer two related questions that come up in this context: Will there ever be robots that have the same subjective experiences as people? And, more practically, will there be artificial systems that can communicate fully in natural language with people?

Two basic lines of reasoning are used to support the notion that computers or robots might eventually fully achieve human language and experience. The more common, and less interesting, argument is based on ever more detailed simulation. To take this to the extreme, suppose a computer system simulated every molecule of your brain and predicted your every measurable behavior and physiological response. Would you accept this as capturing the essence of your experience? When we ask this question in class, almost half the students say, "yes, the simulation would get it all." I haven't been able to determine why they say this; for me, there would still be a huge gap. The philosopher John Searle loves to point out that no simulation of water, however detailed, is actually *wet*. If you are thirsty, simulated water will not help.

But it doesn't much matter whether this idealized simulation would work, because there are plain and fancy reasons why such a computation is impossible. There is no way to get the information on the current state of your brain and the amount of computation involved is not possible with any envisioned computer. We can't even simulate well enough to do weather forecasting. Since the biochemistry of drugs, hormones and neurotransmitters play a central role in human information processing, it is unlikely that a coarser simulation will automatically capture human personal experience.

The other way by which computers might have experience like those of humans is less direct and requires a longer story. As I have stated too often, much of human thought and language concerns the human body, its experience, and its interactions with the world. So we assume our aspiring fluent computer will need interior and exterior senses and an ability to interact with the world, that is, that it is a robot. We could (even now) endow a robot with programs that can interpret internal sense readings (low battery, wheel slippage, etc.) as being good or bad for the robot along various dimensions. Such a robot could come to correlate wet pavements with slippery wheels and legitimately issue the statement, "I hate to go out when it's wet." This would be a statement about the robot's personal experience and might well not be meaningful to a robot with a rather different design.

A robot with a (programmed) sense of itself, goals, desires, and so on would certainly be better able to operate autonomously in the world. But we have no reason to believe it would share human subjective experience. There is a fierce ongoing debate about whether any animals have full humanlike subjective experience, but there is no scientific basis for either side, and we will not worry further about this issue. However, an answer to the following question is central to our goals:

If the meaning of language is based in bodily experience and if computers cannot share our subjective experience, will we ever be able to communicate naturally with computers?

The answer is—*partially*. We all acknowledge that there are strong limitations on the extent to which we can convey understanding across barriers such as gender, age, race, culture, and many others. There are understandings that we share with our colleagues and not with our family and vice versa. If we built an expert computer system that cared how often and successfully it performed, it could well turn out that this system and an expert person could share deeper understanding (and beliefs and desires) within this domain than the person would with most other people. Professional programmers currently come to react that way to their code—a complicated program is treated as a living entity with its own mind. An analogous situation would be a champion horse and rider team, who share understanding and communicate in a way not available to anyone else.

Nevertheless, there is a basic sense in which understanding does involve our shared human experience. And human experience is based in the human body and brain and biochemistry. It seems quite possible (to me, almost certain) that robots that are physically very different from people will, in general, have experience quite different from ours. This does not depend only on particularly animal subjectivity; two robots with radically different sensors and mechanisms would find it hard to communicate about many things.

If understanding depends on shared experience, then this is critically important if one also accepts (as this book obviously does) the bodily grounding of semantics of language. The strong form of the bodily grounding hypothesis is that much of our abstract and theoretical language is interpreted by mappings to this experiential core. To the extent that this is true, robots will find it very hard to communicate with people. People routinely invent new language usage and are usually understood without elaboration. Meaning based on embodied experience provides an explanation. Conceptual extensions that occur automatically in humans would be a mystery to robots with radically different bodies.

The practical take-home lesson for me is the following: A presumption of shared experience is the basis for communication. If we want computer systems to understand or learn natural language well enough to meet AI goals, we need to explicitly account for the human experience that underlies much of language and thought. We could try to do this by building robots and pushing their experience to be as much as possible like ours. We could endow the robots with human image schemas, but they would not connect to the same embodied experiences. While interesting and fun, building robots is not likely to be a realizable solution to human-machine communication.

The alternative is to explicitly view the problem as one of communicating among alien species. Our programs should try to incorporate as much knowledge of humans as needed for the tasks involved. The common way of attempting this is to include lots of *rules about* human knowledge and experience. The story of embodied cognition in this book suggests that this will never be adequate and we must work on *simulations* of human understanding. For example, one should not try to list all the conditions that might cause dizziness, but rather include a vestibular model that is good enough for prediction. Neural computation methods appear to be required because they make it possible to capture the evidential, situational, multifaceted character of human thought and to propose explicit mappings to brain structures. Even so, there are some aspects of human experience that we are unlikely to ever be able to convey to machines. This suggests great caution in using automated systems for teaching certain subjects, for therapy, or for making judgments about people.

Unified Cognitive Science

There are already a large number of intellectual and practical applications of the embodied neural approach to language and thought. Surely additional applications will arise as our field advances, but how should we proceed? I suggest that progress on understanding language, thought, and other aspects of our minds depends on a unified cognitive science. Every chapter in this book depends on insights that cross traditional subdisciplinary lines, and the enterprise would be inconceivable within any one field.

There might seem to already be a unified cognitive science; after all, there is a society that meets annually and publishes a journal. But the cognitive linguists have distinct meetings as do cognitive neuroscientists, neural computationists, and others. And the core of each subdiscipline tends to ignore relevant results expressed in different paradigms. Linguists, even cognitive linguists, pay little attention to behavioral or neural findings on language; there are also psycholinguists and language development specialists who have their own cultures. The journal *Brain and Language* is mainly about clinical studies, and a number of journals now focus on brain-imaging experiments and little else. The ever increasing complexity of each subdiscipline makes it harder and harder for people to keep up with work that is not directly relevant to their own. In self-defense, scientists develop a sophisticated technique of one-line dismissal—What is a simple reason I can ignore this result?

This push toward greater specialization does not arise from some failing of the scientists involved. Developing and maintaining expertise in a particular area of biology, linguistics, computer science, or other field is more challenging than ever, and no one fully grasps the insights of more than a few subareas. The criteria for sound experimental and theoretical work differ widely and must be maintained within a discipline. In my own attempts at synthesis, it was not hard to read the various literatures—the question was what to believe. But this necessary disciplinary rigor does skew all the reward structures toward inward-looking specialization.

The theory of neural computation, which I have argued is necessary for any bridge between brain and language, has evolved in a number of ways that abdicate this unifying role. Like other disciplines, the field is largely focused on internal technical concerns. There are good unified efforts at lower levels of neural organization, and computational models are routine in neuroscience. But the models of higher level behavior are almost all explicitly *suggestive*, with no claim that they could even in principle describe the actual neural circuits and their information processing. This seems to fit a general pattern in which the various subdisciplines prefer articulating theories that provide no external constraints on their internal theorizing.

I have no ready solution to achieving the unified cognitive science needed. To be fair, there has been an outstanding tradition of multidisciplinary work for decades in some subdomains, particularly in vision and motor control. But this has been achieved by largely ignoring the more cognitive aspects of these behaviors. Much of the mechanism needed to understand a story is also required to follow a film of that story, but there is currently virtually no modeling work on embodied image understanding.

One might hope that degree programs at various levels in cognitive science will yield a new generation of more broadly based scientists. This might happen, but many degree programs, including ours at Berkeley, consist mainly of standard classes in traditional disciplines with no explicit unification. Another hope is our greatly increased ability to collaborate through the Internet. This is already leading to online journals and other new means of scientific communication. There are, of course, a large number of news and discussion groups concerned with understanding the brain and mind, but the discourse is highly uneven.

Perhaps the best way to build a unified cognitive science is through intensive and extended workshops. When the current ideas on neural computation were being developed in the 1980s, there were many multidisciplinary workshops and meetings. Not all of these were successful, but some were among my most exciting scientific experiences and demonstrably led to many of the advances discussed here. Workshops of various kinds continue to be held, but apparently not with the same intensity.

What I believe is likely to be most effective is multidisciplinary postdoctoral collaboration. Many postdoctoral programs already exist at individual labs, as well as sabbatical year collaborative groups for more senior scientists at institutes such as the Center for Advanced Study in the Behavioral Sciences. What we don't have is a mechanism for bringing together six to ten recent doctoral graduates across the cognitive sciences for a year of cooperative effort on a topic of shared interest. In my experience, many breakthrough ideas have come from people at about this stage unifying alternative perspectives. Whether through this mechanism or another one, scientists who are driven to really understand how it all works will perforce build a unified science of the mind.

Science has been making amazing progress at revealing how things, including us people, actually work. Many philosophical issues and mysteries of previous eras have become technical subjects of study and application. I hope that you now agree the nature of human language is one of the questions that has made this transition from mystery to scientific discipline. As the unified cognitive science extends our understanding of language and thought, there are unprecedented opportunities for developing intelligent computer systems and for deeper insights into the intelligent systems that we all are.

References and Further Reading

General References

Augustine Saint. *Confessions*. Henry Chadwick, trans. Oxford University Press, 1992, I.8.

Badler N., Erignac C., and Liu Y. Virtual humans for validating maintenance procedures. *Communications of the ACM*, pp. 57–63, 2002.

Bailey D. When push comes to shove: A computational model of the role of motor control in the acquisition of action verbs. PhD thesis, University of California, Berkeley, 1997.

Bailey D., Chang N., Feldman J., and Narayanan S. Extending embodied lexical development. In *Proceedings of the twentieth annual meeting of the Cognitive Science Society COGSCI-98*. Madison, 1998.

Bargh J.A., Chen M., and Burrows L. Automaticity of social behavior: Direct effects of trait construct and stereotype activation on action. *Journal of Personality and Social Psychology*, 71:230–244, 1996.

Bergen B. Probability in phonological generalizations: Modeling optional French final consonants. *Proceedings of the Twenty-Sixth Annual Meeting of the Berkeley Linguistics Society*. Berkeley: Berkeley Linguistics Society, 1999.

Bergen B. and Chang N. Embodied construction grammar in simulation-based language understanding. In J-O. Östman and M. Fried, eds. *Construction Grammar(s): Cognitive and Cross-language dimensions*. John Benjamins, 2005.

Bergen B., Narayan S., and Feldman J. Embodied verbal semantics: evidence from an image-verb matching task. *Proceedings Cognitive Science* 25. Mahwah, NJ: Erlbaum, 2003.

Berlin B., Breedlove D., and Raven P. General principles of classification and nomenclature in folk biology. *American Anthropologist* 74:214–242, 1973.

Berlin B. and Kay P. *Basic Color Terms: Their Universality and Evolution*. Berkeley and Los Angeles: University of California, 1969.

Bickerton D. *Roots of Language*. Ann Arbor: Karoma Publishers, 1981.

Bloom L. *The Transition from Infancy to Language: Acquiring the Power of Expression*. New York: Cambridge University Press, 1993.

Bloom P. *How Children Learn the Meanings of Words*. Cambridge, MA: MIT Press, 2002, chapters 8, 10, and 25.

Boroditsky L., Schmidt L.A., and Phillips W. Sex, Syntax, and Semantics. Language in Mind. In *Advances in the Study of Language and Thought*. Dedre Gentner and Susan Goldin-Meadow, eds. Cambridge, MA: MIT Press, 2003.

Bowker G. and Star S. *Sorting Things Out: Classification and its Consequences* Cambridge, MA: MIT Press, 1999.

Bregler C. Learning and Recognizing Human Dynamics in Video Sequences. *IEEE Conference on Computer Vision and Pattern Recognition*, 1997.

Brooks R. *Flesh and Machines*. Vintage, 2003, chapters 3 and 26.

Bryant J. Constructional Analysis. M.S. report, University of California, Berkeley, 2003.

Bryant J. Towards Cognitive, Compositional Construction Grammar. *ROMAND 2004: Robust Methods in Analysis of Natural language Data*, Geneva, 2004.

Buccino G., Binkofski F., Fink G.R., Fadiga L., Fogassi L., Gallese V., Seitz R.J., Zilles K., Rizzolatti G., and Freund H.-J. Action observation activates premotor and parietal areas in a somatotopic manner: An fMRI study. *European Journal of Neuroscience*, 13:400–404, 2001.

Cacioppo J.T., Priester J.R., and Berntson G.G. Rudimentary determinants of attitudes: II. Arm flexion and extension have differential effects on attitudes. *Journal of Personality and Social Psychology*, 65:5–17, 1993.

Chang F., Dell G.S., Bock K., and Griffin Z.M. Structural priming as implicit learning: A comparison of models of sentence production. *Journal of Psycholinguistic Research*, 29(2):217–229, 2000.

Chang N. Constructing Grammar: A computational model of the acquisition of early constructions. PhD thesis, University of California, Berkeley, 2006.

Chang N., Feldman J., Porzel R., and Sanders K. Scaling cognitive linguistics: Formalisms for language understanding. *Proceedings of SCANALU*, 2002.

Changeaux J.P. *Neuronal Man*. Princeton, NJ: Princeton University Press, 1997, chapters 4–6.

Chomsky N. *Language and Thought*. Moyer Bell Ltd., 1993, chapters 1, 21, and 22.

Churchland P. *Brain-Wise: Studies in Neurophilosophy*. Cambridge, MA: MIT Press, 2002, chapters 1, 3, and 26.

Damasio A. *Looking for Spinoza*. Harvest Books, 2003, chapters 1 and 26.

Damasio A.R. *The Feeling of What Happens: Body and Emotion in the Making of Consciousness*. New York: Harcourt Brace, 2000.

Deacon T.W. *The Symbolic Species: The Co-evolution of Language and the Brain*. New York: W.W. Norton, 1988.

Delancey S. What an innatist argument should look like. In T. Haukioja, M-L Helasvuo, and M. Miestamo, eds. *SKY 1997* (1997 Yearbook of the Linguistic Association of Finland). 1997, pp. 7–24.

Dennett D. *Kinds of Minds*. New York: Basic Books, 1997, chapters 1, 3, and 26.

Dodge E. and Wright A. Herds of Wildebeest, Flasks of Vodka, Heaps of Trouble: An Embodied Construction Grammar Approach to English Measure Phrases. *Proceedings of the Berkeley Linguistics Society*, 2002.

Dowling J. *Creating Mind*. W.W. Norton & Co. Inc., 2000, chapters 4–8.

Duckworth K.L., Bargh J.A., Garcia M., and Chaiken S. The automatic evaluation of novel stimuli. *Psychological Science* 13:513–519, 2002.

Edelman G. et al. *A Universe of Consciousness*. Basic Books, 2001, chapters 1 and 26.

Fauconnier G. and Turner M. *The Way We Think*. New York: Basic Books, 2003, chapters 1, 7–8, 15–17, and 23.

Feldman J.A. An essay concerning robotic understanding. *AI Magazine* 11:12–13, 1990.

Feldman J.A. Dynamic connections in neural networks. *Biological Cybernetics* 46:27–39, 1982.

Feldman J.A. Some decidability results on grammatical inference and complexity. *Information and Control* 20(3):244–262, April 1971.

Feldman J.A. and Ballard D.H. Connectionist models and their properties. *Cognitive Science* 6:205–254, 1982.

Feldman J. and Narayanan S. Embodied meaning in a neural theory of language. *Brain and Language* 89:385–392, 2003.

Fillmore C.J. Grammatical construction theory and the familiar dichotomies. In R. Dietrich and C.F. Graumann, eds., *Language Processing in Social Context*, pp. 17–38. Amsterdam: North-Holland/Elsevier, 1989.

Freud S. *A Project for a Scientific Psychology.* London: Hogarth Press, 1966 (1895).

Gibbs Jr. R. *The Poetics of mind: Figurative thought, language, and understanding.* Cambridge: Cambridge University Press, 1994.

Gold E.M. Language identification in the limit. *Information and Control* 10:447–474, 1967.

Goldberg A. *Constructions: A Construction Grammar Approach to Argument Structure.* Chicago: University of Chicago Press, 1995.

Goodsell D.S. *The Machinery of Life.* Springer, 1997, chapters 2 and 4.

Grady J. Foundations of meaning: Primary metaphor and primary scenes. Dissertation, University of California, Linguistics Department, Berkeley 1997.

Greene B. *The Elegant Universe.* Vintage, 2000.

Gurevich O. On the status of the morpheme in Georgian verbal morphology. *Proceedings of the 29th Annual Berkeley Linguistics Society Conference,* 2003, pp. 161–172.

Harris R.A. *The Linguistics Wars.* Oxford University Press, 1983.

Hauk O., Johnsrude I., and Pulvermüller F. Somatotopic representation of action words in human motor and premotor cortex. *Neuron* 41(2):301–307, 2004.

Hauser M., Chomsky N., and Fitch W. The faculty of language: What is it, who has it, and how did it evolve? *Science* 298:1569–1579, 2002.

Hawkins J. and Balekslee S. *On Intelligence.* Times Books, 2004, chapters 2 and 3.

Hillis D. *Pattern on the Stone.* Perseus Books Group, 1999, chapters 2, 3, and 9.

Jackendoff R. *Foundations of Language.* Oxford University Press, 2003, chapters 2, 21–27.

Johnson C. Constructional grounding: The role of interpretational overlap in lexical and constructional acquisition. Dissertation. University of California, Linguistics Department, Berkeley, 1999.

Johnson M. and Lakoff G. *Metaphors We Live By.* Chicago: University of Chicago Press, 2003, chapters 1, 8, 11, 15, and 16.

Kahneman D. and Tversky A. Prospect theory: An analysis of decision under risk. *Econometrica* 47:263–291, 1979.

Kay P. and Kempton W. What is the Sapir-Whorf Hypothesis? *American Anthropologist* 86:65–79, 1984.

Kay P., Regier T., and Cook R. Focal colors are universal after all. *Proceedings of the National Academy of Sciences* 102:8386–8491, 2005.

Lakoff G. *Moral Politics*. Chicago: University of Chicago Press, 2002, chapter 26.

Lakoff G. *Women, Fire, and Dangerous Things: What Categories Reveal about the Mind.* Chicago: University of Chicago Press, 1987.

Lakoff G. and Johnson M. *Philosophy in the Flesh.* Harper Collins Publishers, 1999, chapters 1, 3, and 26.

Lettvin J.Y., Maturana H.R., McCulloch W.S., and Pitts W.H. What the Frog's Eye Tells the Frog's Brain. *Proceedings of the IRE* 47(11):1940–1951, November 1959.

Levinson S. Language and mind: Let's get the issues straight! In D. Gentner and S. Goldin-Meadow, eds. *Language in Mind: Advances in the Study of Language and Cognition.* Cambridge, MA: MIT Press, 2003, pp. 25–46.

Lewontin R. *The Triple Helix: Gene, Organism, and Environment.* Cambridge, MA: Harvard University Press, 2002, chapter 6.

Lucy J. Language, Culture, and Mind in a Comparative Perspective. *Language, Culture and Mind*, Michel Achard and Suzanne Kemmer, eds. Stanford, CA: CSLI Publications, 2004.

MacWhinney B. The emergence of language from embodiment. In B. MacWhinney, ed. *The Emergence of Language.* Mahwah, NJ: Lawrence Erlbaum, 1999.

McClelland J. and Patterson K. Rules and connections. *Trends in Cognitive Science* 6(11):471, 2002.

Meltzoff A.N. and Prinz W. *The Imitative Mind: Development, evolution, and brain bases.* Cambridge, England: Cambridge University Press, 2002.

Mok E., Bryant J., and Feldman J. Scaling up to mental spaces. *Proceedings of the Second International Workshop on Scalable Natural Language Understanding*, Boston, 2004.

Nadel L., Samsonovitch A, Ryan L., and Moscovitch M. Multiple trace theory of human memory: Computational, neuroimaging and neuropsychological results. *Hippocampus* 10:352–368, 2000.

Narayanan S. KARMA: Knowledge-based action representations for metaphor and aspect. PhD thesis, University of California, Berkeley, 1997.

Narayanan S. Moving right along: A computational model of metaphoric reasoning about events. *Proceedings of the National Conference on Artificial Intelligence* (AAAI '99):121–128, 1999.

Narayanan S. Talking the talk is like walking the walk: A computational model of verbal aspect. *Proceedings of the Nineteenth Annual Meeting of the Cognitive Science Society COGSCI-97*. Stanford, CA: Stanford University Press, 1997.

Narayanan S. and Jurafsky D. Bayesian models of human sentence processing. *Proceedings of Cognitive Science Society*, 752–758, 1998.

Nelson K. *Language in Cognitive Development*. Cambridge University Press, 1998, chapters 6, 8, and 10.

Nisbett R.E. *The Geography of Thought*. New York: The Free Press, 2003. Chapter 6 of this fascinating book focuses on linguistic issues.

Palmer S. *Vision Science: Photons to Phenomenology*. Cambridge, MA: MIT Press, 1999.

Pearl J. Belief networks revisited. *Artificial Intelligence* 59:49–56, 1993.

Pinker S. *How the Mind Works*. W.W. Norton & Company, 1999.

Pinker S. *The Language Instinct*. Perennial Classics, 2000, chapters 1, 8, 10, 15, and 16.

Pinker S. *Words and Rules*. Perennial, 2000, chapters 21–22.

Pinker S. and Jackendoff R. What's special about the human language faculty? *Cognition* 95:201–236, 2005.

Pinker S. and Ullman M. The past and future of the past tense. *Trends in Cognitive Science*, 6(11):456–465, 2002.

Ramachandran V. S. *Phantoms in the Brain*. Perennial, 1999, chapters 4–6, and 26.

Reddy M. The conduit metaphor—A case of frame conflict in our language about language. In Andrew Ortony, ed., *Metaphor and Thought*, pp. 284–324. Cambridge: Cambridge University Press, 1979.

Regier T. *The Human Semantic Potential*. Cambridge, MA: MIT Press, 1996, chapters 2, 3, 11, and 12.

Rensberger B. *Life Itself*. Oxford University Press, 1998, chapter 4.

Richardson D.C., Spivey M.J., McRae K., and Barsalou L.W. Spatial representations activated during real-time comprehension of verbs. *Cognitive Science* 27:767–780, 2003.

Rizzolatti G. and Arbib M. Language within our grasp. *Trends in Neurosciences*, 21(5):188–194, 1998.

Rizzolatti G., Fogassi L., and Gallese V. Neurophysiological mechanisms underlying the understanding and imitation of action. *Nature Neuroscience Reviews* 2:661–670, 2001.

Rosch E. Natural categories. *Cognitive Psychology* 4:328–50, 1973.

Rosch E. and Lloyd B., eds. *Cognition and Categorization*. Hillsdale, NJ: Erlbaum, 1978.

Rosch Heider E. Universals in color naming and memory. *Journal of Experimental Psychology* 93:1–20, 1972.

Sapir E. The status of linguistics as a science. *Language* 5:207–214, 1929. Reprinted in *The Selected Writings of Edward Sapir in Language, Culture, and Personality*, D.G. Mandelbaum, ed. Berkeley: University of California Press, 1958, pp. 160–166.

Schacter D.L. *Searching for Memory.* Basic Books 1997, chapters 5 and 9.

Searle J.R. Minds, brains, and programs. *Behavioral and Brain Sciences* 3(3):417–457, 1980.

Shastri L. Episodic memory and cortico-hippocampal interactions. *Trends in Cognitive Science* 6:162–168, 2002.

Shi J., Smith T.J., Granieri J., and Badler N. Smart avatars in JackMOO. *Proceedings of Virtual Reality '99.* Houston, TX: IEEE Computer Society, March 1999.

Slobin D. Language and thought online: cognitive consequences of linguistic relativity. In *Language in Mind: Advances in the Study of Language and Thought*. Deidre Gentner and Susan Goldin-Meadow, eds. Cambridge, MA: MIT Press, 2003.

Stellwagen D. and Schatz C.J. An instructive role for retinal waves in the development of retinogeniculate connectivity. *Neuron* 33:357–367, 2002.

Talmy L. Force dynamics in language and cognition. *Cognitive Science* 12:49–100, 1988.

Tanenhaus M.K., Leiman J.M., and Seidenberg M.S. Evidence for the multiple stages in the processing of ambiguous words in syntactic contexts. *Journal of Verbal Learning and Verbal Behavior* 18:427–440, 1979.

Tettamanti M., Buccino B., Saccuman M., Gallese V., Danna M., Scifo P. Fazio F., Rizzolatti G. Cappa S., and Perani D. Listening to action-related sentences activates fronto-parietal motor circuits. *Journal of Cognitive Neuroscience* 17:273–281, 2005.

Tinbergen N. On the aims and methods of ethology. *Zeitschrift für Tierpsychologie* 20:410–463, 1963.

Tomasello M. *Constructing a Language: A Usage-Based Theory of Language Acquisition.* Cambridge, MA: Harvard University Press, 2003.

Tomasello M. *First Verbs: A Case Study of Early Grammatical Development.* Cambridge, England: Cambridge University Press, 1992.

Tomasello M. *The Cultural Origins of Human Cognition.* Cambridge, MA: Harvard University Press, 2001, chapters 1, 10, 11, 15, and 26.

Whorf B.L. and Caroll J.B., eds. *Language, Thought, and Reality: Selected Writings of Benjamin Lee Whorf.* Cambridge, MA: MIT Press, 1956.

Novels

Lodge D. *Thinks*. Penguin Books, 2002.

Papadimitriou C.H. *Turing*. Cambridge, MA: MIT Press, 2003.

Powers R. *Galatea 2.2*. Picador, 2004.

Index